Scrollsaw
Toys For All Ages

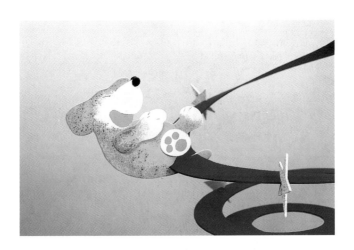

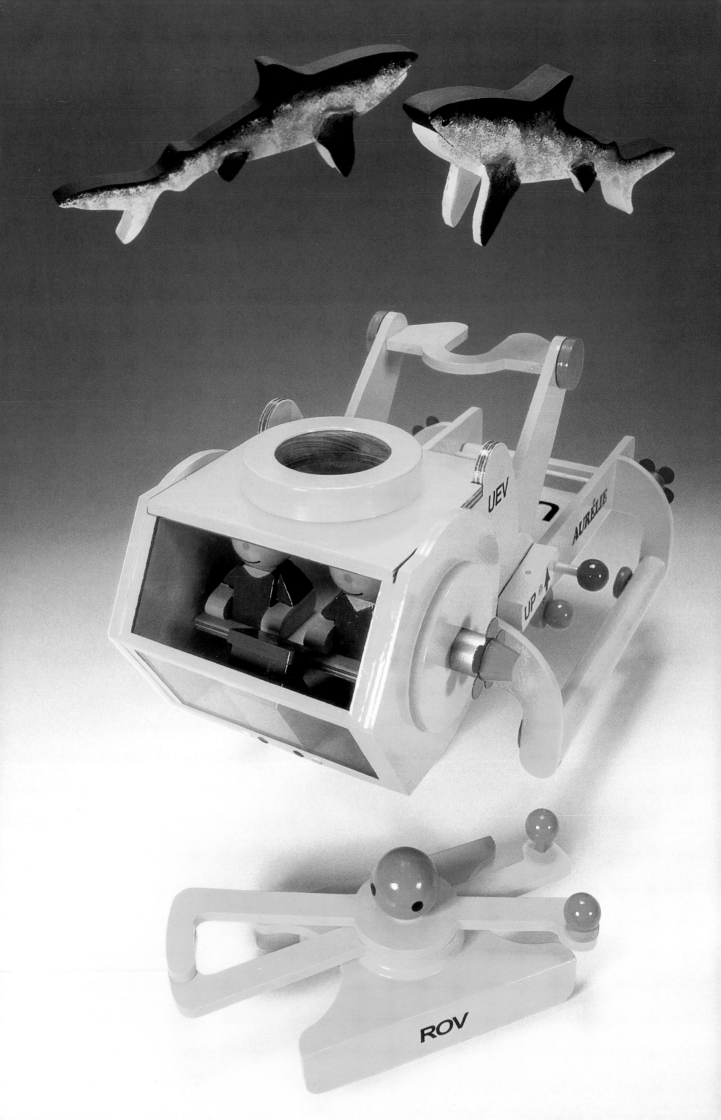

Scrollsaw
Toys For All Ages

IVOR CARLYLE

GUILD OF MASTER CRAFTSMAN PUBLICATIONS LTD

First published 1999 by
Guild of Master Craftsman Publications Ltd,
166 High Street, Lewes,
East Sussex BN7 1XU

ISBN 1 86108 146 4

Photographer, pages 16–17, 22–23, 28–29, 34–35,
42–43, 50–51, 58–59, 66–67, 78–79, 88–89 and
100–101: Zul Mukhida
Editor: Cathy Lowne
Designer: Sarah Theodosiou, based on an original
design by Ian Hunt
Cover designer: Graham Willmott
Typeface: Univers and Rotis
Colour origination by Viscan Graphics (Singapore)
Printed and bound by Kyodo Printing (Singapore) under
the supervision of MRM Graphics, Winslow,
Buckinghamshire, UK

10 9 8 7 6 5 4 3 2 1

CONTENTS

To my wife, Joyce,
who made this book possible.

ACKNOWLEDGEMENTS

Thanks to Georgina Hoare and Christopher and James Horne for acting as photographic models.

Also thanks to my mother-in-law, Mrs Roma Caddy, for making the pop-up bear in Chapter 6.

The publishers would also like to thank Sarah, Clay and Rye Charman, Kitty Clark, Katrina Jane Ming Gray, Yasmin Mukhida and Benjamin Thomas Simpson for acting as photographic models.

INTRODUCTION

It is very satisfying to give a child a toy that you have made yourself and then to see him or her playing with it enthusiastically. The individuality of the finish, the warm, sturdy feel of the wood and the intense glossy colours of the paintwork provide such a different experience from anything the child will get from a commercially available, mass-produced toy. The added advantage is that after years of happy play, the chipped and dented toy can be repaired and made as good as new before once more exercising the child's imagination and helping in his or her development. Even when children get older and no longer play with the toys, they still cherish them and do not throw them away: they may even pass them on to their own children one day.

This is where the increasingly popular powered scrollsaw (or fretsaw) comes in. The underlying principle on which this machine operates is not new, but modern developments have made it an extremely accurate and versatile tool. It is incredibly user-friendly and for this reason is used widely in schools for all kinds of craftwork.

Also, a scrollsaw doesn't take up very much room and will fit into the average spare room, garage or garden shed. With the addition of some tools from a reasonably well-equipped toolkit, such as a hammer and a selection of clamps, the scrollsaw equips an enthusiastic owner to make themselves popular with children of all ages, including the grown-up ones.

METRIC CONVERSIONS

All the measurements used during the design and construction of these toys were metric. The imperial equivalents shown throughout the book are as close to an equivalent as can be made. However it is always a good idea to 'cut to fit' and make allowances for the inevitable variations in the materials and their cutting out. Use either metric or imperial measurements, not a mixture.

CONVERSION FACTORS

1 centimetre = 0.3937 of an inch

1 inch = 25.4 millimetres

METRIC CONVERSION TABLE

INCHES TO MILLIMETRES AND CENTIMETRES

MM = MILLIMETRES   CM = CENTIMETRES

INCHES	MM	CM	INCHES	CM	INCHES	CM
1/8	3	0.3	9	22.9	30	76.2
1/4	6	0.6	10	25.4	31	78.7
3/8	10	1.0	11	27.9	32	81.3
1/2	13	1.3	12	30.5	33	83.8
5/8	16	1.6	13	33.0	34	86.4
3/4	19	1.9	14	35.6	35	88.9
7/8	22	2.2	15	38.1	36	91.4
1	25	2.5	16	40.6	37	94.0
1 1/4	32	3.2	17	43.2	38	96.5
1 1/2	38	3.8	18	45.7	39	99.1
1 3/4	44	4.4	19	48.3	40	101.6
2	51	5.1	20	50.8	41	104.1
2 1/2	64	6.4	21	53.3	42	106.7
3	76	7.6	22	55.9	43	109.2
3 1/2	89	8.9	23	58.4	44	111.8
4	102	10.2	24	61.0	45	114.3
4 1/2	114	11.4	25	63.5	46	116.8
5	127	12.7	26	66.0	47	119.4
6	152	15.2	27	68.6	48	121.9
7	178	17.8	28	71.1	49	124.5
8	203	20.3	29	73.7	50	127.0

TOOLS, TECHNIQUES AND MATERIALS

TOOLS

THE SCROLLSAW

The scrollsaw, as shown in Fig 1.1, is powered by an electric motor, usually of a surprisingly low wattage. This makes the running costs very economical. An adjustable table, which enables you to cut bevelled edges up to a maximum of 45°, adds to its versatility.

BLADES

Apart from wood, the scrollsaw can be used to cut plastic, metal, foam rubber, card, leather and many other materials with ease. The many and varied types of blade available enable you to get the best possible results with the particular material you are using. Buy replacement blades in reasonably large quantities: this is a very cheap way to purchase them and allows you to replace them as soon as they are worn and no longer working efficiently.

The blades that I used the most when making the projects featured in this book are shown in Fig 1.2. The Grade 7 reverse-cut blade is the most useful. As you can see in the magnified section, the teeth at the bottom of the blade point in the opposite direction to those at the top.

This means that the underneath of the cut is as clean as the top, creating a very neat finish and saving you having to clean up any breakout on the underside.

The Grade 0 blade is used for plywood that is 1.5mm (1⁄16in) thick, or thinner, while the machine coping blade, at the other extreme, is used for rip-cutting wood as thick as

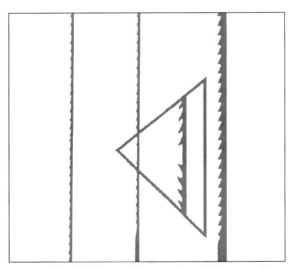

Fig 1.2 The blades used most often in these projects, shown actual size. From left to right: Grade 0 (25 TPI), Grade 7 reverse-cut, and a machine coping blade (11 TPI).

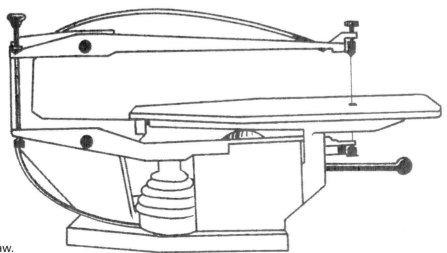

Fig 1.1 A powered scrollsaw.

25mm (1in) or more. The TPI (teeth per inch) figure speaks for itself. These are the blades that suit me; however, there are many types of blade available, so you should experiment with different ones to get the speed and 'feel' of cutting that suits you best, and so obtain the optimum results from your machine.

The scrollsaw's ability to make precise internal cuts enables you to make tongue and slot joints without a hammer and chisel, making them easier and quicker to complete. When purchasing a machine, buy one that has as large a throat capacity as you can afford. This makes it easier to manoeuvre larger pieces of work. The machine used for the projects in this book has a throat capacity of 457mm (18in). Although small and miniature machines are excellent for very fine work in thin woods, they are not particularly suitable for the larger, thicker pieces used to make some toys.

You should consider buying a machine with a variable cutting speed: high speeds produce the best results with wood, but slower speeds are essential when working on plastics and metal.

A vital accessory for the powered scrollsaw is a footswitch control. Not only does this make the machine easier to use, but it increases safety by leaving both of your hands free to control the wood at all times. Good lighting is essential in order to cut accurately along a fine line, so an adjustable desk lamp is a good idea. Scrollsaws do produce a lot of very fine dust, so wear a dust mask and goggles and have a vacuum cleaner on hand so that you can clean up regularly.

DRILLS

In my opinion, an electric drill is essential. When used in conjunction with a drill stand and drill vice, as shown in Fig 1.3, it will enable you to make such things as axle holes very accurately, which will help to ensure that your toys run or work smoothly.

Any basic DIY electric drill with the (now universal) 43mm collar is suitable and, as with the saw, the fastest speed settings produce the cleanest and most efficient results. Stands and drill vices for these tools are now readily available and a suitable model can be acquired for just a modest outlay.

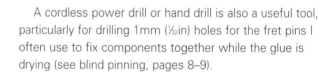

TIP

Before using the stand, fit a long drill bit into the chuck, check with a try square that it is set at 90° to the base and adjust if necessary.

A cordless power drill or hand drill is also a useful tool, particularly for drilling 1mm ($\frac{1}{32}$in) holes for the fret pins I often use to fix components together while the glue is drying (see blind pinning, pages 8–9).

DRILL BITS

Twist drill bits are required for all-purpose drilling, along with the lip and spur bit shown in Photo 1. The spur on the lip and spur drill bit makes it easier to align the bit with the centre mark of the hole, and prevents it wandering. (Warning: wear eye protection!)

PLANES

Conventional woodworking planes are not necessary for these projects. I used a model maker's small balsa plane with a disposable blade (see Photo 2). These are very inexpensive and do not require resharpening: you simply replace the blade when it gets blunt.

KNIVES AND SAWS

General-purpose DIY knives are useful, as are scalpels and craft knives with interchangeable blades. You will need a safety rule and a cutting mat for precision work, such as cutting out masking tape and card templates. A junior

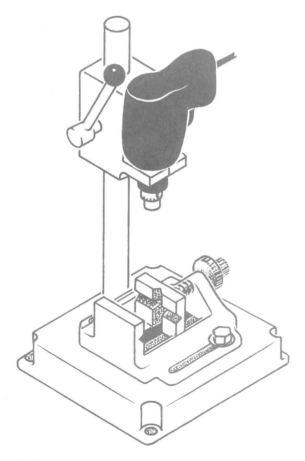

Fig 1.3 An electric drill on a drill stand.

Photo 1 On the left are two twist drill bits which are useful for all-purpose drilling. On the right are three lip and spur drill bits.

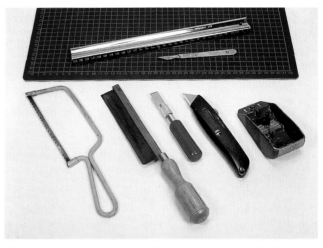

Photo 2 A junior hacksaw, Gent's saw, craft knife, Stanley knife, small balsa plane, safety ruler and scalpel on a cutting mat.

hacksaw is sufficient for cutting steel axle rods. In addition, a 152mm (6in) Gent's saw is ideal for trimming off the ends of small dowels, etc.

HAMMER

You will need a 99gm (3½oz) cross pein hammer for tapping in small fret pins and 3mm (⅛in) dowels (see Chapter 8, Towalong Ladybird, Photo 6.)

CLAMPS, ETC

The combined clamp and saw horse, which is used for all sorts of DIY jobs around the house, is very useful,

especially for clamping the larger items. Apart from this, a collection of G-clamps, F-clamps, fret clamps (very cheap), plastic spring clamps and masking tape, shown in Photo 3, is essential.

Always protect your workpiece by inserting blocks of scrap wood between the work and the clamp itself. To avoid this scrap wood sticking to your work if excess glue leaks out, put polythene between the scrap wood and the workpiece. Masking tape is also useful.

ABRASIVES

Aluminium oxide paper is the most useful general-purpose and long-lasting type of abrasive paper for shaping and

Photo 3 G-clamp, F-clamp, fret clamp, plastic spring clamp and masking tape for keeping a tight grip on everything.

finishing wood as well as rubbing down paint, varnish and metal. Grades 100 through to 220 (the finest) are sufficient for the projects here. You can make a sanding block by attaching the paper to a piece of plywood with double-sided tape.

PENCILS AND PENS

The clearer and finer your cutting line, the easier you will find it to cut accurately with the scrollsaw. This is very important: a thick or variable line is impossible to follow accurately and

TIP

Always sand in the direction of the wood grain, otherwise you will scratch the surface and this will show when it is varnished or painted.

any deviation by the blade is easy to spot afterwards. I like to use a refillable clutch pencil. A 0.9mm ($\frac{1}{16}$in) 2B lead – the softest available – leaves a fine black line to follow, especially if you bring the projecting lead to a sharp point by rubbing it against a sanding block, as I have done in Photo 5.

DRAWING INSTRUMENTS

All you need are the standard drawing instruments shown in Photo 4, such as rulers, T-square, try-square and set squares. Also shown in the photograph is a Japanese mitre square, which is extremely useful for checking the 45° setting of the scrollsaw blade. A pair of compasses that will hold a variety of drawing instruments is particularly useful, as is one that will accept an extension bar. A plastic circle marker with a variety of diameters from 2mm ($\frac{3}{32}$in) upwards saves a lot of work when marking out rounded corners. A 'flexible curve' is very handy for drawing curves.

BRUSHES

The brushes you need (Fig 1.4) are sold in art and craft shops and although they may seem a little more expensive, they will last many years if you look after them. The

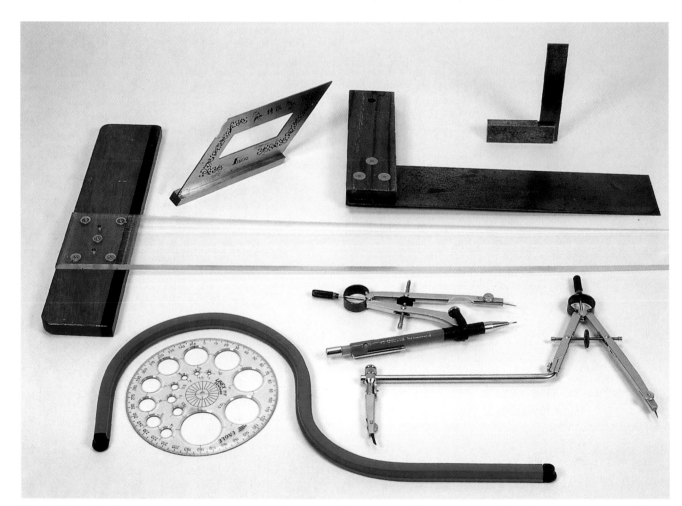

Photo 4 Drawing instruments: two try-squares, a Japanese mitre square, a T-square, two pairs of compasses – one with an extension bar, a flexible curve and a plastic circle marker.

synthetic sable brushes that are available now, sometimes sold as student ranges, are very good value. For general application brushes that are 16–20mm (⅝–¾in) wide are ideal. A flat 50mm (2in) brush is perfect for large areas that need covering quickly; smaller sizes are better for the more detailed work. After cleaning the brushes with the appropriate thinner, give them a gentle wash with water and washing-up liquid or some liquid soap. This keeps them clean, soft and springy and prolongs their life.

OTHER TOOLS

Apart from the tools listed above, the contents of the average DIY toolbox will be sufficient. Throughout the book, I only specify tools that you are not likely to have to hand.

HEALTH AND SAFETY

You'll need a vacuum cleaner to clean up the dust. As mentioned, when using the drill and looking very closely at the drill bit to align it on the workpiece do use eye protection such as goggles. Also, wear a dust mask to avoid breathing in the very fine dust from the saw. The dust-clearing blower on most scrollsaws throws the dust forward. You should avoid breathing it in, especially the dust from man-made boards which contain adhesives.

TECHNIQUES

TRANSFERRING THE DESIGNS

I have provided working drawings for all of the toys. I recommend drawing the designs onto the wood using the dimensions that I have provided. If you prefer to photocopy the drawings and use them as templates, note that they have been reproduced at different scales, because many of them are too large to be shown full size. The percentage to which they have been reduced is indicated in the captions, and some mathematics skills are required to establish the correct enlargement when photocopying! Be aware that photocopies are not completely accurate and can distort by up to 10%.

MAKING TEMPLATES

Making templates is a good idea if the item is complicated or is repeated a number of times. Trace, or photocopy, the shape onto paper, then stick this onto thin card and cut it out with a sharp knife. Then, using a sharp pencil, draw around the template onto the wood, and mark the positions for drill holes and attachments.

Photo 5 The pencil kept sharp with the sanding block on the left makes for accurate marking (on the right).

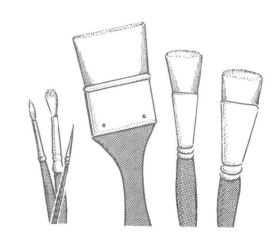

Fig 1.4 A selection of brushes.

MARKING UP CIRCLES AND ROUND CORNERS

This can be time-consuming and fiddly, so to speed up the process and ensure accuracy, use a plastic circle marker.

TIP

You can mark the centre of a hole, especially on a template, with a small pin chuck containing a pin (on the left in Photo 5). The pin can be sharpened on the sanding block.

MARKING UP AND CUTTING OUT JOINTS

I often use cross halving and slot and tongue joints in these toys. A simple way to help to ensure that these joints fit accurately is to use a piece of wood of the correct width as a guide (see the slot and tongue joint I am marking up in Photo 5). Then cut to the inside, or 'waste', side of the line, as shown in Fig 1.5. This will give you a slot of the exact width.

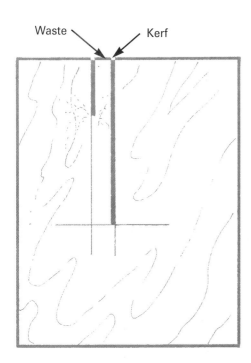

Fig 1.5 Cutting to a waste line.

FRETTING OUT

To make internal cuts (a technique known as fretting out), first drill a pilot hole through the waste wood near to your cutting line. Release the scrollsaw blade and pass one end of it through the hole. Clamp the blade back into the machine and cut out the waste area. To remove the wood, simply release the blade again.

CUTTING DUPLICATE PARTS

Another method that you can use to cut out exact duplicate pieces is to stick two or more pieces of wood or ply together with double-sided tape, then cut round your marked line. You can then separate them again.

DRILLING DOWELS

To drill holes in dowels accurately, you need a vee block held in a drill vice, as shown in Fig 1.6.

TIP

If you do not have a vee block, it is a simple matter to make one on your scrollsaw. Cut through a piece of MDF or plywood about 9mm (⅜in) thick at a 45° angle. Glue and pin the two parts to another piece of scrap to form a vee groove.

DRILLING AND CUTTING WOODEN BALLS

Cutting and drilling wooden balls can be extremely difficult, if not a little hazardous. To overcome this, you can use simple jigs. To make a drilling jig, cut a hole the same diameter as the ball in a piece of 9mm (⅜in) thick wood with an exit cut to one side. When you place the ball in it and squeeze the exit cut with the drill vice, it is firmly gripped, as shown in Photo 6.

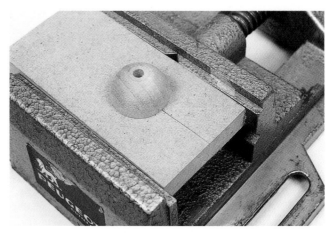

Photo 6 A wooden ball held safely in a drilling jig.

In order to cut a ball in half (see Chapter 8, Towalong Ladybird), cut a hole slightly smaller in diameter than the ball into a piece of wood at least half as thick as the diameter of the ball, e.g., for a 25mm (1in) ball, your wood must be at least 12mm (½in) thick. Push the ball firmly into place, allowing the jig to grip it hard, and then strap the ball in with masking tape, lining up the edge of the tape with the exit cut to act as a guide for the cutting line, as shown

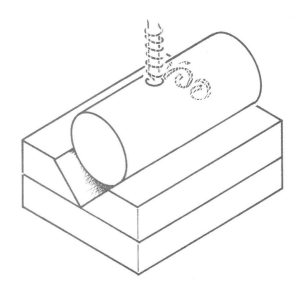

Fig 1.6 For drilling dowel safely, place it in a vee block which is itself held in a drill vice.

Photo 7 The masking tape not only holds the ball in the jig, but also acts as a cutting guide.

in Photo 7. The scrollsaw blade reaches the ball by travelling through the centrally positioned exit cut in the jig. Do not cut through the jig.

CUTTING LONG PIECES OF WOOD

To cut out long pieces of wood on a scrollsaw, you will have to cut in a sideways direction (see Chapter 7, Mountain Passenger Lift). To do this, you need to twist the ends of the blade through 90° with a pair of pliers, as shown in Photo 8, before fitting it onto the scrollsaw. The cutting action will not be as smooth as usual, but will still produce an acceptable result.

Photo 8 Twisting the scrollsaw blade through 90° so that it will cut long pieces of wood.

CUTTING DOWELS

To make a safe and accurate cut through dowelling, make a simple jig from two pieces of scrap joined together to form a step, as shown in Photo 9. The step stops the dowel rolling while you are cutting it.

TIP

If you need to cut a number of pieces of dowelling to the same length, fix a small nail into position on the jig to act as a stop gauge.

Photo 9 Save time and fingers by making a simple jig to hold dowelling that needs to be cut.

CUTTING ACRYLIC SHEETING

To cut acrylic sheeting, leave its protective covering in place and mount it onto scrap ply or hardboard with double-sided tape (see Chapter 12, Mars Pathfinder game, Photo 8). Mark your cutting line on the film with a fine ballpoint pen. The blade that you usually use will cut acrylic, but you will need to run the saw at about half speed, or the acrylic will melt. Bear in mind that acrylic blunts blades rapidly, so they will need replacing more often. To finish off, polish the edges with rubbing compound, as shown in Photo 10, jeweller's rouge or metal polish.

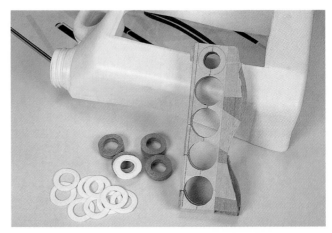

Photo 11 Plastic washers can be made by sandwiching plastic between scraps of plywood before cutting out.

Photo 10 Rubbing compound used to polish the cut edges on the acrylic.

MAKING PLASTIC WASHERS

To make plastic washers, sandwich plastic from containers (such as flat-sided liquid containers) between pieces of scrap plywood, drill out the holes then cut out the circles (see Photo 11). Always wash the containers thoroughly before use.

CUTTING FOAM PLASTIC

To slice foam plastic to the required thickness, clamp a block of wood to the scrollsaw table at the required distance from the blade. Pass the blade through the plastic foam while sliding the foam gently and evenly against the wooden fence as seen in Photo 12.

GLUING AND FIXING

When gluing the parts together with PVA glue, clamp them together as snugly as possible. Holding plywood edges together while the glue sets can be a problem, so I use a method known as blind pinning (Fig 1.7), in which brass fret pins hold the pieces until the glue has set and are then removed. First, drill a 1mm (½in) pilot hole. Push the brass

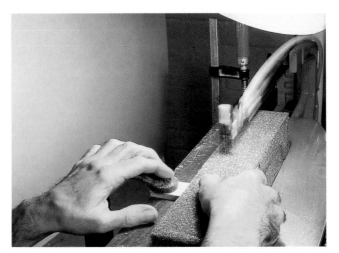

Photo 12 Using a wooden fence to cut foam plastic to the required thickness.

fret pin through a small piece of thick card as in step 1 (this makes it easier to hold in place) and then hammer it into place. When the glue has set, rip the piece of card away as shown in step 2. Then use a pincers to pull the fret pin out by its exposed head as in step 3. You can also use masking tape to bind parts together, so keep some to hand.

When using epoxy resin adhesive, make sure that you roughen up the surfaces to be joined, especially if they have been painted. If you find the adhesive is stiff and difficult to manage, warm it up with a hairdryer until it starts to flow more easily. This trick is also good for when you want the adhesive to flow into holes. Smears or excess resin can be cleaned up with a cloth dabbed in methylated spirits, so keep these on hand when using the resin.

MAKING SCREW HOLES

Before inserting any screw, drill a suitable pilot hole in the wood. This will prevent the wood from splitting. The pilot hole should be the same diameter as the central part of the screw, without the threads. Compare the drill bit to the screw by holding them up to the light.

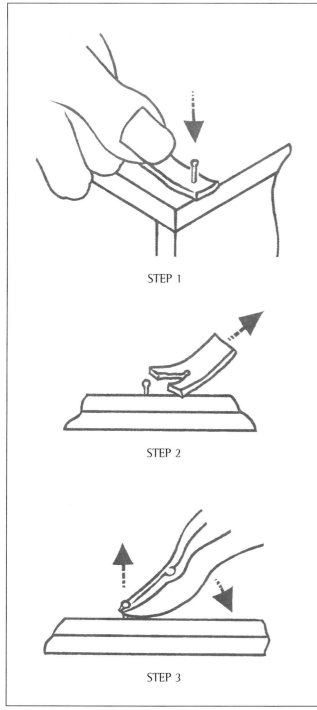

STEP 1

STEP 2

STEP 3

Fig 1.7 Inserting and removing a temporary fret pin with the aid of a thick piece of card.

REINFORCING JOINTS

These toys will need to withstand some hard knocks over the years, so it is a good idea to strengthen the joints by inserting dowels. For 6mm (¼in) ply, use 12mm (½in) lengths of 3mm (⅛in) dowel. When the joint is assembled, drill a 12mm (½in) deep hole into it with a 3mm (⅛in) bit. Apply the glue and gently tap the dowel into place. For an example of joints reinforced with dowels, see Photo 8 of the Shape Sorter on page 48.

MATERIALS

PLYWOOD

The principal material used for these projects is birchwood multiply. When cut efficiently it has a clean, hard edge which is free of splinters. Birch multiply is available in thicknesses from about 0.5mm (½₂in) upwards. The most economical way to buy the plywood 6mm (¼in) or more thick is from a timber merchant. It comes in 2440 x 1220mm (8 x 4ft) sheets, but the timber merchant will cut it into more convenient sizes, although he may charge you a modest fee for this service. Cladding or builders' plywood, which is 5mm (³⁄₁₆in) thick, can often be obtained as scrap off-cuts that have been thrown away. You can use these for backing very thin plywood or acrylic sheet, and for sandwiching foam plastic when you need to cut it out. Bear in mind that '6mm (¼in)' is a nominal thickness and the actual size is often nearer to 6.5mm (⁹⁄₃₂in), so allow for this when marking up (see Marking up and cutting out, page 5).

PINE

When selecting ready-prepared pinewood, make sure it is of good quality and free from twisting, splitting and any other faults. A good timber yard will give you advice and may be able to supply suitable off-cuts, which will prove more economical.

TIP

The measurements on the project cutting lists are the finished dimensions: allow 15–20mm (⅝–¾in) around and between items when working out how much wood you need.

HARDWOOD

Beech is commonly used for toys and furniture, and small offcuts are easy to find. I used remnants from some old school desks for the projects. Maple performs a similar role in the USA.

MOULDINGS AND DOWELS

Miniature dowels, 3mm (⅛in) in diameter and upwards, are available from hobby and model suppliers.

ADHESIVES

PVA wood glue is perfect for making wooden toys and gives an incredibly strong joint when the wood surfaces are brought tightly together. It is easy to clean up with a damp cloth while it is still wet, because it is water soluble until it dries.

Two-part epoxy resin adhesives are very effective and convenient for gluing together non-wood surfaces or wood to anything else. These adhesives are also very good at filling gaps. Some set slowly, others are rapid. Whichever you use, handle with care.

Use a cyanoacrylate adhesive or 'super glue' to fix rubber to plastic, as you will for the Mars Pathfinder game in Chapter 12.

A hot-melt glue gun is extremely useful for sticking foam rubber to plastic or wood (see Chapter 2, Paint stamps, Photo 5). Aerosol cans of spray mount are useful for sticking paper patterns to wood.

SCREWS

The most reliable screws to use with composite materials, such as plywood, are those with a constant shank diameter, a shallow pitch and a double spiral cutting thread, the most common of which are known as chipboard screws. Their particular features avoid splitting, crumbling or breakout from the material. The small automotive self-tapping screws sold in car accessory shops are similar and very useful for the same reasons. I recommend the 'pozidrive' type of head, because there is less chance of the screwdriver slipping and marking the wood. Before you insert a screw, drill a suitable pilot hole in the wood. This will prevent splitting.

PINS

You will need 14mm (½in) long brass fret pins for blind pinning (see page 8).

ACRYLIC SHEETING

Pieces of 2mm (³⁄₃₂in) acrylic sheeting (known as Perspex in the UK and Plexiglass in the USA) are available from DIY stores as a glazing material. If you need anything thicker than this, go to a signmaker or glazier, who may be able to let you have offcuts fairly cheaply.

READY-MADE FITTINGS

You can get the various sizes of wooden balls, ready-made wooden wheels, steel axle-rods and snap-on hub caps necessary for these projects fairly cheaply from hobby and craft suppliers. Multi-stranded nylon cord in various sizes and colours can be found in hardware and camping supplies shops.

WASHERS

Steel washers are available from hardware shops and their size usually denotes the size of the hole for most everyday purposes. I also make my own from plastic, because they are lighter and more versatile. Also, you are not restricted to the commercially available sizes. The dimensions of the washers vary and are given in the cutting lists for each project. The simple technique for making them is shown in Photo 11 on page 8.

FOAM PLASTIC/FOAM RUBBER

For the paint stamps you can use the large sponges that decorators use, available from DIY stores. The black plastic foam as used in the Mars Pathfinder project can be obtained from tool and photographic shops – it is used to make the spacers for equipment boxes. You will find foam plastic suppliers in the telephone directory. They may sell offcuts, which can be cheaper.

LETTERING

The lettering and graphics used with the projects are laser cut and self adhesive. They are found in specialist model shops for use on model aeroplanes, etc. The type styles are limited, but many specialist logos, flags and markings are available. You can find addresses for mail order suppliers in specialist aeromodelling magazines.

PAINT AND VARNISHES

It is the duty of the toymaker to ensure that all finishes are suitable for children to use. Fortunately, there are many types of paints and varnishes now available for toymaking and these are clearly marked with a CE logo or reference to the necessary BS standards (UK and Europe).

ENAMELS

The hardest and most durable paints are the oil-based enamel paints. They produce the deep shiny colours that give the hand-made toy its unique quality. Many colours are available and they also come in little 14ml (2fl. oz.) tins of special colours.

Photo 13 Mixing acrylic paint and acrylic varnish allows the pattern and texture of the wood to show through.

ACRYLIC PAINT

Acrylic paints are also available in forms approved for use on toys and they come in very convenient small containers. They dry quickly and are easy to use. You can thin them and clean up afterwards with water.

Use acrylic paint mixed with acrylic varnish if you want the texture and pattern of the wood to show through the colour, as shown in Photo 13. Mix together one part paint to five parts varnish: test the mix on a piece of scrap wood first and adjust the amounts if necessary.

ACRYLIC VARNISH

Gloss, silk and matt acrylic varnishes are available and, because they are water soluble they are easy to thin and cleaning brushes afterwards is a relatively simple operation. The varnish is transparent and neutral in colour. Many acrylic varnishes sold in DIY stores have a colour tint added, so you may have to go to a specialist store to obtain a totally neutral type (such as Rustins, which is also certified suitable for use on toys). These varnishes dry quickly; they can be touch dry in as little as 30 minutes.

FINISHING

Painting the finished toy can be as much fun as making it in the first place, and a good paint job really does enhance the toy, so it is worth spending time and effort to get this stage exactly right.

First, rub down all the wooden surfaces with Grade 200–220 aluminium oxide abrasive paper, then remove all traces of dust with a vacuum cleaner, in reverse operation to blow the dust away – if your machine has this option – as this is the most effective method of removing the loose dust: it is best done out of doors. Decide which areas you are going to leave natural, simply protected by a

TIP

If necessary, thin the enamel paint slightly with white spirit to maintain a good, flowing consistency. Some colours require a really good stir to mix the pigments fully with the medium, but do this carefully to avoid building up an air-filled froth.

Most ranges of enamel paint have a matching transparent lacquer that is compatible with the opaque colours.

Photo 14 Masking allows you to create interesting and detailed effects, such as the camouflaging on the 'come apart' car.

transparent lacquer finish. Thin the lacquer, if necessary, to get a good, flowing consistency and cover the areas required and a little of the area around them. When the lacquer is dry, rub it gently with Grade 220 abrasive paper and remove the dust with a cloth moistened with white spirit. Recoat, and when it is dry, mask it off with masking tape and paint the other surfaces with a white, non-toxic primer after masking out the edges of the lacquered areas with tape. You should use this primer when you are applying opaque coloured paint finishes. You may need two coats of the top coat, depending on its opacity which varies from one colour to another, so more than one coat may be needed. An undercoat or primer is necessary whether you are using enamel or acrylic paints, except where you want a translucent finish, for example on the Mars Pathfinder game in photo 13 on page 11.

Masking can be used to great effect for the details on the toys (see Photo 14). To paint or varnish small, fiddly pieces, mount them onto the ends of sharp panel pins that have been hammered through pieces of scrap wood from the other side, as shown in Photo 15.

Make templates of the figures' faces out of thin card and use these to make pencil guide marks as shown in Photo 16. Then fill in the eyes and mouth of each with a permanent marker. Finish them off with coats of varnish. When you have finished all the painting and varnishing, leave the toys to dry and harden for as long as possible before passing them onto those waiting to play.

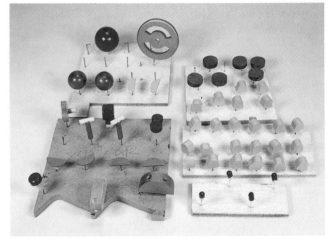

Photo 15 Small, fiddly pieces will resist your best efforts to paint them unless they are skewered by panel pins.

Photo 16 Using a template to transform the surface of a wooden ball into a face.

THE PROJECTS

PAINTSTAMPS

2

Many designs and motifs can be made in stamp form and the possibilities are almost endless. The advantage of paintstamps is that you can apply any type of paint to almost any kind of surface – smooth, textured, flat or curved. The cost of making the stamps is minimal, so you can experiment freely. They add an exciting extra dimension to the finish of toys such as the Windmill Mouse House, Shape sorter and Mars Pathfinder game. They can also be used to decorate children's rooms. An effective and popular example is constellations of stars on the walls and ceiling. You can use either plywood or acrylic sheet to back the stamps.

MATERIALS

STAMPBLOCKS

Stamps	Foam rubber (car wash or decorator's sponges)
Cutting support/backing	5–6mm (³/₁₆–¹/₄in) plywood
Backing	2mm (³/₃₂in) acrylic sheet
Handles	12mm (¹/₂in) dowelling

MISCELLANEOUS

Screws (4)	no 8 chipboard	12–25mm (¹/₂–1in)
Masking tape		
Double-sided tape		
Drawing paper		
Pencil		
Cross-head screwdriver		
Scissors		
EXTRA TOOLS		
Hot-melt glue gun with multi-purpose glue sticks		
Electric carving knife (optional)		

CONSTRUCTION

Decorator's sponges from a DIY store should be big enough for any of the designs in this book. They can hold a large amount of paint, so you can vary the density of the print and achieve interesting textures, although you should avoid overloading them with paint or it might run. Use an electric carving knife to cut sponges down to half thickness (see also Cutting foam plastic on page 8). This doubles the number of stamps, and economises on paint. The instructions below are for one stamp.

1 Photocopy or trace your stamp designs onto the drawing paper.

2 Cut two pieces of plywood so that they are about 20mm (³/₄in) larger all round than the piece of foam.

3 Stick the two pieces of ply together with double-sided tape and drill a 3mm (¹/₈in) hole in each corner, as shown in Photo 1. Separate them and mark them so that they can be reassembled in the same order and position.

Photo 1 Drilling a 3mm (¹/₈in) through the two pieces of ply that will hold the sponge.

4 If you are using the plywood as backing for the stamp, glue the foam to one piece. Do not glue the foam to the ply if you are going to use the acrylic for backing. The advantage of using acrylic sheet for backing is that it can be washed, while the plywood cannot, so use acrylic if you intend to use the stamp over and over again.

TIP

When using oil-based paints, leave the paint to dry and then slice off the hardened surface with the electric carving knife before reusing the stamp.

5 Screw the two pieces of plywood together, sandwiching the foam between them as shown in Photo 2 and Fig 2.1.

6 Cover the screw heads with masking tape to avoid scratching the scrollsaw table. Turn the sandwich over.

7 Using double-sided tape, fix the stamp outline to the top of the sandwich as shown in Fig 2.1 and Photo 3. If there is room, you can cut more than one stamp out of a sandwich.

TIP

The paint surface of a stamp must be laterally reversed if the design is not symmetrical, otherwise it will print back to front.

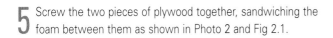

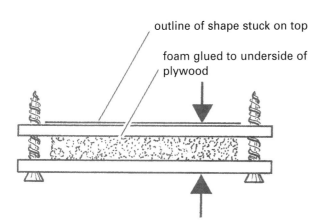

Fig 2.1 A cross-section of the sandwich. The screws are tightened until the foam is fully compressed.

outline of shape stuck on top

foam glued to underside of plywood

Photo 2 Screwing the two pieces of plywood together so that the foam is tightly sandwiched between them.

Photo 3 Fixing the stamp outline to the top of the plywood and sponge sandwich.

8 Cut out the shape. Do not cut in from the edge but drill a hole somewhere near the outline as seen in Photo 4 and insert the saw blade through it (see Fretting out on page 6). You may need to tease the foam apart with a nail in order to insert blade. Then cut out your stamp.

Photo 4 Cutting out the paintstamp. Start from a hole drilled near to the outline.

9 Undo the sandwich. Stick the foam onto the acrylic backing, or reinforce the foam-to-wood join, if necessary, with the hot-melt glue gun and attach the dowel or scrap-wood handles as shown in Photo 5. Very small stamps, such as the little wedges used to produce the fur effect on the Tumbling cats in Chapter 4, can be attached directly to their handles as shown in Fig 2.2 and Photo 5.

10 You can produce a compound design with multiple stamps. The flower shapes used to decorate the Windmill mouse house in Chapter 10, as shown in Fig 2.3, are a good example. Do not stick the sponge to the ply before you cut the shapes out, but arrange and glue the cut-out stamps onto another piece of ply or acrylic.

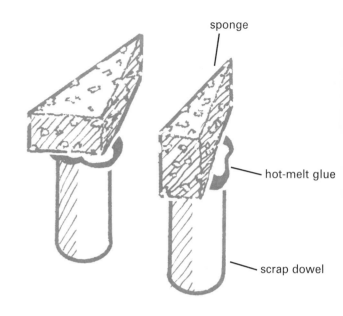

sponge

hot-melt glue

scrap dowel

Fig 2.2 A small paintstamp can be stuck directly to its handle.

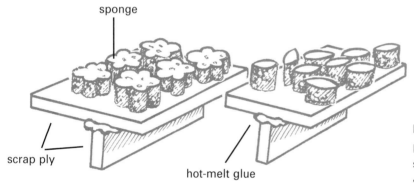

sponge

scrap ply

hot-melt glue

Fig 2.3 Compound paintstamps made by sticking several foam shapes to one piece of ply.

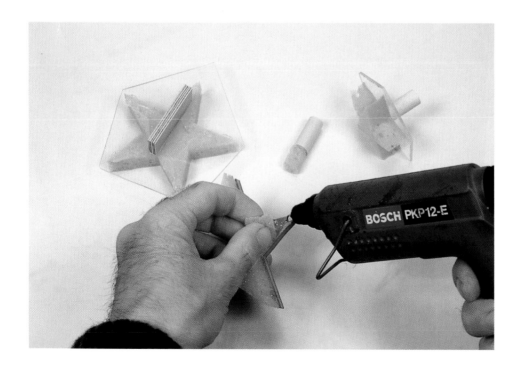

BOSCH PKP12-E

Photo 5 Making sure that the foam is stuck to the plywood with hot-melt glue. Smaller stamps need no backing, just a handle.

NURSERY RHYME MOBILE

Hey diddle, diddle,
The cat and the fiddle,
The cow jumped over the moon,
The little dog laughed to see such fun,
And the dish ran away with the spoon.

Mobiles look very attractive hanging from the ceiling of the nursery room and are visually stimulating for babies and the very young. The zany characters in this nursery rhyme are full of fun and you can recite to the child while you both watch the mobile slowly turning around in rising warm air currents. Do not be put off by the complexity of the finish of the characters: I have designed them carefully so that their features are easy to reproduce.

CUTTING LIST

NURSERY RHYME MOBILE

SUPPORT

Spiral (1)	1.5mm (¹/₁₆in) ply	300 x 300mm (11¹³/₁₆ x 11¹³/₁₆in)

CAT

Cat (1)	1.5mm ply	126 x 92mm (4¹⁵/₁₆ x 3⁵/₈in)
Face (1)	1.5mm ply	35 x 40mm (1³/₈ x 1⁹/₁₆in)
Violin (1)	1.5mm ply	19 x 44mm (³/₄ x 1³/₄in)
Arm (1)	1.5mm ply	14 x 26mm (⁹/₁₆ x 1in)
Bow (1)	1.5mm ply	6 x 65mm (¹/₄ x 2⁹/₁₆in)
Nose (1)	6mm (¹/₄in) dowel	4mm (³/₁₆in) long

DOG

Dog (1)	1.5mm ply	150 x 83mm (5¹⁵/₁₆ x 3¹/₄in)
Nose (2)	1.5mm ply	6mm diameter (¹/₄in diameter)
Arms (2)	1.5mm ply	24 x 50mm (¹⁵/₁₆ x 2in)
Paws (2)	1.5mm ply	30 x 26mm (1³/₁₆ x 1in)

COW

Cow (1)	1.5mm ply	88 x 161mm (3¹/₂ x 6⁵/₁₆in)
Nose (2)	1.5mm ply	23 x 19mm (⁷/₈ x ³/₄in)
Eye and horns (2)	1.5mm ply	18 x 22mm (¹¹/₁₆ x ⁷/₈in)

DISH AND SPOON

Dish and spoon (1)	1.5mm ply	81 x 105mm (3³/₁₆ x 4¹/₈in)
Dish eyes (1)	1.5mm ply	11 x 18mm (⁷/₁₆ x ¹¹/₁₆in)
Spoon eyes (1)	1.5mm ply	7 x 9mm (¹/₄ x ⁹/₃₂in)
Spoon head and dish arm (1)	1.5mm ply	43 x 33mm (1¹¹/₁₆ x 1⁵/₁₆in)
Dish hand (1)	1.5mm ply	14 x 10.5mm (⁹/₁₆ x ⁷/₁₆in)
Dish back (1)	1.5mm ply	42mm diameter (⁹/₁₆in diameter)

MOON

Moon (1)	1.5mm ply	207 x 150mm (8¹/₈ x 5⁷/₈in)

STARS

Stars (9)	1.5mm ply	47mm diameter (1⁷/₈in diameter)

FINISHING

White acrylic primer

Acrylic craft paints (suggested colours: ultramarine blue, white, pink, red, yellow, black, orange,

light brown, dark brown, silver, gold and grey)

Sponge

Old toothbrush and piece of scrap wood

Small paintbrushes

Fine permanent black marker

MISCELLANEOUS

Ready-made hardwood wheel (1)   25mm (1in) diameter

Dark blue embroidery thread

'Invisible' nylon thread

EXTRA MATERIALS AND TOOLS

Scrap cladding or builder's plywood   5mm ($^{11}/_{16}$in)

Water-soluble PVA adhesive

Double-sided tape

Bulldog clip

CONSTRUCTION

1 Mark up the spiral onto the ply. This is easily done by marking out with a pair of compasses the four concentric semi-circles that make up the top circles as shown in Fig 3.1 from the centre (A). Then from centre (B) 15mm ($^5/_8$in) apart from centre (A) draw the bottom four semi-circles and the complete innermost circle and also complete the outermost perimeter to make a perfect spiral. The areas around the cat's and the dish and spoon's suspension holes can be drawn with a plastic circle marker. Cut it out using a 2/0 grade blade (approx. 34 teeth per inch). Drill the 1mm ($^1/_{32}$in) diameter holes for the threads. If you decide to use a relatively soft 5mm ($^3/_{16}$in) cladding or builder's plywood as backing to assist cutting out, then this thin blade will not only manage the task well, but also give a clean edge.

2 Make templates for the moon, stars and the parts for the cat, dog, cow, dish and spoon from Fig 3.2 and cut them out. Mounting the 1.5mm ($^1/_{16}$in) ply onto some scrap cladding or builder's plywood will greatly assist in the cutting out as shown in Photo 1. Drill the 1mm ($^1/_{16}$in) holes for the hanging threads. To make the internal line cuts for the features, first make a 1mm ($^1/_{32}$in) pilot hole for the scrollsaw blade, as shown in Photo 2.

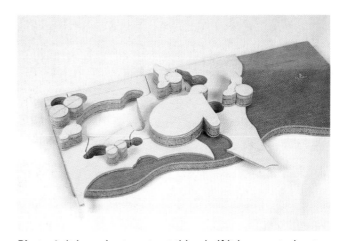

Photo 1 It is easier to cut out thin ply if it is mounted onto some scrap cladding or builder's plywood first.

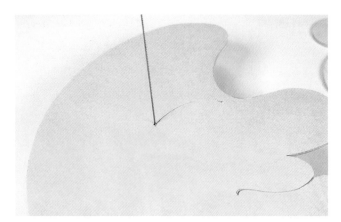

Photo 2 Making the internal cuts for the features.

3 Round off the end of a piece of 6mm (¼in) dowel and then cut it to length for the cat's nose.

4 Drill three 1mm (½2in) holes for the threads to go through at equal intervals around the edge of the hardwood wheel.

5 Cut out all of the parts (see photo 3). You can now partially assemble the dish and spoon, and cat and fiddle, before painting them, along with the dog and cow.

Glue the dish back and spoon head and arm sections onto the back of the dish and spoon. Glue on the dish hand to the front.

Temporarily tape the cat's face and violin onto the body.

Photo 3 The characters, cut out and ready for assembly.

Photo 4 Assembling the cat and the dish and spoon.

Check exactly where the bow will sit and, to enable it to fit between the cat's body and arm, make a notch on the back of the bow where it rests on his hip as it passes behind his hand. Then, using the face and violin as a guide, glue the arm on, as shown in Photo 4. Once the glue is dry, remove the violin and face.

6 Prime all parts with white acrylic primer, allow to dry and then paint the cow, the spoon, the violin and bow, the dog's paw and the base colour of the fur on the cat and dog. For extra effect, sponge gold and silver acrylic paint onto the moon and give the stars extra sparkle by using a toothbrush to fleck them with silver paint as shown in Photo 5. To add texture to the fur on the dog and cat, sponge on the second colour. Give the dish's face a pink blush. Paint the spiral and wheel dark blue.

7 Clean the thread holes out with a 1mm (½2in) drill bit held in a pin chuck. Glue the cat's nose into the hole in the face. Clamp the violin and bow to the rest of the cat with a bulldog clip while the glue is setting on them as shown in Photo 6. Glue the eyes, arms, paws, noses and horns into place on the other figures, including the duplicates of the features on the cow and dog so that they can be seen from the other side.

Photo 5 Using a toothbrush to fleck the stars with silver.

8 Add the eye dots to the cow, dish and spoon using a permanent black liner pen as shown in Photo 6. No varnishing is required.

9 Tie lengths of invisible nylon thread through holes 1, 2, 3 and 4 on the spiral, then tie the thread from hole 1 to one of the holes in the hardwood wheel, making sure that the distance between them is 250mm (9⅞in). Thread the invisible thread from hole 2 through the hole in the cow's eye, and then through the same hole in the wheel, so that the cow will face in the right direction. Tie the other two invisible nylon threads to the other holes in the wheel so the spiral is level when suspended.

10 Tie a large knot into the end of the embroidery thread and pass the thread up through the axle hole of the wheel. Using invisible thread, suspend the moon from the centre of the wheel, attaching it to the knot in the embroidery thread, then tie the dish and spoon to the hole at the bottom of the spiral and the cat to hole 1. Clip the dog – by its tail – into its notch on the spiral and glue the stars to the other nine notches.

Attach the top end of the embroidery thread to a hook in the ceiling (or whatever you have decided to hang it from). Young children, even when they are confined to cot, are naturally curious and can reach a surprisingly long way. Make sure that you suspend the mobile well out of reach.

Photo 6 Adding eye dots to the dish and spoon.

TUMBLING CATS 4

This simple toy will amuse very young children as it rolls first one way then the other for some time before stopping. Starting it off provides the child with practice in their manual co-ordination and the fun of watching the tireless cats in their never-ending game.

CUTTING LIST

DISC

Tumbling cats disc (1)	6mm (¼in) plywood	216mm (8½in) diameter
Faces (4)	6mm (¼in) plywood	52mm (2¹⁄₁₆in) semi circle
Cheeks (4)	1.5mm (¹⁄₁₆in) plywood	37 x 20mm (1½ x ¾in)
Noses (4)	6mm (¼in) dowel	11mm (⁷⁄₁₆in) long
Axle (1)	12mm (½in) dowel	65mm (2⁹⁄₁₆in) long
Hubs (2)	12mm (½in) plywood	25mm (1in) diameter

BASKET

Basket sides (2)	6mm (¼in) plywood	458 x 175mm (18 x 6⅞in)
Brackets (2)	6mm (¼in) plywood	165 x 124mm (6½ x 4⅞in)
Base (1)	6mm (¼in) plywood	369 x 40mm (14½ x 1⁹⁄₁₆in)

OTHER TOOLS AND MATERIALS

Thin card for templates (cereal packets)

Paint brushes

Small sanding block

Oil-based white wood primer

Enamel paints (suggested colours: black, white, red, dark green, light green, orange, yellow and transparent lacquer)

PVA wood glue

Epoxy resin glue

Photo 1 A card template, made from Fig 4.1, can be used to mark up the plywood.

CONSTRUCTION

1 Trace out or photocopy Fig 4.1 and make a card template to assist with marking up as shown in Photo 1.

2 Cut out the tumbling cats disc and make the cut lines for the paws and tails. For the inner outlines of the legs make 1mm (½₂in) pilot holes for inserting the scrollsaw blade as can be seen in Photo 1. Make pilot holes and fret out the faces (see Fretting out on page 6).

3 Cut out the cheeks from 1.5mm (¹⁄₁₆in) plywood. (Note that in Photo 1 I am testing the nose, face and cheeks for fit; do not glue at this stage.)

4 To make each of the four noses, round off the end of a length of 6mm (¼in) dowel and cut it to length. (See Cutting Dowels on page 7.)

5 Join two pieces of plywood for the basket sides together with double-sided tape and cut out around the outline (Fig 4.2), except for the top edge. Separate the two pieces of plywood and cut out the top edges to a 5° bevel. This will reduce resistance for the tumbling cats axle.

Photo 2 Assembling the brackets and base from Fig 4.3 to the basket sides.

TIP

To ensure perfect symmetry make a template of the basket side half section and use it to mark out both ends.

6 Cut out the brackets and base (Fig 4.3) and assemble and glue the basket as shown in Photo 2. Make sure that the highest edge of the bevels on the basket sides is on the inside. Clamp well while the glue is setting as shown in Photo 3. Use a small sanding block to smooth the junction between bevelled edge and the straight surface.

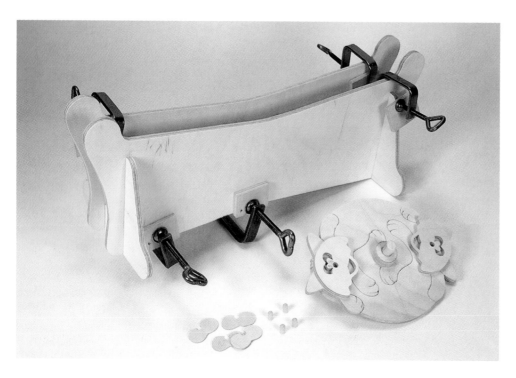

Photo 3 Clamping the basket together while the glue dries.

7 Cut the axle dowel to length and round off the ends.

8 Glue the axle into the fighting cats disc, making sure it is at exactly 90°. Glue the hubs (Fig 4.4) to each side with their bevelled surface facing out from the disc.

9 Glue the faces to the disc as in Photo 1. Do not glue on the cheeks until the painting is complete.

10 Prime all the surfaces that are to be painted. Use at least two coats of enamel paint, sanding them down and wiping thoroughly between coats. The outline cuts of the limbs will help you to produce neat outlines. See Step 9, page 20, for how to produce the fur effect as seen in Photo 4. Apply at least two coats of oil-based varnish to give a good, hard-wearing finish. When the varnish is completely dry, rub the bevelled edge on the top of the basket sides, as well as the rolling surfaces of the axle, with abrasive paper to provide traction for the disc.

11 Finally glue the noses into the holes in the faces and use epoxy resin to glue on the cheeks.

Photo 4 The completed, painted cats.

THE FISHERMAN'S TALE

5

This rattling and clanking automaton amuses adults as much as it does children. When you pull down the lifebelt and haul up the fish, the fisherman rocks to and fro in his boat, and try as he might to haul in his catch it just gets further away. This project is an ideal showpiece for aunts, uncles or grandparents, who can amuse young visitors with the fisherman's antics.

CUTTING LIST

MAIN FRAME

Back (1)	6mm (¼in) plywood	360 x 204mm (14³⁄₁₆ x 8in)
Cloud and front (1)	6mm (¼in) plywood	165 x 204mm (6½ x 8in)
Wave front (1)	6mm (¼in) plywood	88 x 204mm (3½ x 8in)
Wave (1)	6mm (¼in) plywood	75 x 220mm (2¹⁵⁄₁₆ x 8⅝in)
Sides (2)	6mm (¼in) plywood	110 x 70mm (4⁵⁄₁₆ x 2¾in)
Frame dowels (2)	6mm (¼in) dowel	108mm (4¼in) long
Plastic washers (2)	20mm (²⁵⁄₃₂in) with 6mm (¼in) holes.	

MECHANISM

Drive axle (1)	12mm (½in) dowel	85mm (3⅜in) long
Spigot disc (1)	6mm (¼in) plywood	40mm (1⁹⁄₁₆in) diameter
Cam (1)	6mm (¼in) plywood	54mm (2⅛in) x 40mm (1⁹⁄₁₆)
Spigot (1)	3mm (⅛in) dowel	17mm (¹¹⁄₁₆in) long
Lifebelt (1)	6mm (¼in) plywood	60mm (2⅜in) diameter
Discs (3)	6mm (¼in) plywood	40mm (1⁹⁄₁₆in) diameter
Plastic washers (3)	20mm (²⁵⁄₃₂in) with 12mm (½in) holes.	

BOAT

Boat with fisherman (1)	6mm (¼in) plywood	167mm (6⁹⁄₁₆) x 162mm (6³⁄₈in)
Boat peg (1)	6mm (¼in) dowel	20mm (¹³⁄₁₆in) long
Boat retainer (1)	6mm (¼in) plywood	12mm (½in) x 32mm (¼in)
Hull side (1)	2mm (³⁄₃₂in) balsa	124 x 53mm (4⅞ x 2³⁄₃₂in)
Fishing rod (1)	3mm (⅛in) dowel	21mm (¹³⁄₁₆in) long
Stiff thread for fishing line.		
Plastic washers (3)	20mm (²⁵⁄₃₂in) with 6mm (¼in) hole.	

FISH

Sides (2)	6mm (¼in) plywood	153 x 71mm (6 x 2¾in)
Eyes (2)	12mm (½in) dowel	12mm (½in) long
Inner section (1)	12mm (½in) plywood	168 x 94mm (6⅝ x 3¹¹/₁₆in)
Steel nuts		
Braided nylon cord	2mm (³/₃₂in) approx.	

MISCELLANEOUS

White acrylic primer

Acrylic paints (suggested colours: cobalt blue, duck egg blue, white, red, sienna, pink, yellow, green, black and grey)

Matt acrylic varnish

PVA wood glue

Wax candle (for lubricating moving parts)

FIXING

Round-headed screw (1)	No 8 x 38mm (1½in)
Wallplug or cavity wall fixing for a No 8 screw (1)	

CONSTRUCTION

1 Cut out all the parts.

2 Join back and cloud front (Fig 5.1) together with double-sided tape and drill the central 12mm (½in) hole through both of them. Attach the wave front (Fig 5.2) with more double-sided tape. Turn the assembly over so that the wave front is on your work surface, and drill the two 6mm (¼in) holes through the back and cloud front, but stopping short of piercing the wave front as shown in Photo 1. Separate and mark the parts so that you can reassemble them the same way round later. Fret out the boat peg hole in the cloud front and the wall mounting screw hole in the back as shown in Photo 2 (see Fretting out on page 6). The dimensions for the wall mounting hole are suitable for a No 8 size screw.

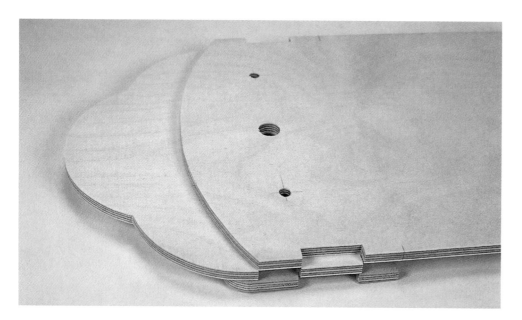

Photo 1 The back, cloud and wave, face down on the work surface with the 12mm (½in) and 6mm (¼in) diameter holes.

Photo 2 Gluing the spigot disc to the cam, with the hole opposite the peak of the cam.

3 Drill out the 12mm (½in) holes in the cam and discs before cutting out. Drill out the 3mm (⅛in) hole in the spigot disc. Glue the spigot disc (Fig 5.4) to the cam (Fig 5.4) with the hole opposite the peak of the cam as can be seen in Photo 2. Round off the edges of the cam before gluing in the spigot.

4 Assemble the main frame by gluing and clamping the back, cloud front, wave front and sides (Fig 5.2) together as shown in Photo 3. Insert the drive shaft and frame dowels temporarily to keep the frame aligned while the glue is setting.

5 Fret out the interior of the boat and fisherman (Fig 5.5). Counterbore a 6mm (¼in) hole in from the back for the dowel boat peg and a 3mm (⅛in) hole in from the front for the fishing rod (Fig 5.5). Round off the exterior edges and the outer surface of the balsa boat hull so that they form a smooth curve (Fig 5.5, Photo 4) before gluing the latter into place. Glue the boat peg into its hole.

6 To make each fish eye (Fig 5.6) round off the end of a piece of 12mm (½in) dowel then cut it to length. Drill 12mm (½in) holes in the fish sides for the eyes, and a 3mm (⅛in) hole in its mouth (in the inner section) for the cord.

7 Round off the edges of the fish sides (Fig 5.6) before gluing one into position on the fish inner section (Fig 5.6). Fix the nuts inside the fish with epoxy resin. Make a loop of braided nylon cord, knot the ends together and thread it through the fish's mouth as shown in Photo 5, Add the other side of the fish. An overall weight of 4¾oz (135 grammes) gives the ideal rate of descent.

Photo 4 The fretted out boat, with rounded exterior edges, and boat peg ready to be glued into position.

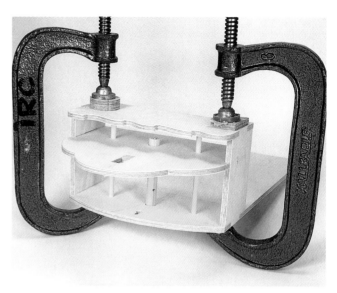

Photo 3 The back, cloud front, wave front and sides glued and clamped.

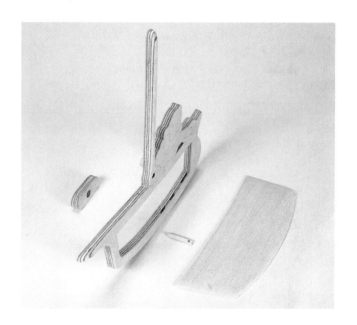

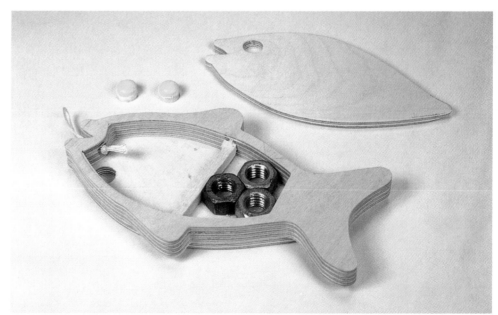

Photo 5 The inside of the fish, showing the nuts that give it the ideal weight.

8 Fret out the central hole of the lifebelt (Fig 5.6).

9 Paint everything, except the moving components, with acrylic primer and paints. Use a piece of sponge to make a foaming sea effect shown in Photo 6. Glue the fish eyes into their holes, and then cover all the painted areas with a matt acrylic varnish if desired.

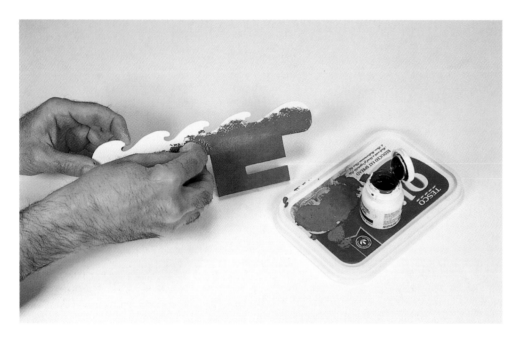

Photo 6 Using a sponge to create the foaming sea effect.

10 Fit the cam, disc assembly, discs and the drive axle into the frame as shown in Photo 7, using the three 12mm (½in) washers to reduce friction against the frame. Glue the discs into place on the axle. I suggest that you use epoxy resin for the cam to ensure a strong fit. Do not allow the axle to protrude from the back or later it will rub on the wall behind. Rubbing a thin layer of candle wax on the moving parts will help to ensure smooth running.

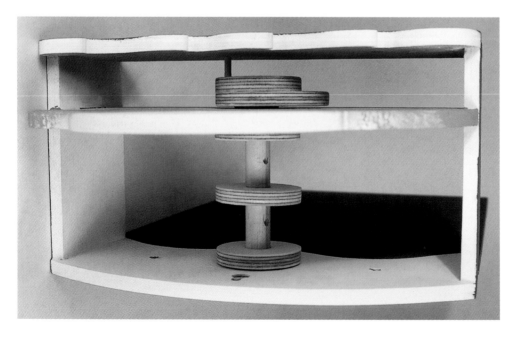

Photo 7 The cam-and-spigot disc assembly, discs and drive axle in the frame.

11 Place the wave into position. Secure it by pushing the frame dowels through from the back as shown in Photo 8, securing them with glue, remembering to slip the 6mm (¼in) washers just in front of the wave.

12 Glue the fishing rod, with a little stiff thread for the line added, to the boat. Place a 6mm (¼in) washer on the peg at the back of the boat before inserting it through the boat peg hole in the cloud front. Glue the boat retainer horizontally onto the boat peg using the counterbored hole in it to locate it on the peg.

13 Thread cord through the hole at the rear of the axle and wind it up before attaching the lifebelt (Fig 5.6). Attach one end of another cord to the front of the axle and attach the fish to the other end. Note that the length of the cord will depend on how high the automaton is mounted on the wall and how far down you want to pull the lifebelt. The longer the thread, the longer the action will work. Fix the wall mounting screw securely, using a wallplug, or cavity fixing if you have plasterboard walls, and hang the completed automaton on it.

Photo 8 The wave, secured by frame dowels coming through from the back.

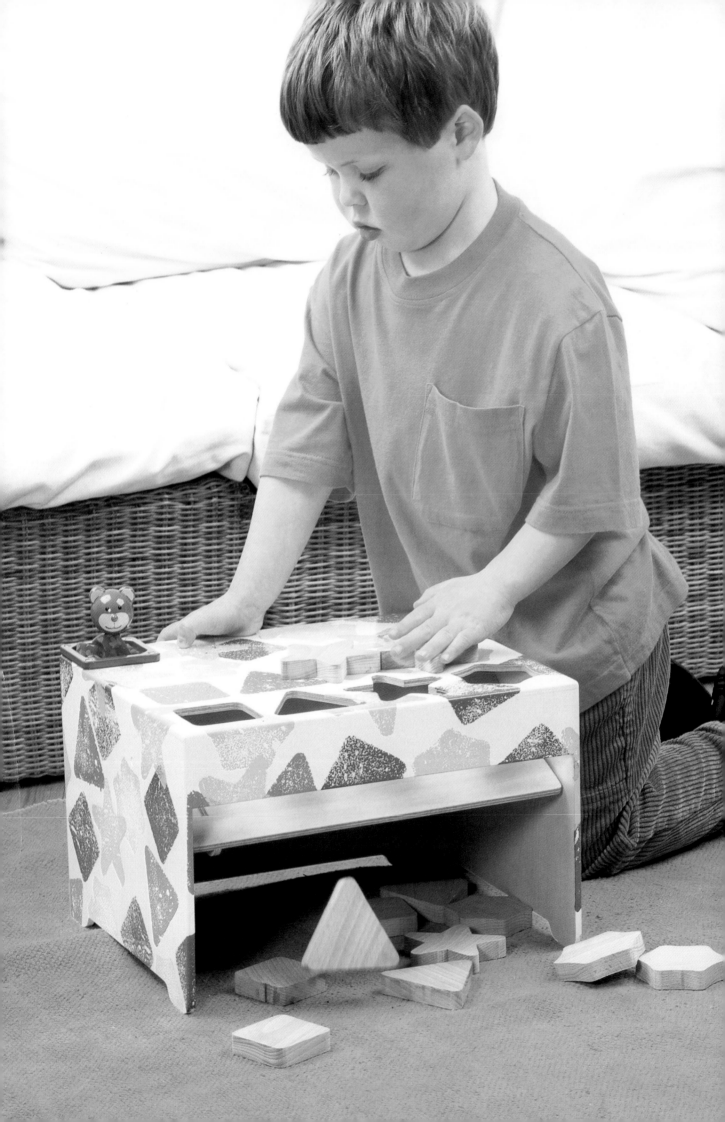

SHAPE
SORTER

6

For the toddler, sorting shapes introduces visual and spatial comparisons. In this challenging version of the toy the shapes must be aligned correctly before they will fall through the holes. The shapes are big enough for the child to manoeuvre with both hands and, with a little help, he or she will soon acquire this skill. As a reward for getting it right, a little bear pops up! The blank areas of the box's surface provide plenty of room for decorating with paintstamps, while the beech shapes make a contrast to the brightly coloured box and have the warm, solid feel that only wood can provide.

CUTTING LIST

BOX

Sides (2)	6mm (¼in) plywood	305 x 230mm (12 x 9¹⁄₁₆in)
Back (1)	6mm (¼in) plywood	355 x 230mm (14 x 9¹⁄₁₆in)
Top (1)	6mm (¼in) plywood	355 x 305mm (14 x 12in)
Front (1)	6mm (¼in) plywood	355 x 61mm (14 x 2³⁄₈in)
Rest bar (1)	6mm (¼in) plywood	355x 46mm (14 x 1¹³⁄₁₆in)
Ramp (1)	6mm (¼in) plywood	355 x 70mm (14 x 2¾in)
Flap (1)	6mm (¼in) plywood	355 x 117mm (14 x 4⅝in)
Flap lever (1)	6mm (¼in) plywood	337 x 168mm (13¼ x 6⅝in)
Flap arm (1)	6mm (¼in) plywood	245 x 46mm (9⅝ x 1¹³⁄₁₆in)
Fillet (1)	6mm (¼in) plywood	36 x 18mm (1³⁄₈ x ¹¹⁄₁₆in)
Hole rim (1)	6mm (¼in) plywood	70 x 70mm (2¾ x 2¾in)

Steel nuts or weights (2) adding up to 43 grammes (1½ oz)

BEAR

Ears (2)	6mm (¼in) plywood	16mm (⅝in) diameter
Nose (1)	6mm (¼in) dowel	10mm (⁷⁄₁₆in) long
Figure (1)	lightweight silk or polyester 200sq cm (30sq in)	
		155 x 120mm (6⅛ x 4¾in)
Rod (1)	12mm (½in) dowel	95mm (3¾in) long
Head (1)	Hardwood ball	37mm (1⁷⁄₁₆in) diameter

SHAPES

Squares (3)	16mm (⅝in) beech	60 x 60mm (2³⁄₈ x 2³⁄₈in)
Triangles (3)	16mm (⅝in) beech	90 x 74mm (3½ x 2⅞in)
Pentagrams (3)	16mm (⅝in) beech	116mm (4⁹⁄₁₆in) diameter
Hexagons (3)	16mm (⅝in) beech	84mm (3⁵⁄₁₆in) diameter

MISCELLANEOUS

Card for templates

3mm (⅛in) dowel (for reinforcing joints)   450mm (17¾in)

Plastic washers (2)   32mm (1¼in) diameter with 6mm (¼in) diameter hole.

2mm (³⁄₃₂in) braided nylon cord   150mm (5⅞in)

Screws (4)   No 4 countersunk brass   12mm (½in)

Paint (oil-based primer and coloured enamels for exterior surfaces, suggested colours: white, pink,

blue, red, yellow and, for the bear, brown, buff and black)

Permanent ink liner pen

Satin acrylic varnish (for interior surfaces)

PAINTSTAMPS

Scrap plywood 5mm (³⁄₁₆in)

Foam plastic

Offcuts of dowel or wood

CONSTRUCTION

1 Cut all the parts out, remembering to cut the 30° bevel on the top edge of the flap lever (note that the bevel should be facing you when you view the flap lever as it is shown in Fig 6.1). Cut out all the internal slots (see Fretting out on page 6).

2 Trim the pivots on the flap carefully with a knife (Fig 6.1) down to 6mm (¼in) in diameter. Test their operation in a 7mm (⁹⁄₃₂in) hole drilled in a piece of scrap as shown in Photo 1.

3 Drill 3mm (⅛in) holes in the flap lever and flap arm where indicated (Fig 6.1).

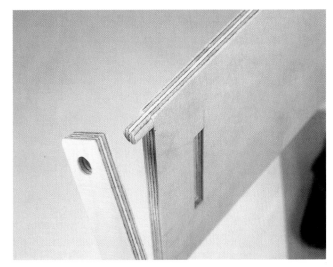

Photo 1 Test that the pivots on the flap are working properly by inserting them into 7mm (⁹⁄₃₂in) holes drilled into scrap wood.

4 Glue together the flap, flap lever, flap arm and fillet (Fig 6.1). The fillet is positioned about 6mm (¼in) in from the edge of the assembly as shown in Fig 6.1. Use masking tape and clamps to hold these parts together while the glue sets, as shown in Photo 2.

5 Round off the middle of the flap assembly where the parts meet and rub the join smooth. Now you can varnish this assembly.

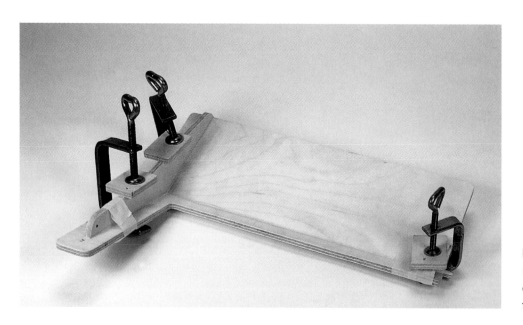

Photo 2 The flap, flap lever, flap arm and fillet clamped together while the glue sets.

6 Stick the steel nuts to the flap lever with epoxy resin as shown in Photo 3, positioned as shown on Fig 6.1.

7 Drill a 3mm (⅛in) hole into the rod for the bear (Fig 6.2) and stick the cord into it with epoxy resin. (Note that the 12mm (½in) dowel I used for the rod was a little narrower than usual due to stock variation, so I had to glue a piece of paper around it to make a tight fit into the head).

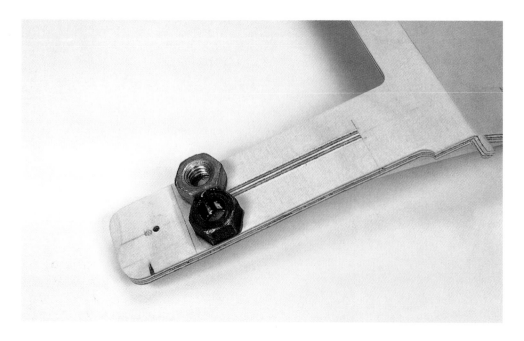

Photo 3 The steel nuts stuck to the flap lever.

8 To make the bear's head (Fig 6.2), drill three 6mm (¼in) holes and one 12mm (½in) hole into the 37mm (1⁷⁄₁₆in) diameter hardwood ball (see page 6). For the nose, round off a piece of 6mm (¼in) dowel and cut it to length. Round off the peg section of each ear (Fig 6.2). Glue on the ears and smooth off the edges.

9 Countersink the 3mm (⅛in) holes in the hole rim (Fig 6.2) and smooth off its top edges. Put the piece of material for the bear right sides together, and stitch the edges of the figure together as indicated in Fig 6.2, remembering to leave a gap for the rod to pass through. Turn it right side out. All the parts for the bear are shown in Photo 4.

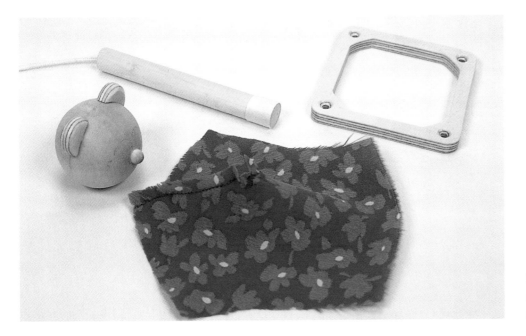

Photo 4 The parts that make up the bear for the shape sorter.

10 Drill a 13mm (¹⁷⁄₃₂in) hole in the rest bar for the rod (Fig 6.3) and enlarge it to the shape shown with abrasive paper wrapped around a 12mm (½in) dowel.

11 Make card templates of the sorter shapes (Fig 6.4) making sure they are symmetrical. Use them to mark up the holes in the top of the sorter (Fig 6.5) and

Photo 5 Testing that the beechwood shapes fit snugly into the holes cut into the top.

also the beechwood shapes as shown in Photo 5. On the top, cut to the outside of the lines. When cutting the beechwood shapes, cut inside the lines. This will ensure that the former should fit into the latter smoothly.

12 Take the sides, front (Fig 6.5), back, rest bar, ramp (Fig. 6.3) and flap assembly seen in Photo 6, and dry assemble these with the plastic washers (you will need to trim these to fit) in place round the pivots, as shown in Photo 7. Check the top for fit and make sure that the flap swings freely. Also check that the rod, with the bear's head temporarily in place, slides up and down in the hole in the

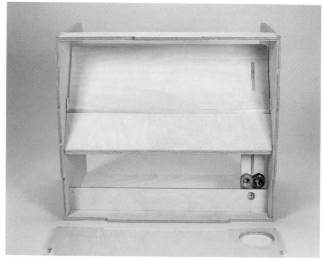

Photo 7 A dry assembly of the parts shown in Photo 6, to make sure that the top fits and the flap swings.

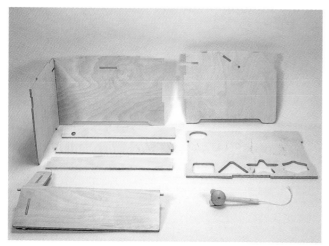

Photo 6 The sides, front, back, rest bar, ramp and flap assembly ready to be put together.

rest bar. The flap assembly should be counterbalanced so that the bear's head is flush with the top and will pop up as soon as any weight is placed on the flap. Carefully mark the parts with a pencil to ensure that you reassemble the pieces in the correct order.

Photo 8 The main assembly complete, with front and back corners reinforced with dowels.

13 Rub candle wax on the pivots and washers. Glue together everything except the top and bear. Hold top in place for now with masking tape. Reinforce the front and back corners with 12mm (½in) long 3mm (⅛in) dowels as can be seen in Photo 8 (see Reinforcing joints on page 9).

14 When the glue is set, remove the top and varnish the interior, avoiding areas around the pivot, the hole for the rod and where the top will be glued on. Also varnish the underside of the top, again avoiding the areas to be glued. When the varnish is completely dry, glue the top into place and reinforce the joints with 3mm (⅛in) dowels.

15 Round off the edges of the top to a radius of about 3mm (⅛in) with a balsa plane and smooth them off with a sanding block as shown in Photo 9.

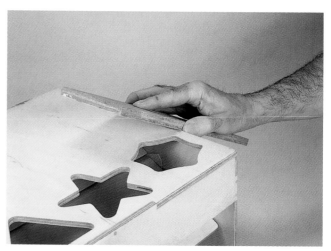

Photo 9 Rounding and smoothing off the edges makes them more comfortable to lean against and safer for toddlers who are still finding their feet.

16 Paint the bear, hole rim and the box exterior with oil-based enamels. Use the shape templates to make paintstamps (see Chapter 2) for the box decoration as seen in Photo 10. The beechwood shapes have a pleasant feel to them if finished with a satin acrylic varnish. Beech is a hardwood traditionally used for toys and can be left unfinished. However, a couple of coats of satin acrylic varnish will help to keep it clean and yet still retain a natural appearance and finish. Good quality modern enamels sold for finishing toys are very durable and do not normally need overcoating with lacquer. It can be done, but it does slightly reduce the brilliance of the colours.

17 Place the rod in the hole in the rest bar and pass its cord through the 3mm (⅛in) holes in the flap lever and flap arm and tie it in place.

18 Holding the hole rim in place with masking tape as a guide, drill pilot holes into the top for the screws.

19 Gather up the edges of the figure and stick it to the underneath edge of the hole rim with double-sided tape as shown in Photo 11, making absolutely sure that the seam is the right way round. Pass the rod up through the figure and screw the assembly onto the top. Glue the figure to the rod, leaving enough room for the head. Finally glue on the head.

Photo 10 The paintstamps for decorating the sorter.

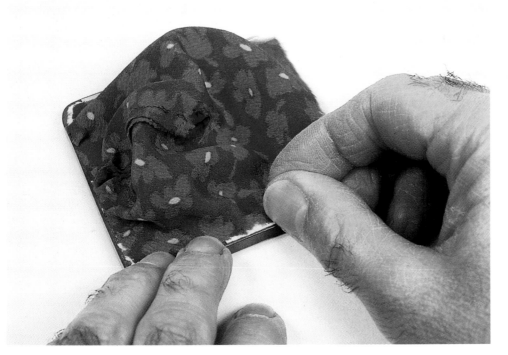

Photo 11 Gathering up the edges of the bear's 'cloth body' and sticking them to the hole rim with double-sided tape.

MOUNTAIN PASSENGER LIFT

7

This crank-operated overhead passenger railway transports its passengers from one end to the other in two cars which travel in opposite directions. The rounded feet enable it to operate at almost any angle so it can be set up in all sorts of interesting situations. Other loads can be hooked or tied onto the holes in the car seats making it useful for transporting all sorts of cargo.

CUTTING LIST

FRAME AND TRACK

Top (1)	6mm (¼in) plywood	1220 x 100mm (48 x 3¹⁵/₁₆in)
Bottom rail (1)	6mm (¼in) plywood	1220 x 100mm (48 x 3¹⁵/₁₆in)
Centre divider (1)	6mm (¼in) plywood	1014 x 40mm (39¹⁵/₁₆ x 1¹⁹/₃₂in)
Pillars (2)	6mm (¼in) plywood	297 x 203mm (11¹¹/₁₆ x 8in)
Pillar feet (2)	22mm (⅞in) dowel	203mm (8in) long
Fillets (4)	6mm (¼in) plywood	64 x 71mm (2⁹/₁₆ x 2¹³/₃₂in)
Track supports (6)	6mm (¼in) plywood	60 x 36mm (2⅜in x 1⁷/₁₆in)

PULLEY SYSTEM

Pulley rims (2)	6mm (¼in) plywood	80mm (3⅛in) diameter with a 7mm (⁹/₃₂in) diameter hole.
Hexagonal pulley interior (1)	12mm (¾in) plywood	62mm (2½in) diameter
Hexagonal pulley shaft (1)	6mm (¼in) dowel	52mm (2in) long
Pulley rims (2)	6mm(¼in) plywood	80mm (3⅛in) diameter with a 6mm (¼in) diameter hole.
Pulley interior (1)	12mm (½) plywood	60mm (2⅜in) diameter
Pulley shaft (1)	6mm (¼in) dowel	40mm (1¹⁹/₃₂in) long
Crank (1)	12mm (½in) plywood	70 x 85mm (2¾ x 3¹¹/₃₂in)
Crank handle (1)	6mm (¼in) dowel	18mm (¾in) long
Crank handle knob (1)	hardwood ball 19mm (¾in)	
Plastic washers (5)	20mm (¹³/₁₆in diameter with a 6mm (¼in) diameter hole.	
2mm (³/₃₂in) braided nylon braided cord		3.048m (10ft)

CARS

Car arms (2)	6mm (¼in) plywood	133 x 120mm (5¼ x 4¹¹/₁₆in)
Car seats (2)	6mm (¼in) plywood	120 x 43mm (4¹¹/₁₆ x 1¹¹/₁₆in)
Car bogies (2)	6mm (¼in) plywood	103 x 100mm (4¹/₁₆ x 3¹⁵/₁₆)
Car pivot caps (2)	6mm (¼in) plywood	25mm (1in) diameter
Car pivots (2)	6mm (¼in) dowel	30mm (¼in) long
Bogie wheel axles (4)	3mm (⅛in) dowel	27mm (1¹/₁₆in) long
Wheels (8)	hardwood	25mm (1in) diameter
Plastic washers (8)	20mm (¹³/₁₆in) diameter with a 3.5mm (⅛in) diameter hole.	
Pivot spacers (2)	12mm (½in) plywood	25mm (1in) diameter

PEOPLE

Bodies (6)	18mm (¾in plywood)	43 x 27mm (1¹¹/₁₆ x 1¹/₁₆in)

Arms (12)	6mm (¼in) plywood	27 x 19mm (1¹⁄₁₆ x ¾in)
Neck joints (6)	6mm (¼in) dowel	18mm (¾in)
Heads (6)	hardwood balls	25mm (1in) diameter

MISCELLANEOUS

| Joint reinforcers (20) | 3mm (⅛in) dowel | 12mm (½in) long |

Oil-based primer, lacquer and coloured enamels (suggested colours: blue, orange, silver, yellow, brown, pink, black and green. Use matt flesh for the heads of the passengers, and give them a coat of lacquer after you have drawn on the faces with a permanent liner pen)

CONSTRUCTION

1 Cut out all the components, but see Step 2 below for some of the details on cutting out the top and bottom rail. Counterbore the 6mm (¼in) holes in the pivot caps and drill the holes in the pivot spacers before you cut them out. To make the long cuts (Fig 7.1) you will need to use a blade twisted through 90° (see Cutting long pieces of wood, page 7).

2 Join the top and bottom rail strips together with double-sided tape and fret out the centre slots. Cut out the notches on the ends and also drill the pulley holes. Separate the two strips and carefully mark them with a pencil for later reassembly. Fret out the other slots from the bottom rail and the notches in the sides as seen in Photo 1.

3 Check that the centre divider (Fig 7.1 and Photo 1) fits the top and bottom rail and mark all three with a pencil for reassembly.

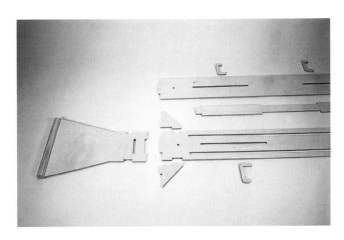

Photo 1 The components ready for assembly.

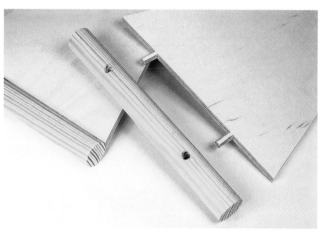

Photo 2 One pillar and pillar foot assembled, another ready for assembly – studs trimmed to 6mm (¼in) diameter.

Photo 3 The completed pulley wheels and the dowel crank handle ready for fitting.

4 Trim the studs at the base of the pillars (Fig 7.2) with a knife to a 6mm (¼in) diameter section. Glue the two pillar feet (Fig 7.2) onto the pillars as shown in Photo 2.

5 Glue together the pulley wheel (Fig 7.3) components as shown in Photo 3. Note the round pulley has a 7mm (⁹⁄₃₂in) diameter hole and the hexagonal pulley has a 6mm (¼in) one. Counterbore the two 6mm (¼in) holes into the crank (Fig 7.4), remembering that they enter from opposite sides. Check that the hexagonal pulley shaft fits into the central hole on the crank but do not glue it. Drill a hole in to the 19mm (¾in) wooden ball (see Drilling and cutting wooden balls, page 6). Glue the dowel crank handle into this hole (Photo 3) and into the second hole on the crank.

6 Glue the centre divider onto the bottom rail and make sure it is square. Clamp them together firmly until the glue is set (Photo 4). Reinforce the joints with 3mm (⅛in) dowels through the bottom rail and into the centre divider (see Reinforcing joints, page 9). Repeat the process with the top making sure that the pulley holes match. Glue on the pillars and the fillets (Fig 7.5) and reinforce these joints with 3mm (⅛in) dowels (Photo 5).

7 Glue the car seats, pivot spacers and car pivots (Fig 7.6) to the car arms (Photo 6).

8 Glue one 25mm (1in) wheel to one end of each of the four 3mm (⅛in) axles (Photo 6, top right).

Photo 4 The centre divider clamped to the bottom rail while the glue sets.

Photo 5 The pillars and fillets in position and the joints reinforced with 3mm (⅛in) dowels.

9 Make the plastic washers (see page 8).

10 Glue the arms and bodies (Fig 7.7) together. You can sit the people in the holes in the seats to get the arms level. When the glue is set, trim the tops of the arms at the shoulders with a Gent's saw and finish off with a sanding block. Drill 6mm (¼in) holes between the shoulders and into the 25mm (1in) wooden balls (see page 6). Glue the 6mm (¼in) neck joints into them.

11 Carefully rub candle wax onto all the moving parts, but avoid areas that are to be glued. Paint the crank, track supports, cars, car pivot caps, car bogies and people with oil-based enamels. Then varnish the areas that are not waxed and will not be glued.

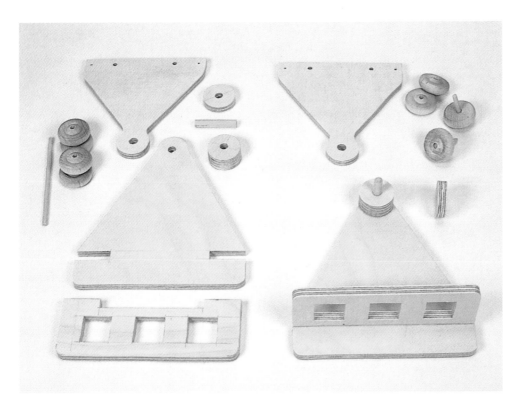

Photo 6 The components for the car seats ready for assembly.

12 Attach a washer with a 6mm (¼in) hole to each side of the pulley wheel with the round inner section using double-sided tape. Place the pulley wheel in position at the end of the track with the 6mm (¼in) hole and insert the 6mm (¼in) pulley shaft. Check whether the pulley wheel rotates freely: if necessary, take it out sand down the plastic washers a little. Glue the pulley shaft to the top and the bottom rail only.

13 Glue the hexagonal pulley shaft into the crank and place another washer on it. Tape a washer each side of the hexagonal pulley wheel as you did for the round one. Insert the pulley wheel between the top and the bottom rail, insert the pulley shaft into the 7mm (%₃₂in) hole until the crank is in position, and check that it runs freely. If not, sand the washers down a little. Place some glue in to the pulley's hole before reinserting it and then feed through the pulley shaft until the crank is in position. Do not glue the shaft to the top or bottom rail.

14 Thread a small-holed washer over each of the wheel axles. Insert the car bogies through the slot in the bottom rail (one either side of the centre rail) and push the wheel axles through the 3.5mm (⅛in) diameter holes from behind (Photo 7). To aid access, the track can be moved. Add rest of the washers and glue on the outer wheels.

15 Glue three track supports (Fig 7.8) onto each side with epoxy resin. One goes exactly in the middle and the others 305mm (12in) in from each end.

16 Insert the car pivots through the holes in the car bogies. Glue the car pivot caps onto the pivots, making sure that you do not get any glue on the bogies, or the cars will not swing.

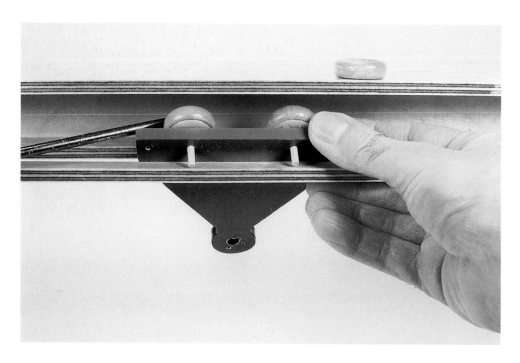

Photo 7 Fixing a car bogie to the rail.

17 Fasten the car bogies in the centre of the track. Pass the end of a piece of 2mm (³⁄₃₂in) nylon cord through a hole in the car bogey and make a knot. Pass it around the circular section pulley and tie it onto the car bogie on the other side by passing it through the 2mm (³⁄₃₂in) hole so the knot is again at the back. Fit another cord to the other 2mm (³⁄₃₂in) hole in the first car bogie and pass it twice around the hexagonal pulley before fastening it with moderate tension to the other bogey via its remaining 2mm (³⁄₃₂in) hole. Check that everything runs smoothly and that cars both travel as far as they can in each direction (Photo 8).

Photo 8 Checking that the cars move freely along the tracks.

TOWALONG LADYBIRD

8

This pullalong toy provides lots of fun and action for young children. The busy ladybird spins her wings and makes an insect rattling sound as she goes along. It has been designed so that if anything (such as small fingers) does get in the way of the rotating wings they will stop.

CUTTING LIST

BODY

Body section (2)	19mm (¾in) pine	302 x 158mm (11⅞ x 6¼in)
Body sides (2)	6mm (¼in) plywood	302 x 158mm (11⅞ x 6¼in)
Eyes (2)	one hardwood ball	37mm (1⁷⁄₁₆in) diameter
Antennae ends (2)	hardwood balls	25mm (1in) diameter
Antennae (2)	Plastic-covered curtain wire	105mm (4⅛in)
Nose cord wedge (1)	3mm (⅛in) dowel	12mm (½in)
Braided nylon cord	2mm (³⁄₃₂in) approx.	1.5m (59in)

MECHANISM

Drive wheel section (1)	19mm (¾in) pine	140mm (5½in) diameter
Drive wheel sides (2)	6mm (¼in) plywood	140mm (5½in) diameter
Drive wheel spacers (2)	1.5mm (¹⁄₁₆in) plywood	50mm (2in) diameter
Drive wheel axle (1)	6mm (¼in) dowel	51mm (2in) long
Wooden beads (22)		14mm (⁹⁄₁₆in) diameter
Plastic washers (2)		30mm (1³⁄₁₆in) diameter with 6mm (¼in) holes

WINGS

Wings (2)	6mm (¼in) plywood	88 x 100mm (3¹⁵⁄₃₂ x 3¹⁵⁄₁₆in)
Wing hubs (2)	6mm (¼in) plywood	54mm (2⅛in) diameter
Wing axle (1)	6mm (¼in) dowel	178mm (7in)
Wing axle covers (4)	1.5mm (¹⁄₁₆in) plywood	52 x 19mm (2¹⁄₁₆ x ¾in)
Rubber tap washer (1)		18mm (¾in) diameter
Plastic washers (2)		30mm (1³⁄₁₆in) diameter with 6mm (¼in) holes

LEGS

Leg sections (6)	19mm (¾in) pine	34mm (1¹¹⁄₃₂in) diameter
Leg sections (6)	19mm (¾in) pine	26mm (1in) diameter
Leg sections (6)	19mm (¾in) pine	20mm (²⁵⁄₃₂in) diameter
Leg dowels/wheel axles (3)	6mm (¼in) dowel	208mm (8³⁄₁₆in) long
Wheels (6)	16mm (⅝in) beech	30mm (1³⁄₁₆in) diameter
Wheel hub caps (6)	6mm (¼in) plywood	20mm (²⁵⁄₃₂in) diameter

MISCELLANEOUS

Handle (1)	hardwood ball	37mm (1⁷⁄₁₆in) diameter
Brass fret pins	12mm (½in)	
Oil-based primer		
Gloss enamels (suggested colours: red, white, black, metallic blue and silver)		
Lacquer		
Candle		

CONSTRUCTION

1 Glue and clamp together the two pieces of 19mm (¾in) thick pine to make the 38mm (1½in) thick body section (Fig 8.1). Laminating two pieces of pine in this way gives a stronger and more stable softwood section.

2 Line up the body template (Fig 8.1) with its base along the bottom edge of the laminated wood. Mark up the cutting lines. Cut out only the cavity for the drive wheel (as has already been done in Photo 1).

3 Sandwich the pine section between the two pieces of 6mm (¼in) plywood for the body sides as follows. Line up the smooth, prepared edge of one of the sheets of plywood along the bottom edge of the pine stock and glue it in place (Photo 1). Mark up the outline and axle hole positions onto the second sheet of plywood (also shown in Photo 1) and glue it on. To make sure that the pieces do not slip while you are gluing and clamping, tap a few brass fret pins into the waste area from either side. Allow the glue to dry.

4 Cut out around the body exterior line (Photo 2). As the assembly has an overall width of 50mm (2in) you will need a coarse blade. Make test cuts in the waste area to choose the best blade for the job.

5 Drill the 6mm (¼in) holes through the body for the leg axles and drive wheel axle. Drill a hole through one of the centres shown for the wing axle hole on Fig 8.1 and then enlarge it with a file or abrasive paper wrapped around a 4mm (¾in) dowel to the shape shown.

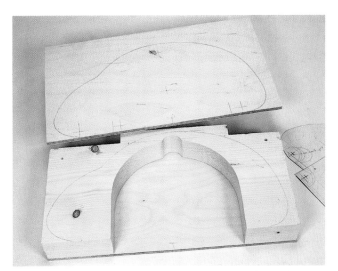

Photo 1 The pine and plywood that make up the main body of the ladybird. The drive wheel cavity already cut.

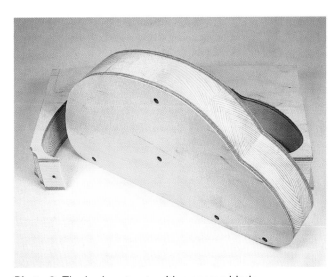

Photo 2 The body cut out, with a coarse blade.

6 Mark the positions for the eyes. Cut a 37mm (1⁷⁄₁₆in) hardwood ball in half (see Drilling and cutting wooden balls, page 6) to make the eyes and glue one half on each side of the head (Photo 3).

7 Drill the 5mm (⁷⁄₃₂in) holes for the antennae into the head at an angle of 45 degrees (Photo 3). These should be 20mm (¾in) deep. Drill 5mm (⁷⁄₃₂in) holes into the 25mm (1in) wooden balls for the antennae (see Drilling and cutting wooden balls, page 6).

8 Drill the 3mm (⅛in) hole in the nose for the pull cord and drill the 8mm (⁵⁄₁₆in) and 3mm (⅛in) holes in to a 37mm (1⁷⁄₁₆in) hardwood ball to make the handle (Fig 8.3).

9 Mark up and drill the axle holes for the leg sections in the pine (Fig 8.2) before cutting the circles out. Glue the 6mm (¼in) leg dowels through the holes in the body (make sure that they are positioned symmetrically) and then glue on the leg sections (Fig 8.2) as shown in Photo 4.

10 Mark up the 98mm (3⅞in) drive wheel section interior circle onto one of the pieces of 6mm (¼in plywood) for the drive wheel sides (see Fig 8.2). Drill out the 6mm (¼in) hole in the centre. Mark up the same 98mm (3⅞in) drive wheel interior circle onto the 19mm (¾in) pine and cut it out. Glue the pine onto the plywood as shown in Photo 5, aligning its inner edge with the circle marked on the plywood. Use fret pins in the waste areas to secure the parts while clamping and gluing.

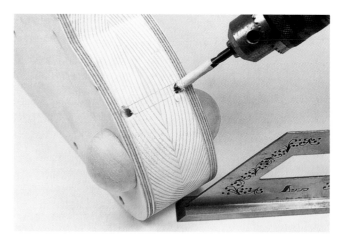

Photo 3 Drilling the holes for the antennae, eyes in place.

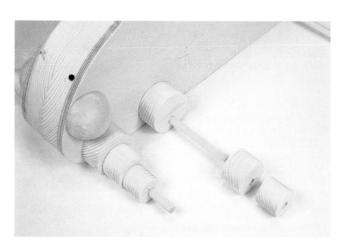

Photo 4 Gluing on the leg sections.

Photo 5 The pine – minus the drive wheel interior circle – about to be sandwiched between two pieces of plywood.

Photo 6 Checking the alignment of the axle holes and that the axle itself is at 90° to the drive wheel.

11 Onto the other piece of plywood for the drive wheel side mark up the outer 140mm (5½in) circle and drill out the 6mm (¼in) hole in the centre (Photo 5). Place the wooden beads into the drive wheel's internal cavity. Glue on the second plywood side. Before clamping, check the alignment of the axle holes by inserting a 6mm (¼in) dowel through them and making sure that it is at a right angle with a try-square, as shown in Photo 6. To prevent the pieces slipping during clamping, tap fret pins into the waste areas from either side.

12 When the glue is set, cut out around the outer edge of the drive wheel assembly as shown in Photo 7. I used a grade 7 blade for this, but check that this works for you and use a coarser blade if necessary.

Photo 7 The completed drive wheel after cutting out around the outer edge.

13 Cut out the two drive wheel spacers from the 1.5mm (1⁄16in) ply (Fig 8.2). Drill 6mm (1⁄4in) holes through their centres and glue one to each side of the drive wheel (Fig 8.2).

14 If the hole in the tap washer is less than 6mm (1⁄4in), stick it to a piece of wood with double-sided tape and place it in a drill vice. Insert a drill bit the same size as the hole in the washer into the drill chuck. Align the drill bit and washer hole. Lift the drill carefully and replace this drill bit with the larger 6mm (1⁄4in) drill bit and drill the washer. Twist drill bits and a fast drill speed are best for this job.

15 Mark up and drill out the axle holes in the wheels (Fig 8.2) and counterbore the holes for the wheel hubs (Fig 8.3), before cutting them out.

16 Cut out the wings, wing hubs, and wing axle covers (Fig 8.3). Glue the wings into the hubs, making sure that the axle holes are aligned, and then add a wing axle cover to each side of the wing (Photo 8).

17 Paint the outside of the ladybird with oil-based white primer, gloss enamels, and then varnish it for a tough finish. Sponge silver patterns onto the one side of the wings only.

18 Cut the wing axle out from 6mm (1⁄4in) dowel a little longer than required and make a point at one end. Push the axle through the hole at the top of the body pointed end first, through the tap washer and out through the other side. Centre the washer in the hole and mark on the axle with a pencil where it exits the body sides. The axle should fit tightly into the washer, but you can glue them if you want.

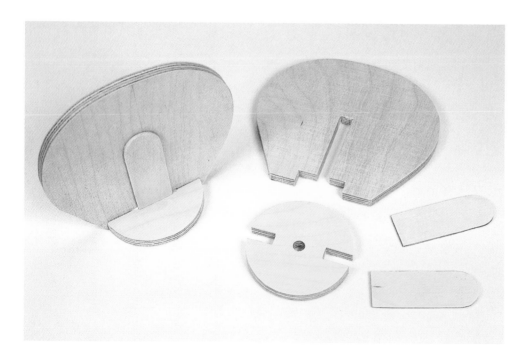

Photo 8 Two wings – one assembled.

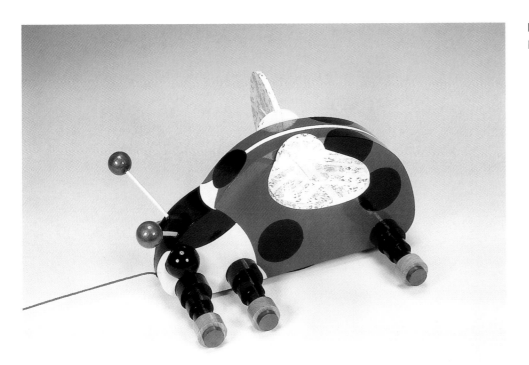

Photo 9 The completed ladybird.

19 Make the plastic washers (see page 8). Stick one round the axle hole on each side of the drive wheel with double-sided tape. Rub the axle holes and washers with candle wax. Insert the drive wheel into the cavity and push the drive wheel axle through from the side. Test that the drive wheel moves freely and that the wing axle can both rotate and ride up and down in its hole to disengage the drive wheel, before you glue the axle to the body sides.

20 Position the wing axle using the pencil marks made previously and cut it to the correct length on each side of the body. Candle wax the washers slipping them onto the wing axle and then glue the wings to the wing axle, at right angles to each other as shown in Photo 9.

21 Rub candle wax onto the wheel axles only where the wheels run. Fit the wheels and then stick the wheel hub caps on with epoxy resin.

22 Stick the curtain wire antennae into the holes in the head and attach the 25mm (1in) hard wood balls onto the ends as shown in Photo 9 using epoxy resin. Insert the 2mm (³⁄₃₂in) nylon cord into the hole in the nose with some epoxy resin and secure it with a 3mm (⅛in) dowel wedge. Allow the resin to set, then cut the dowel flush. The length that the cord needs to be depends on the height of the child but I suggest a minimum of 1 metre (39in). Pass the cord through the hole in the handle, make a knot and tug it back into the countersunk hole.

UNDERWATER EXPLORATION VESSEL

Deep-sea exploration by specialised submersibles has revealed everything from sunken wrecks to underwater volcanoes and has captured the imagination of children and adults alike. The 'Aurélie' has a crew of two and a cradle for carrying its own remote controlled ROV (Remotely Operated Vehicle) which is launched from the mother craft after diving. The ROV is equipped with scissor-action callipers for picking up samples and other tasks. The sharks add a little extra bit of danger and excitement for the crew to tackle during their underwater missions. I named the UEV after a French marine biologist who stayed with us while she was at Southampton University for an Anglo-French exchange.

CUTTING LIST

UEV

Hatch (1)	6mm (¼in) plywood	138 x 125mm (5⁷⁄₁₆ x 4¹⁵⁄₁₆in)
Porthole top (1)	1.5mm (¹⁄₁₆in) plywood	92mm (3⅝in) diameter
Porthole (1)	15mm (¹⁹⁄₃₂in) pine	92mm (3⅝in) diameter
Front bulkhead and legs (1)	6mm (¼in) plywood	237 x 108mm (9¹¹⁄₃₂ x 4¼in)
Upper front bulkhead (1)	6mm (¼in) plywood	138 x 70mm (5⁷⁄₁₆ x 2¾in)
Cabin floor (1)	6mm (¼in) plywood	138 x 96mm (5⁷⁄₁₆ x 3¹³⁄₁₆in)
Hull sides (2)	6mm (¼in) plywood	438 x 142mm (17¼ x 5¹⁹⁄₃₂in)
Rear bulkhead and legs (1)	6mm (¼in) plywood	237 x 100mm (9¹¹⁄₃₂ x 3¹⁵⁄₁₆in)
Hull base (1)	6mm (¼in) plywood	411 x 138mm (16³⁄₁₆ x 5⁷⁄₁₆in)
Cabin sides (2)	6mm (¼in) plywood	134 x 143mm (5¼ x 5⅝in)
Cabin discs (2)	6mm (¼in) plywood	83mm (3¼in) diameter
Hardwood wheels (4)	25mm (1in) diameter	
Wheel axle screws (4)	Brass countersunk	No 6 x 25mm (1in)
Skids (2)	22mm (⅞in) dowel	240mm (9⁷⁄₁₆in) long
Skid locating pegs (4)	6mm (¼in) dowel	16mm (⅝in) long
Skid pegs (4)	3mm (⅛in) dowel	12mm (½in) long
Cradle arms (2)	6mm (¼in) plywood	181 x 93mm (7⅛ x 3²¹⁄₃₂in)
Cradle cranking dowel hubs (2)	20mm (²⁵⁄₃₂in) pine	32mm (1¼in) diameter
Cradle cranking dowel (1)	6mm (¼in) dowel	165mm (6½in) long
Cradle pegs (2)	3mm (⅛in) dowel	10mm (⅜in) long
Yoke (1)	6mm (¼in) plywood	134 x 69mm (5⁵⁄₁₆ x 2¹¹⁄₁₆in)
Yoke hub caps (2)	6mm (¼in) plywood	30mm (1³⁄₁₆in) diameter
Console panel (1)	6mm (¼in) plywood	40 x 26mm (1⁹⁄₁₆ x 1in)
Console base (1)	20mm (²⁵⁄₃₂in) pine	65 x 33mm (2⁹⁄₁₆ x 1⁵⁄₁₆in)
Console top (1)	20mm (²⁵⁄₃₂in) pine	33 x 20mm (1⁵⁄₁₆ x ¾in)
Spinners (4)	15mm (¹⁹⁄₃₂in) pine	20mm (¾in) diameter
Rear thruster shafts (2)	6mm (¼in) dowel	27mm (1¹⁄₁₆in) long
Side thruster shafts (2)	6mm (¼in) dowel	43mm (1¹¹⁄₁₆in) long
Thrusters (4)	15mm (¹⁹⁄₃₂in) pine	20mm (¾in) diameter
Crank handles (1)	wooden ball	19mm (¾in)
Crank latch handle (1)	wooden ball	19mm (¾in)
Crank handle dowel (1)	6mm (¼in) dowel	35mm (1⅜in) long
Crank latch handle dowel (1)	6mm (¼in) dowel	10mm (⅜in) long
Skid locating pegs (4)	6mm (¼in) dowel	16mm (⅝in) long

Skid pegs (4)	3mm ($\frac{1}{8}$in) dowel	12mm ($\frac{1}{2}$in) long
Crank (1)	15mm ($\frac{19}{32}$in) pine	60 x 20mm ($2\frac{3}{8}$ x $\frac{3}{4}$in)
Crank latch (1)	6mm ($\frac{1}{4}$in) plywood	49 x 24mm ($1\frac{15}{16}$ x $\frac{15}{16}$in)
Locking hub (1)	22mm ($\frac{7}{8}$in) dowel	20mm ($\frac{25}{32}$in) long
Top window (1)	5mm ($\frac{7}{32}$in) clear acrylic	138 x 66mm ($5\frac{7}{16}$ x $2\frac{19}{32}$in)
Bottom window (1)	5mm ($\frac{7}{32}$in) clear acrylic	138 x 72mm ($5\frac{7}{16}$ x $2\frac{27}{32}$in)
Porthole window (1)	2mm ($\frac{3}{32}$in) clear acrylic	68mm ($2\frac{11}{16}$in) diameter
Cradle bar (1)	6mm ($\frac{1}{4}$in) dowel	124mm ($4\frac{7}{8}$in) long
Cradle locking dowels (2)	3mm ($\frac{1}{8}$in) dowel	10mm ($\frac{3}{8}$in) long
Screw eye (1)		
Crank locking dowel (1)	3mm ($\frac{1}{8}$in) dowel	10mm ($\frac{3}{8}$in) long
Washers for wheels (4)	mild steel	4mm ($\frac{5}{32}$in) hole
Brass screws (4)	countersunk	No 6 x 25mm (1in)
Plastic washers (2)		20mm ($\frac{25}{32}$in) diameter with 6mm ($\frac{1}{4}$in) holes
Propellers (4)	plastic	42mm ($1\frac{21}{32}$in) diameter
Mild steel ballast minimum		113 grammes (4oz)

ROV

Top (1)	6mm ($\frac{1}{4}$in) plywood	150 x 100mm ($5\frac{15}{16}$ x $3\frac{15}{16}$in)
Outer sides (2)	6mm ($\frac{1}{4}$in) plywood	150 x 30mm ($5\frac{15}{16}$ x $1\frac{3}{16}$in)
Inner sides (2)	6mm ($\frac{1}{4}$in) plywood	102 x 24mm (4 x $\frac{15}{16}$in)
Centre disc (1)	6mm ($\frac{1}{4}$in) plywood	62mm ($2\frac{7}{16}$in) diameter
Axles (4)	3mm ($\frac{1}{8}$in) dowel	24mm ($\frac{15}{16}$in) long
Hardwood wheels (4)	25mm (1in) diameter	
Callipers (2)	6mm ($\frac{1}{4}$in) plywood	227 x 70mm ($8\frac{15}{16}$ x $2\frac{3}{4}$in)
Calliper handles (2)	wooden balls	19mm ($\frac{3}{4}$in)
Calliper handle dowel (1)	6mm ($\frac{1}{4}$in) dowel	21mm ($\frac{13}{16}$in) long
Calliper handle dowel (1)	6mm ($\frac{1}{4}$in) dowel	15mm ($\frac{19}{32}$in) long
Centre shaft (1)	6mm ($\frac{1}{4}$in) dowel	40mm ($1\frac{9}{16}$) long
Top of centre shaft (1)	wooden ball	37mm ($1\frac{7}{16}$in)
Plastic washer (1)		20mm ($\frac{25}{32}$in) diameter (with 6mm ($\frac{1}{4}$in) hole

CREW

Heads (2)	wooden balls	37mm ($1\frac{7}{16}$in)
Neck joints (2)	6mm ($\frac{1}{4}$in) dowel	25mm (1in) long
Arms (4)	12mm ($\frac{1}{2}$in) plywood	37 x 30mm ($1\frac{7}{16}$ x $1\frac{3}{16}$)
Bodies (2)	24mm ($\frac{15}{16}$in) pine	67 x 37mm ($2\frac{5}{8}$ x $1\frac{7}{16}$in)

SHARKS

Pectoral fins (4)	6mm (¼in) plywood	49 x 36mm (1¹⁵⁄₁₆ x 1³⁄₈in)
Pelvic fins (4)	6mm (¼in) plywood	28 x 18mm (1⅛ x ¹¹⁄₁₆in)
Body (2)	18mm (¹¹⁄₁₆in) pine	288 x 70mm (11⁵⁄₁₆ x 2¾in)
Eye rod (2)	4mm (⁵⁄₃₂in) dowel	23mm (²⁹⁄₃₂in) long

MISCELLANEOUS

2mm (³⁄₃₂in) braided nylon cord

12mm (½in) fret pins (4)

Oil-based primer

Lacquer

Oil-based gloss enamels (suggested colours: yellow, orange, red, silver, blue, green, brown, white and cream)

Matt paint (suggested colours: flesh, dark grey, light grey and white) available in 14ml tins. Note that the matt flesh colour will need an overcoat of gloss lacquer on the figures.

Candle

Model-maker's lettering

Fine abrasive paper

CONSTRUCTION

1 Cut out the hatch (Fig 9.1) and round off the pivots to fit a 6mm (¼in) hole (check it in a hole drilled in a piece of scrap wood). Fret out the porthole circle in it (see Fretting out, page 6). Mark up the outer and inner circles for the porthole top (Fig 9.1) onto a piece of 1.5mm (¹⁄₁₆in) plywood. Find the centre and push a fret pin through it. Turn it over, and again use a pair of compasses to draw a circle the same diameter as the inner circle of the porthole on the reverse. Mark the inner circle of the porthole on a piece of the 15mm (¹⁹⁄₃₂in) pine, then cut out the inner parts from both components. Glue the porthole and porthole top together using the circle on the reverse of the ply to position the pinewood. Tap brass fret pins through waste areas to hold the pieces in position while the glue is setting. Once the glue is dry, cut out around the outer circle marked on the plywood as shown in Photo 1.

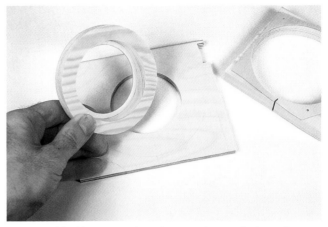

Photo 1 Marking up and cutting out the porthole and porthole top.

2 Join two pieces of 6mm (¼in) plywood together with double-sided tape and cut out two identical hull sides (Fig 9.2) cabin sides and cabin discs (Fig 9.3). Cut out the slots and drill out any holes before you separate them.

3 Cut out the front and rear bulkheads with legs, upper front bulkhead (Fig 9.4) cabin floor (Fig 9.5) and hull base (Fig 9.6) out of 6mm (¼in plywood), remembering the 30° bevel in the front of the hull base. Cut any slots and drill any holes.

4 Lay the pieces out as in Photo 2. Dry assemble the hull sides, cabin floor, upper front bulkhead and front bulkhead with legs while inserting the hatch assembly to check it for fit.

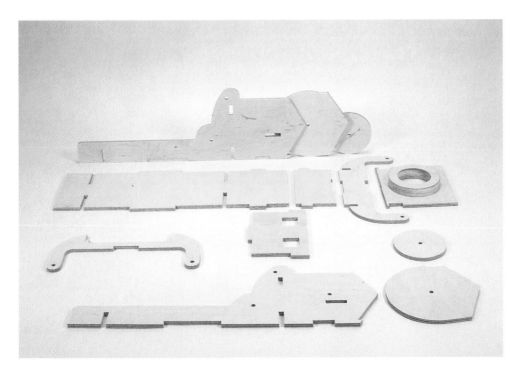

Photo 2 The hull sides, cabin floor, upper front bulkhead and front bulkhead with legs ready for a dry assembly.

5 Glue the porthole to the hatch. Give the hatch pivots a thorough coating of candle wax so that the hatch will open and close smoothly. Glue on the upper front bulkhead, the front bulkhead with legs, the cabin floor and the hull sides. Clamp together and leave to dry (Photo 3).

6 When the glue has set, add the rear bulkhead with legs followed by the hull base. The bevel at the front of the hull base goes underneath and must line up with the hull sides. Clamp, tape and wedge the parts firmly into place while the glue sets as shown in Photo 4. Check that the assembly sits evenly on its legs while on a flat surface and gently weigh it down to prevent it twisting while the glue is setting.

Photo 3 The hatch and upper front bulkhead in place.

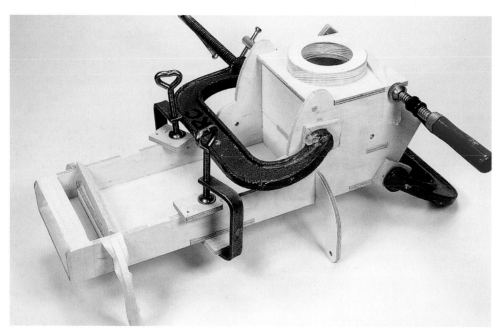

Photo 4 Rear bulkhead with legs and hull base in position and clamped while the glue sets.

7 Glue and clamp the cabin sides into place, using 6mm (¼in) dowels pushed through the centre holes to help keep them aligned while the glue is setting. Then glue on the cabin discs as shown in Photo 5, again aligning them on the 6mm (¼in) dowels.

8 Countersink the axle holes already in the wooden wheels, firmly holding them in a self-grip wrench under the drill. Put tape around the jaws of the wrench to prevent them marking the wheels.

9 Cut the 22mm (⅞in) dowel to length for the skids (Fig 9.7) and drill the 6mm (¼in) holes in each end, as well as the 3mm (⅛in) pilot holes for the wheel axle screws. Fit the wheels temporarily to check the alignment with a try-square as shown in Photo 6. Mark the positions of the skids on to the legs. Glue the skids onto the legs. Glue in the 6mm (¼in) skid locating peg dowels at each end. Extend the 3mm (⅛in) holes in the legs into the skids and insert 3mm (⅛in) skid peg dowels to lock them into position. Once this is set, remove the wheels.

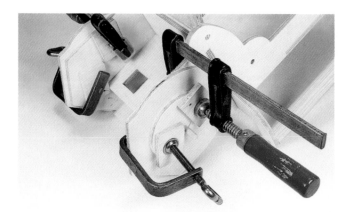

Photo 5 A cabin disc aligned with the 6mm (¼in) dowel and clamped while the glue sets.

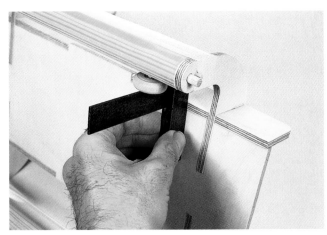

Photo 6 Checking the alignment of the wheels with a try-square (see Step 9).

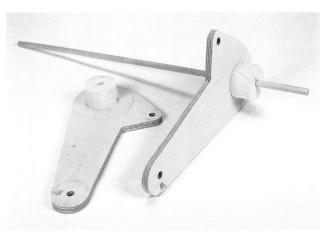

Photo 7 Gluing the cranking dowel hubs and the cradle pegs onto the cradle arms.

10 Tape two pieces of 6mm (¼in) plywood together for the cradle arms (Fig 9.8) and mark one of them up. Drill out the three sets of 6mm (¼in) holes, then cut out the two arms. Drill the 3mm (⅛in) holes at the apex for the locking pegs and the counterbored 3mm (⅛in) holes for the cradle pegs (on the inner face of each arm). Glue the cranking dowel hubs (Fig 9.8) and the 3mm (⅛in) cradle pegs onto the cradle arms as shown in Photo 7. Insert a length of 6mm (¼in) dowel temporarily to align the hubs while the glue sets.

11 Cut out the yoke (Fig 9.8) and round off the pivots to a 6mm (¼in) round section as you did for the hatch. Counterbore the 6mm (¼in) holes into 6mm (¼in) plywood for the yoke hub caps (Fig 9.8) and then cut these out.

12 Cut out the ROV top, outer and inner sides and centre disc, and make the bevel on the centre disc (Fig 9.9). Glue them all together. The inner sides are glued edge-on to the top in the positions indicated in Fig 9.9. Use masking tape to bind and hold them together while the glue is setting. Insert 3mm (⅛in) dowels in the axle holes (through the wheels as well) and a 6mm (¼in) dowel in the top and the centre disc, to aid alignment, while you glue on the centre disc, as shown in Photo 8.

13 Tape together two pieces of plywood for the callipers (Fig 9.10) and drill out the centre 6mm (¼in) hole. Then cut the callipers out. Counterbore the 6mm (¼in) holes in the handle sections on opposite sides of the arms to produce right- and left-hand versions. Drill 6mm (¼in)

Photo 8 Dowels inserted temporarily to aid alignment of the ROV parts.

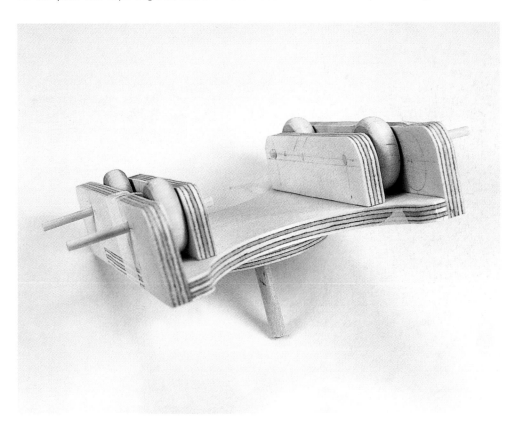

holes 7mm (⁹⁄₃₂in) deep into two 19mm (¾in) wooden balls (see Cutting and drilling wooden balls, page 6) for the handles and glue the handle dowels into them.

14 Cut out the console parts (Fig 9.11), round off the corners of the console panel and glue the three pieces together.

15 Cut out the spinners and thrusters (Fig 9.12). Drill 6mm (¼in) holes through the the thrusters, and counterbore 6mm (¼in) holes in the spinners. Glue the dowel thruster shafts into the spinners (Fig 9.12) and cut out the propellers (Fig 9.12) from plastic in the same way as the plastic washers (see Making plastic washers, page 8).

16 Counterbore one 6mm (¼in) hole in the two 19mm (¾in) wooden balls for the crank handle and crank latch handle and glue in their dowels. Counterbore a 6mm (¼in) hole 20mm (²⁵⁄₃₂in) into a 37mm (1⁷⁄₁₆in) wooden ball for the centre shaft of the ROV and glue in the 6mm (¼in) centre shaft. Counterbore two more 37mm (1⁷⁄₁₆in) wooden balls for the crew's heads and glue in the neck joints.

17 Cut out the crank and crank latch (Fig 9.13) and drill the countersunk and counterbored holes in them. Drill a 1.5mm (¹⁄₁₆in) hole through the cradle cranking dowel (Fig 9.16) and counterbore the 3mm (⅛in) hole in it for locking on the crank. Cut out the locking hub and drill a 6mm (¼in) hole through it.

18 Glue the arms onto the bodies (Fig 9.14) and place into the holes in the cabin floor to check alignment. Drill 6mm (¼in) holes between the shoulders and trim the shoulders to shape. Glue on the heads. Paint with oil-based

primer, enamels and lacquer all the parts which require a durable finish. Note that it is best to leave the cradle cranking dowel until after it is in position, because the lacquer will make it hard to get through the holes.

19 Cut the porthole window out from the 2mm (³⁄₃₂in) acrylic (see Cutting acrylic, page 8) and glue it into the hatch assembly with epoxy resin. Wipe off any smears with methylated spirits before the resin sets. Cut out the top and bottom windows (Fig 9.15). Glue in the bottom window with epoxy resin and and allow this to set. Then glue in the control console, as shown in Photo 9, with epoxy resin and allow this to set. To avoid any possibility of cut fingers, round off and smooth the top edge of the top window before gluing it into place When all is set, smooth off the window joint where the two parts meet. Mask out the window frame and paint in the window frame area to match the rest of the UEV as shown in Photo 9. I had finished the cradle and crank assembly before this stage, but I suggest you fit the windows now, because it will make handling the toy while fitting the windows less difficult.

20 Fit the wheels onto the ROV and glue the axles into place. Glue the calliper handle balls onto the calliper arms, following the arrangement in Photo 10. Thread a plastic washer onto the centre shaft, then push through the centre holes in the callipers (check that they are still in the correct order) and glue it into the top of the ROV. The callipers should move freely, but not be loose.

21 Fit the wheels onto the skids. Place a 4mm (⁵⁄₃₂in) washer between the skid and wheel and screw these into place with the No 6 25mm (1in) axle screws.

Photo 9 The control console in position.

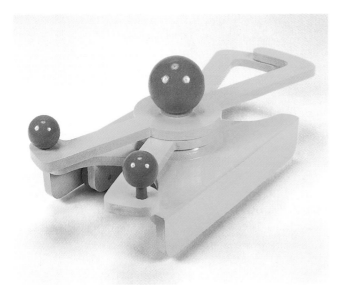

Photo 10 The completed ROV.

Photo 11 The yoke and cradle arms in position.

22 Place the yoke between the cradle arms and slip a plastic washer over each of the pivots followed by the yoke hub caps, which are glued to the pivots with epoxy resin. The yoke should be able to rotate freely. Also join the two cradle arms together at their apex with the cradle bar dowel (Photo 11). Drill a little way into the dowel with a 3mm (⅛in) drill via the 3mm (⅛in) holes in the cradle arms. Glue in the 3mm (⅛in) locking dowels.

23 Fit the screw eye onto the back of the cabin (Fig 9.4). Fit the cradle cranking dowel into the 6mm (¼in) counterbored hole in the crank and lock into place with a 3mm (⅛in) dowel as seen in Photo 12 and 13. Insert plastic washers between the cradle and the hull sides as you lower the cradle into position. A certain amount of give in the assembly will enable you to hold the washers in place

with a pair of tweezers. Alternatively, you could stick them in place with double-sided tape. Insert the cradle cranking dowel through the hole in the left side of the hull, slip the locking hub over it, and then push it out through the right side of the hull. Glue the locking hub onto the cradle cranking dowel to hold the assembly in place as shown in Photo 12.

24 Fit the crank latch to the hull with a No 4 x 12mm (½in) countersunk screw. Put a little epoxy resin on the screw to hold firmly in place, as shown in Photo 13.

25 Tie a knot in the end of a length of 2mm (³⁄₃₂in) nylon cord then thread it through the hole in the cradle cranking dowel, then through the screw eye and tie it onto the cradle bar as seen in Photo 12.

Photo 12 The locking hub fixed to the cradle cranking dowel.

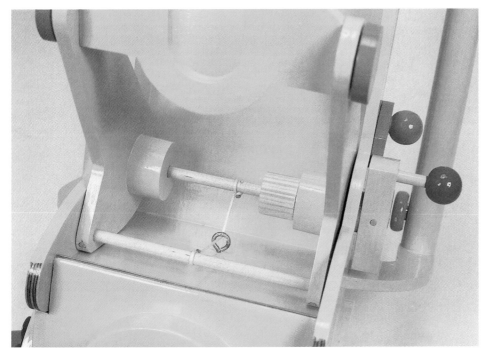

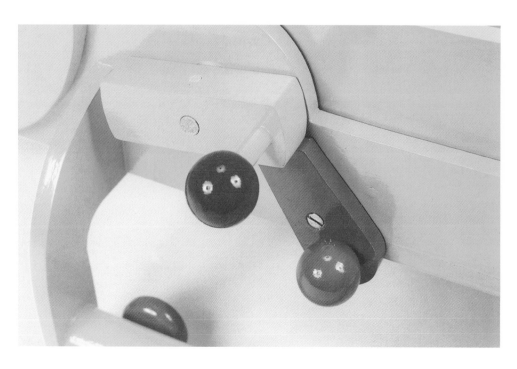

Photo 13 The crank latch is
fitted to the hull with a
countersunk screw.

26 Thread the propellers and the thrusters onto the
thruster shafts. Glue the side thruster shafts into the
holes in the cabin sides. Glue the rear thrusters onto the
rear legs with epoxy resin and hold them in place with tape
(Photo 14) until the resin has set.

27 Glue the ballast onto the hull behind the rear bulkhead
and between the rear thrusters as shown in Photo 15.
I used a piece of hexagonal mild steel bar cut to length.
Square or round section rod would serve just as well.

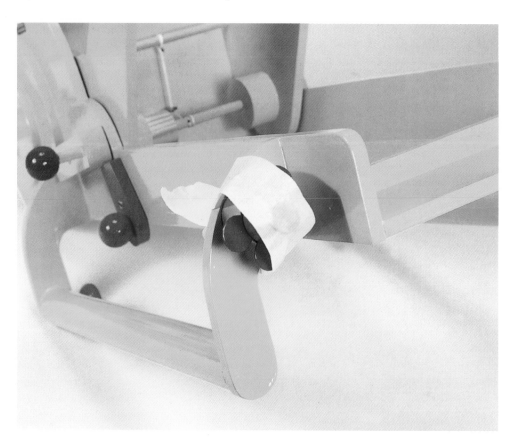

Photo 14 Holding the rear
thrusters in place with tape
while the epoxy resin sets.

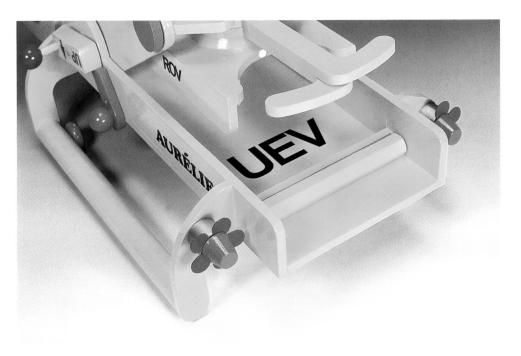

Photo 15 The ballast is glued onto the hull between the rear thrusters.

28 Apply the lettering according to the manufacturer's instructions.

29 Cut out the sharks, and glue the fins to the bodies (Fig 9.17). Round the eye rods off at each end and paint them with black gloss paint. Paint the sharks and glue the eye rods in (Photo 16).

Photo 16 Just when you thought it was safe to go back into the workshop!

WINDMILL
MOUSE HOUSE

10

This compact, open-backed play house is based on a kind of windmill known as a smock windmill. It is inhabited by lots of mice. They furnish their home with all the sorts of things that people leave lying around. This makes it easy for the young windmill owners to furnish it with anything that they think the mice would find useful.

CUTTING LIST

WINDMILL

Base (1)	6mm ($\frac{1}{4}$in) plywood	432 x 344mm (17 x 13$\frac{9}{16}$in)
First floor (1)	6mm ($\frac{1}{4}$in) plywood	432 x 304mm (17 x 11$\frac{31}{32}$in)
Ground floor fronts with doors (2)	6mm ($\frac{1}{4}$in) plywood	172 x 172mm (6$\frac{25}{32}$ x 6$\frac{25}{32}$in)
Ground floor sides (2)	6mm ($\frac{1}{4}$in) plywood	172 x 172mm (6$\frac{25}{32}$ x 6$\frac{25}{32}$in)
Floor supports (4)	6mm ($\frac{1}{4}$in) plywood	33 x 33mm (1$\frac{5}{16}$ x 1$\frac{5}{16}$in)
Tower fronts (2)	6mm ($\frac{1}{4}$in) plywood	350 x 172mm (13$\frac{25}{32}$ x 6$\frac{25}{32}$in)
Tower sides (2)	6mm ($\frac{1}{4}$in) plywood	350 x 172mm (13$\frac{25}{32}$ x 6$\frac{25}{32}$in)
Tower top (1)	18mm ($\frac{23}{32}$in) pine	145 x 134mm (5$\frac{23}{32}$ x 5$\frac{9}{32}$in)
Tower top cap (1)	6mm ($\frac{1}{4}$in) plywood	174 x 132mm (6$\frac{7}{8}$ x 5$\frac{7}{32}$in)
Second floor (1)	6mm ($\frac{1}{4}$in) plywood	215x 192mm (8$\frac{15}{32}$ x 7$\frac{9}{16}$in)
First floor front skirting (2)	18mm ($\frac{23}{32}$in) pine	160 x 14mm (6$\frac{5}{16}$ x $\frac{17}{32}$in)
First floor back skirting (2)	18mm ($\frac{23}{32}$in) pine	170 x 14mm (6$\frac{5}{16}$ x $\frac{17}{32}$in)
Door hinge covers (4)	1.5mm ($\frac{1}{16}$in) plywood	30 x 10mm (1$\frac{3}{16}$ x $\frac{3}{8}$in)
Cap base (1)	15mm ($\frac{19}{32}$in) pine	89 x 80mm (3$\frac{1}{2}$ x 3$\frac{5}{32}$in)
Cap front (1)	15mm ($\frac{19}{32}$in) pine	80 x 80mm (3$\frac{5}{32}$ x 3$\frac{5}{32}$in)
Cap rear (1)	15mm ($\frac{19}{32}$in) pine	60 x 80mm (2$\frac{3}{8}$ x 3$\frac{5}{32}$in)
Sail shaft (1)	12mm ($\frac{1}{2}$in) dowel	137mm (5$\frac{3}{8}$in) long
Cap first top (1)	18mm ($\frac{21}{32}$in) pine	90 x 42mm (3$\frac{9}{16}$ x 1$\frac{21}{32}$in)
Cap second top (1)	15mm ($\frac{19}{32}$in) pine	75 x 42mm (2$\frac{31}{32}$ x 1$\frac{21}{32}$in)
Cap sides (2)	18mm ($\frac{23}{32}$in) pine	83 x 56mm (3$\frac{1}{4}$ x 2$\frac{7}{32}$in)
Sails (2)	6mm ($\frac{1}{4}$in) plywood	500 x 100mm (19$\frac{11}{16}$ x 3$\frac{15}{16}$in)
Sail locking peg (1)	3mm ($\frac{1}{8}$in) dowel	12mm ($\frac{1}{2}$in) long
Sail boss (1)	15mm ($\frac{19}{32}$in) pine	40mm (1$\frac{19}{32}$in) diameter
Hub cap (1)	15mm ($\frac{19}{32}$in) pine	40mm (1$\frac{19}{32}$in) diameter
Plastic washers (2)	24mm ($\frac{15}{16}$in) diameter with 12mm ($\frac{1}{2}$in) holes	
Door handles (2)	6mm ($\frac{1}{4}$in) dowel	10mm ($\frac{3}{8}$in) long

MICE (FOR EACH PAIR)

Female body (1)	38mm (1$\frac{1}{2}$in) pine	44mm (1$\frac{23}{32}$in) diameter
Male body (1)	38mm (1$\frac{1}{2}$in) pine	38mm (1$\frac{1}{2}$in) diameter
Female legs (1)	19mm ($\frac{3}{4}$in) pine	23 x 32mm ($\frac{29}{32}$ x 1$\frac{1}{4}$in)
Male legs (1)	19mm ($\frac{3}{4}$in) pine	23 x 38mm ($\frac{29}{32}$ x 1$\frac{1}{2}$in)

Noses (2)	6mm (¼in) dowel	8mm (¹¹⁄₃₂in) long
Heads (2)	hardwood balls	25mm (1in) diameter
Neck joints (2)	3mm (⅛in) dowel	19mm (¾in) long
Hands inner sections (4)	6mm (¼in) plywood	15 x 15mm (⅝ x ⅝in)
Hand outsides (8)	1.5mm (¹⁄₁₆in) plywood	15 x 15mm (⅝ x ⅝in)
Feet (2)	6mm (¼in) plywood	32 x 32mm (1¼ x 1¼in)
Foot dowels (2)	3mm (⅛in) dowel	12mm (½in)
Ears (4)	6mm (¼in) plywood	16mm (⅝in) diameter
Arms	red and blue crepe cord	

Gumstrip paper for preventing cord from unravelling

MISCELLANEOUS

PVA wood glue

Clear and tinted satin acrylic varnish

Colours for tints (white and duck egg blue)

Opaque acrylic paints (mauve, yellow, light green, dark green, brown, dark blue)

Oil-based primer

Oil-based enamel paints for the mice (red, crimson, orange, dark green, ultramarine, cobalt blue and matt flesh)

Black permanent liner for facial features

CONSTRUCTION

1 Join two pieces of 6mm (¼in) plywood together with double-sided tape for the base and first floor. On one piece of ply mark up the cutting lines for both (Fig 10.1) and cut around the base outline. Fret out the slots for the ground floor sides and fronts. Separate the two pieces of plywood. Trim the rear portion of the marked-up piece of plywood for the first floor. Drill the 6mm (¼in) pivot holes for the doors in the base, as can be seen in Photo 1.

2 Join two pieces of plywood together and mark up the ground floor fronts with doors and ground floor sides (Fig 10.2). Cut around the perimeter except for the bevelled edges and the doors which must be cut out after separation and the bevelled edges have been cut so that the doors have matching bevels (see Photo 2). The two fronts can be either joined back together again for cutting out the doors or cut separately. Note that for the ground floor front and door there are right- and left-hand versions.

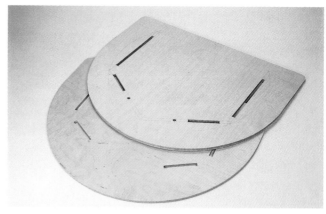

Photo 1 The base of the windmill with the pivot holes for the doors.

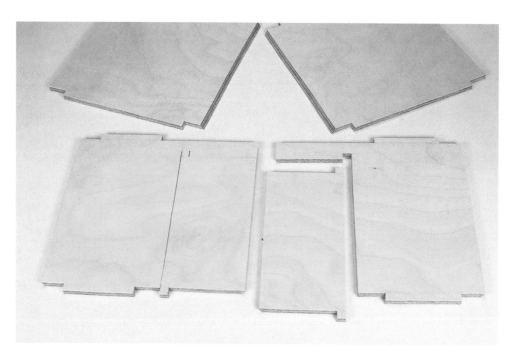

Photo 2 The ground floor fronts and sides.

3 Dry assemble the base, first floor, ground floor fronts and ground floor sides as shown in Photo 3 and adjust as necessary. Mark all the pieces with a pencil to make sure that you glue them in the same order.

4 Cut out the floor supports (Fig 10.3) and trim the locating pegs to a diameter of 6mm (¼in) with a sharp knife.

5 Mark the tower fronts and sides onto 6mm (¼in) plywood (Fig 10.4): you will need to cut them individually to make the bevels. Mark up the windows, but do not cut them out yet. Drill the 6mm (¼in) holes for the floor supports.

Photo 3 A dry assembly of the base, first floor, ground floor fronts and ground floor sides.

6 Mark up the tower top (Fig 10.5) onto 18mm (²³⁄₃₂in) pine and cut it out. Temporarily fit the floor supports onto the tower fronts and sides. Dry assemble the tower fronts and sides with the tower top, using masking tape to hold them together. Place the tower on top of the slots in the first floor to aid alignment, as shown in Photo 4. Use fret clamps and blocks of wood to hold it in place while you make any necessary adjustments. To make sure that the second floor (Fig 10.5) fits accurately, check the dimensions and angles against the tower and make any adjustments before cutting it out.

7 Dismantle the whole thing and fret out the windows in the tower and ground floor fronts and sides. Fret out the windows in the doors, and counterbore the 6mm (¼in) holes for the door handles.

8 Mark up the cutting and guide lines on the tower top cap (Fig 10.5) onto 6mm (¼in) plywood and cut it out. Glue the tower top to the tower cap using the guide line to align it.

9 Glue the base, first floor and ground floor sides and ground floor fronts together. Make sure that the join above the door is accurately aligned by clamping it while the glue is setting (Photo 5).

10 Glue the floor supports into the tower fronts and sides. Join the tower fronts and sides together again. Lay them down on the workbench in the correct order (from left to right this is right side, right front, left front and left side) with their outsides facing up. Run a length of masking tape along each join from top to bottom, making hinges. Turn the whole thing over. Place glue into the three 'V' shaped grooves of the open joins. Carefully fold them together and glue in the tower top and cap assembly. Add the second floor and bind the tower firmly with masking tape, as shown in Photo 6. Wipe off any excess glue.

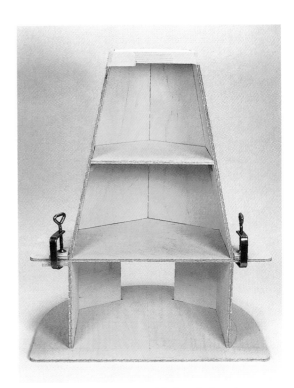

Photo 4 The tower assembled and placed on top of the slots in the first floor to aid alignment.

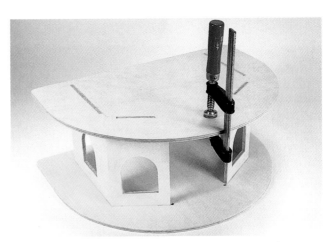

Photo 5 The first floor glued and clamped.

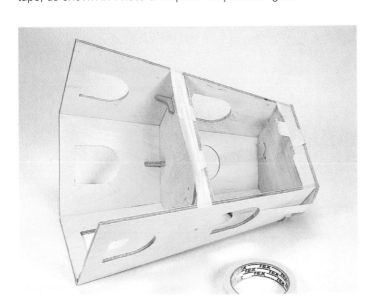

Photo 6 The tower firmly bound together with masking tape while the glue sets.

11 Once the glue has set tidy up the tower. Fill any gaps with balsa slivers and smooth them flush and smooth with abrasive paper.

12 Mark up the first floor skirting (Fig 10.6), check the measurements against the tower, make any adjustments necessary and cut it to fit. Put the tower into place on the first floor, and dry assemble the skirting to make any necessary final adjustments. Remove the skirting and glue the tower onto the first floor using fret clamps to keep it aligned. Place polythene under the clamps to avoid the glue sticking the scrap plywood load spreaders to the windmill. Glue the first floor skirting into place. Place a heavy weight carefully on top of the tower to hold everything together firmly while the glue is setting, as shown in Photo 7.

13 Mark up and cut out the four door hinge covers (Fig 10.7) onto 1.5mm (¹⁄₁₆in) plywood. Glue two of them onto the insides of the ground floor fronts covering the pivot holes as indicated in Fig 10.2. Shorten the door pivots by about 1mm (¹⁄₃₂in) and round them off with abrasive paper. Also round off the back edge of the doors, Test fit the doors into the holes in the base to see if you get a smooth opening and closing action. If not, check where the problem lies and round them off a little more. Cut pieces of 6mm (¼in) dowel to length for the door handles.

14 Mark up and cut out all the pieces for the cap (Figs 10.8 and 10.9) and drill the holes and cut a notch for the sail shaft. Glue the cap base, cap front and cap rear together with the sail shaft inserted temporarily through the holes to help align them. Add the sides and the first and second top parts and leave the glue to set as shown in Photo 8. Remove the sail shaft. Hold the cap assembly in a vice and cut off the waste areas as seen in Photo 9 before shaping with a balsa or block plane. Shape the front to the curve shown in the plan view in Fig 10.8. Finish off with sanding blocks.

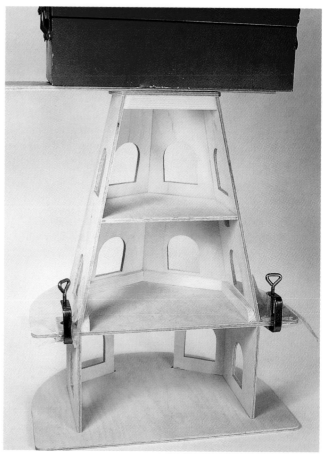

Photo 7 A heavy weight is used to hold the tower and first floor steady while the glue sets.

Photo 8 The components that make up the cap glued together with the sail shaft inserted to align them.

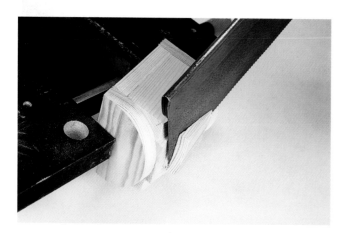

Photo 9 Hold the cap assembly in a vice to cut off the waste areas and shape it.

15 Glue and clamp the cap onto the top of the tower as shown in Photo 10.

16 Join the two pieces of plywood for the sails together with double-sided tape and mark these out (Fig 10.9). Drill the 12mm (½in) hole before cutting them out. Insert a piece of 12mm (½in) dowel into the hole in the sails and line them up to form a cross. Clamp them in this position and drill the 3mm (⅛in) hole for the sail locking peg.

17 Mark up the sail boss and hubcap (Fig 10.9) and drill the holes before cutting them out. Dry fit the sail shaft into the cap and add the sail boss, then a plastic washer followed by the sails with the locking dowel glued into one sail only for now. Add another plastic washer and finally the hubcap. Adjust the length of the sail shaft as necessary.

18 To make the mouse bodies, glue together two pieces of 19mm (¾in) pine to make a 38mm (1½in) laminated stock. Mark up the wood 9mm (⅜in) from its edge with centres for the 6mm (¼in) arm holes and on the base the circle for the body shapes (Fig 10.10) as seen in Photo 11. Cut out around the circles at the angle required (see Fig 10.10). Smooth out any unevenness with a sanding block. Drill a 3mm (⅛in) hole 15mm (⅝in) into the top of each body section. Note how the waste material from the wood cut to make the bodies has a piece of plywood fixed to it in order that the body can be reinserted in to it to hold it steady. While it is being held, cut off the top of the body 6mm (¼in) above the arm hole with a Gent's saw as seen in Photo 12. Rotate the body around to avoid having to cut in to the jig.

Photo 10 Gluing and clamping the cap to the top of the tower.

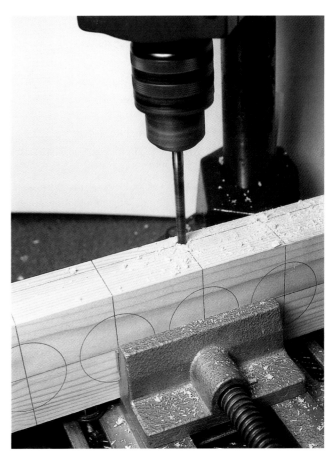

Photo 11 Drilling the arm holes.

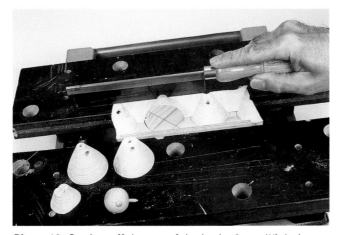

Photo 12 Cutting off the top of the body, 6mm (¼in) above the arm holes with a Gent's saw.

19 Mark up the leg shapes (Fig 10.10) onto 19mm (¾in) pine and cut them out at a 24° angle for the female or 32° for the male leg. I found it much easier to cut out the legs upside-down around the shape of where they meet the feet and leave the scrollsaw to dictate the final shape of the top of the legs as indicated by the light perimeter lines shown on Fig 10.10. Clean up any irregularities with abrasive paper.

20 Drill the 6mm (¼in) and 3mm (⅛in) holes into the 25mm (1in) hardwood balls for the heads as shown in Fig 10.10. For each nose, round off the end of a piece of 6mm (¼in) dowel and cut it to a length of 8mm (¹¹⁄₃₂in) and glue into the head. For the neck joints, sharpen the end of a piece of 3mm (⅛in) dowel before cutting it to a length of 19mm (¾in). Glue it into the head, point outwards.

21 For the hands, cut 9 x 6mm (⅜ x ¼in) notches into the edge of a strip of 6mm (¼in) plywood at least 25mm (1in) apart. Make a sandwich by gluing this plywood between two layers of 1.5mm (¹⁄₁₆in) ply as seen in Photo 13. Mark up the laminated plywood with a template of the hands (Fig 10.10) and then cut them out (also Photo 13).

22 Mark up the feet (Fig 10.10) onto 6mm (¼in) plywood and drill the 3mm (⅛in) holes into them. Glue the feet onto the legs and when the glue is dry, extend the 3mm (⅛in) holes up to 6mm (¼in) farther into the legs. Glue in a 3mm (⅛in) foot dowel.

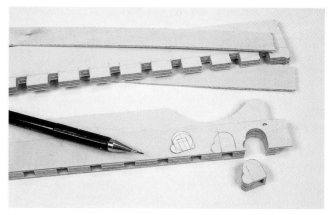

Photo 13 The hands are cut out of a sandwich of 6mm (¼in) ply glued between two layers of 1.5mm (¹⁄₁₆in) ply.

23 Glue the bodies and legs together so that the toes are in line with the front of the body and temporarily fit the heads onto the bodies. Mark up and cut out the ears from 6mm (¼in) plywood (Fig 10.10). Glue on the ears with epoxy resin, using masking tape to hold them in place while the resin is setting. When it has set, but not fully hardened, trim any excess resin with a sharp knife as shown in Photo 14.

24 Paint the windmill and its parts with tinted and clear satin acrylic varnish. You can add texture with a wavy-sponge-and-plank paintstamp as seen in Photo 15. Climbing plants can also be simulated with paintstamps on the ground floor.

Photo 14 Trimming excess resin from the glued mice.

25 Glue the door handles in to the counterbored 6mm (¼in) holes in the doors before fitting them in place and gluing on the exterior door hinge covers. After painting, reassemble the sails as you did in Step 17 and glue the sail shaft into the cap and the hub cap onto the sail shaft.

26 Paint the mice with oil-based enamels as they will receive a lot of handling. Cut the coloured crepe cord into 72mm (2²⁷⁄₃₂in) lengths for the arms. Wrap pieces of gumstrip paper tightly around the cut ends as in Photo 16. This will prevent them unravelling and make it easier to insert them into the arm holes. Do not use self adhesive tape. Insert the cord part way into the body as seen in Photo 16. Put a dab of epoxy resin on the exact middle of the cord before pulling it into position. Glue the neck joint dowel into the neck hole, also with epoxy resin. The pointed end of the dowel skewers the arm cord, holding it firmly in place. Glue the hands onto the ends of the arms with epoxy resin. Finish the mice off by painting the glue round the neck joint when it has set.

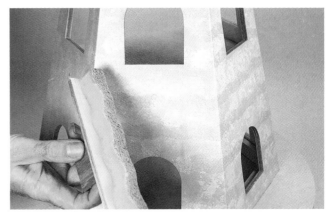

Photo 15 Adding texture to the paintwork with a long wave-shaped paintstamp.

Photo 16 Wrapping gumstrip paper around the cut ends of the arms.

ZEBRA 4WD 'COME APART' VEHICLE

11

This tough four-wheel drive vehicle is the ideal workhorse for the game warden patrolling his territory in remote areas. The Zebra 4WD has lots of features that the young motor enthusiast will appreciate, such as the wheels which can be removed and changed. The engine is accessible allowing the spark plugs and air cleaner to be checked. For major overhauls the engine and radiator can be entirely removed for servicing back at base camp. The boot also opens and holds the jack and wheel spanner with plenty of room for additional items.

CUTTING LIST

Chassis sides (2)	6mm (1/4in) plywood	378 x 134mm (14 7/8 x 5 1/4in)
Front floor (1)	6mm (1/4in) plywood	202 x 204mm (7 15/16 x 8in)
Front bulkhead (1)	6mm (1/4in) plywood	204 x 103mm (8 x 4 1/16in)
Rear bulkhead (1)	6mm (1/4in) plywood	204 x 115mm (8 x 4 9/16in)
Rear floor (1)	6mm (1/4in) plywood	204 x 156mm (8 x 6 5/32in)
Sides (2)	6mm (1/4in) plywood	342 x 129mm (13 7/16 x 5 1/8in)
Seat front (1)	6mm (1/4in) plywood	204 x 25mm (8 x 1in)
Inner wheel arch (2)	6mm (1/4in) plywood	48 x 43mm (1 29/32 x 1 11/16in)
Rear crosspiece (1)	6mm (1/4in) plywood	204 x 56mm (8 x 2 7/32in)
Bonnet dash crosspiece (1)	6mm (1/4in) plywood	216 x 15mm (8 1/2 x 19/32in)
Front mudguard top (2)	6mm (1/4in) plywood	88 x 55mm (3 15/32 x 2 5/32in)
Rear mudguard top (2)	6mm (1/4in) plywood	67x 55mm (2 5/8 x 2 5/32in)
Rear mudguard corners (2)	6mm (1/4in) plywood	46 x 42mm (1 13/16 x 1 21/32in)
Boot lid top (1)	6mm (1/4in) plywood	119 x 93mm (4 11/16 x 3 21/32in)
Boot lid end (1)	6mm (1/4in) plywood	119 x 34mm (4 11/16 x 1 11/32in)
Bonnet lid (1)	6mm (1/4in) plywood	110 x 121mm (4 11/32 x 4 25/32in)
Radiator (1)	6mm (1/4in) plywood	105 x 60mm (4 5/32 x 2 3/8in)
Radiator hose (1)	6mm (1/4in) plywood	105 x 44mm (4 5/32 x 1 3/4in)
Radiator cap (1)	6mm (1/4in) plywood	20mm (25/32in) diameter
Fan (1)	6mm (1/4in) plywood	30mm (1 3/16in) diameter
Engine sides (2)	6mm (1/4in) plywood	50 x 50mm (1 31/32 x 1 31/32in)
Engine block base (1)	6mm (1/4in) plywood	58 x 28mm (2 9/32 x 1 3/32in)
Engine block back and front (2)	6mm (1/4in) plywood	58 x 35mm (2 9/32 x 1 3/8in)
Distributor (1)	6mm (1/4in) plywood	50 x 10mm (1 31/32 x 31/32in)
Air cleaner disc (1)	6mm (1/4in) plywood	20mm (25/32in) diameter
Exhaust plate (1)	6mm (1/4in) plywood	32 x 25mm (1 1/4 x 1in)
Exhaust stub block (1)	6mm (1/4in) plywood	70 x 40mm (2 3/4 x 1 9/16in)
Steering wheel (1)	6mm (1/4in) plywood	60mm (2 3/8in) diameter
Steering wheel hub (1)	6mm (1/4in) plywood	16mm (5/8in) diameter
Spare wheel latch discs (2)	6mm (1/4in) plywood	14mm (9/16in) diameter
Jack inner section (1)	6mm (1/4in) plywood	45 x 25mm (1 3/4 x 1in)
Jack outer sections (2)	6mm (1/4in) plywood	55 x 25mm (2 3/16 x 1in)
Jack foot (1)	6mm (1/4in) plywood	52 x 25mm (2 1/16 x 1in)

Brake hubs (4)	6mm (¼in) plywood	76mm (3in) diameter
Wheels (5)	6mm (¼in) plywood	120mm (4²³⁄₃₂in) diameter
Emergency wheel tyre (1)	6mm (¼in) plywood	120mm (4²³⁄₃₂in) diameter
Hinge covers (4)	1.5mm (¹⁄₁₆in) plywood	25 x 12mm (1 x ½in)
Jack inner section (1)	1.5mm (¹⁄₁₆in) plywood	45 x 25mm (1¾ x 1in)
Wheel tyres (4)	15mm (¹⁹⁄₃₂in) pine	120mm (4²³⁄₃₂in) diameter
Front wing fillets (2)	15mm (¹⁹⁄₃₂in) pine	42 x 28mm (1²¹⁄₃₂ x 1⅛in)
Front chassis crosspiece (1)	15mm (¹⁹⁄₃₂in) pine	108 x 27mm (4¼ x 1¹⁄₁₆in)
Bumper sides (2)	15mm (¹⁹⁄₃₂in) pine	78 x 32mm (3³⁄₃₂ x 1¼in)
Engine block (1)	15mm (¹⁹⁄₃₂in) pine	70 x 50mm (2¾ x 1³¹⁄₃₂in)
Transmission blocks (2)	15mm (¹⁹⁄₃₂in) pine	50 x 25mm (1³¹⁄₃₂ x 1in)
Air cleaner (1)	15mm (¹⁹⁄₃₂in) pine	65 x 45mm (2⁹⁄₁₆ x 1¾in)
Steering pillar (1)	15mm (¹⁹⁄₃₂in) pine	41 x 16mm (1⅝ x ⅝in)
Gear unit (1)	15mm (¹⁹⁄₃₂in) pine	40 x 20mm (1⁹⁄₁₆ x ²⁵⁄₃₂in)
Socket handle (1)	15mm (¹⁹⁄₃₂in) pine	20 x 28mm (²⁵⁄₃₂ x 1⅛in)
Bumper (1)	22mm (⅞in) dowel	108mm (4¼in) long
Silencer (1)	22mm (⅞in) dowel	67mm (2⅝in) long
Hubs (4)	16mm (⅝in) beech	30mm (1³⁄₁₆in) diameter
Generator (1)	12mm (½in) dowel	18mm (¹¹⁄₁₆in) long
Drive shaft (1)	12mm (½in) dowel	197mm (7¾in) long
Exhaust pipe (1)	12mm (½in) dowel	181mm (7⅛in) long
Fan shaft (1)	6mm (¼in) dowel	15mm (¹⁹⁄₃₂in) long
Air cleaner dowel (1)	6mm (¼in) dowel	27mm (1¹⁄₁₆in) long
Air cleaner dowel (1)	6mm (¼in) dowel	23mm (⅞in) long
Generator mount (1)	6mm (¼in) dowel	10mm (⅜in) long
Spark plugs (4)	6mm (¼in) dowel	20mm (²⁵⁄₃₂in) long
Exhaust pipe stub (1)	6mm (¼in) dowel	15mm (¹⁹⁄₃₂in) long
Gear stick handles (2)	6mm (¼in) dowel	18mm (¹¹⁄₁₆in) long
Gear sticks (2)	6mm (¼in) dowel	28mm (1³⁄₃₂in) long
Steering shaft (1)	6mm (¼in) dowel	20mm (²⁵⁄₃₂in) long
Spare wheel latch shaft (1)	6mm (¼in) dowel	24mm (¹⁵⁄₁₆in) long
Spare wheel locating posts (2)	6mm (¼in) dowel	17mm (⅝in) long
Bottom seat cover (1)	17mm (²¹⁄₃₂in) balsa wood	202 x 60mm (7¹⁵⁄₁₆ x 2⅜in)
Top seat cover (1)	17mm (²¹⁄₃₂in) balsa wood	202 x 54mm (7¹⁵⁄₁₆ x 2¹⁄₈in)
Windscreens (2)	5mm (⁷⁄₃₂in) acrylic	82 x 37mm (3¼ x 1⁷⁄₁₆in)

Plastic nuts and bolts (12)	car number plate fixings	
Front and rear axles (2)	mild steel axle rod	6mm (¼in) diameter
Spring caps (4)		6mm (¼in)
Steel washers (4)		6mm (¼in)
Plastic washers (4)		20mm (²⁵⁄₃₂in) with 6mm (¼in) diameter holes
Neoprene tubing		6mm (¼in) internal diameter
Spanner socket (1)		11mm (¹⁵⁄₃₂in)
Cotton material	off-cut from old clothing	
Sheet metal screws (4)		12mm (½in)
Card		
Spark plug leads (4)	plastic-coated cable	2mm (³⁄₃₂in)
Differential (1)	hardwood ball	37mm (1⁷⁄₁₆in) diameter

DRIVER

Arms (2)	6mm (¼in) plywood	95 x 24mm (3¾ x ¹⁵⁄₁₆in)
Shoulder discs (2)	6mm (¼in) plywood	18mm (²³⁄₃₂in) diameter
Lower legs (2)	6mm (¼in) plywood	68 x 29mm (2¹¹⁄₁₆ x 1⁵⁄₃₂in)
Upper legs (4)	6mm (¼in) plywood	76 x 24mm (3 x ¹⁵⁄₁₆in)
Feet (4)	6mm (¼in) plywood	29 x 12mm (1⁵⁄₃₂ x ½in)
Neck (1)	6mm (¼in) plywood	16mm (⅝in) diameter
Body (1)	22mm (⅞in) dowel	78mm (3¹⁄₁₆in) long
Neck joint (1)	6mm (¼in) dowel	20mm (²⁵⁄₃₂in) long
Knee joints (2)	3mm (⅛in) dowel	12mm (½in) long
Head (1)	hardwood ball	37mm (1⁷⁄₁₆in) diameter
Hip and shoulder joints (1)	nylon cord	2mm (³⁄₃₂in)

MISCELLANEOUS

Self-adhesive lettering

Oil-based primer

Enamel paints (suggested colours: black, white, silver, red, blue, metallic blue and lime green)

Matt paints for driver (suggested colours: flesh, brown, black, olive green and buff)

Permanent liner pen (for driver's facial features)

Note: Be aware that some of the components of this toy may present a choking hazard to children of 36 months and under.

CONSTRUCTION

1 Join two pieces of 6mm (¼in) plywood together with double-sided tape and cut out two identical chassis sides (Fig 11.1) as well as cutting out the front floor, rear floor (Fig 11.2), front bulkhead and rear bulkhead (Fig 11.3) as seen in Photo 1. Make a 3mm (⅛in) deep by 6mm (¼in) wide groove for the wheel axle on the underside of the front floor by making two parallel cuts with a Gent's saw and then prising out the waste with a chisel-shaped craft knife blade. Fret out the slot and large hole in the front floor, and drill any holes.

2 Dry assemble and test fit the chassis parts before gluing them together as shown in Photo 2. Note the position of the bevels on the rear floor and rear bulkhead. Fit the axles temporarily to get the alignment correct. Blind pin at strategic points and use clamps and tape to hold the pieces together while the glue is setting.

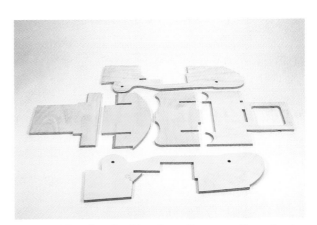

Photo 1 The chassis sides, front floor, rear floor, front bulkhead and rear bulkhead ready for assembly.

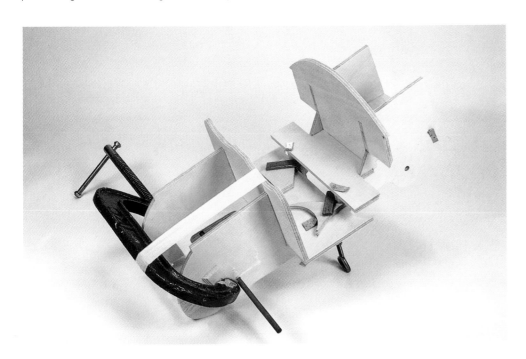

Photo 2 The chassis parts clamped while the glue sets.

Photo 3 When the seat front and inner wheel arches have been fitted, the area indicated here needs to be rounded off.

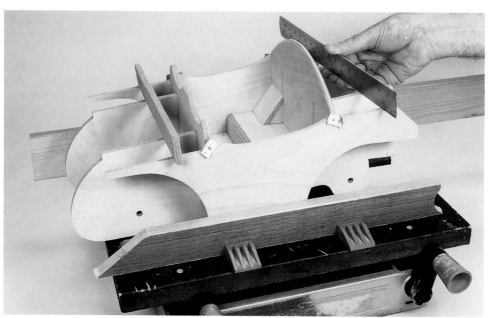

Photo 4 Using a straight edge to check that the top edges of the sides line up with the chassis.

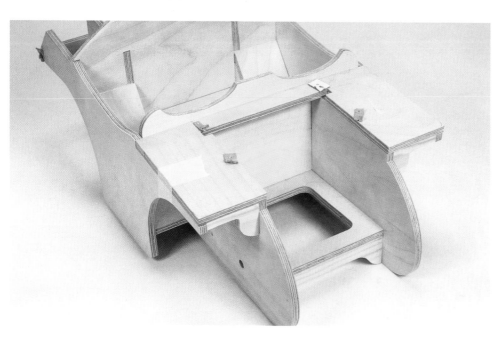

Photo 5 The front wing fillets, front chassis crosspiece, bonnet dash crosspiece and front mudguard tops in place.

3 Cut out the seat front and inner wheel arches (Fig 11.4) Glue them into place as seen in Photo 3. Round off and smooth out the area on the underside that I am indicating in Photo 3.

4 Join two pieces of plywood together with double-sided tape and cut out two identical sides (Fig 11.5). Round off the top edge of the rear bulkhead and the front edge of the seat with a balsa plane and rub smooth. Clean up around the cab area before gluing on the sides as shown in Photo 4. Blind pin and clamp the assembly together. Use straight edges to check that the top edges of the sides line up with the chassis.

5 Mark up and cut out the front wing fillets, front chassis crosspiece, bonnet dash crosspiece and front mudguard tops (Fig 11.4). Glue them in place as shown in Photo 5. Note the position of the notches in the front mudguard tops.

6 Cut out the rear crosspiece, rear mudguard tops and rear mudguard corners (Fig 11.4), and glue them in position, as shown in Photo 6. Note the position of the notches in the rear mudguard tops.

7 Mark up the boot lid top, the boot lid end and the bonnet lid (Fig 11.6), and cut them out. Drill the central 6mm (¼in) hole in the boot lid for the spare wheel latch, but not the two holes for the spare wheel location posts. Round off the pivots on the boot lid top to a 6mm (¼in) diameter together with the edge facing the rear bulkhead before gluing the boot lid top to the boot lid end. Check that they fit into the boot opening and that they open smoothly, as shown in Photo 7. Round off the pivots on the bonnet lid together with the edge facing the cab and the front edge. Check that it fits and opens and shuts smoothly.

8 Mark up and cut out the radiator, hose and cap (Fig 11.7). Round off the hose where it protrudes above the radiator to fit into the counterbored hole in the cap. Glue them together.

9 Mark up the bumper sides (Fig 11.1) using the end of the dowel for the bumper to ensure an accurate fit. Round off the top inner edge of the bumper sides before gluing them into place with the bumper as shown in Photo 8. Temporarily insert the radiator assembly (this needs to lift out smoothly, so if it looks as if it won't once it has been painted and varnished, trim it down a little) to help with the alignment. When you are satisfied this is correct, remove and put aside.

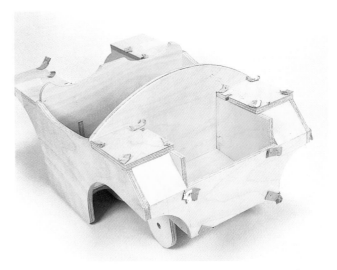

Photo 6 The rear crosspiece, rear mudguard tops and rear mudguard corners in position.

Photo 7 The boot lip top, boot lip end and bonnet lid in position and working smoothly.

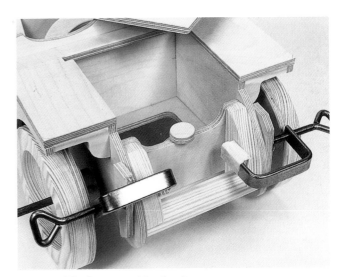

Photo 8 The bumper sides in place.

10 Mark up and cut out the engine block, base, back, front and sides and transmission block (Fig 11.7), and drill all the holes in them. Mark up the distributor (Fig 11.7) and drill the 3mm (⅛in) holes for the spark plug leads before cutting it out. Glue together the engine block, base, back, front and sides as shown in Photo 9 and tape and clamp them together until the glue has set.

11 Counterbore a 6mm (¼in) hole to hold the spark plugs (Fig. 11.7) in a block of wood held in the drill vice. Replace the drill bit with a 3mm (⅛in) drill bit and insert a spark plug into the hole in the wood block. Grip it with a pair of pliers and counterbore the cable hole into it (see also Chapter 12, Mars Pathfinder Game, Fig 12.9).

12 Cut out the fan (Fig 11.7), exhaust stub block, air cleaner and air cleaner disc (Fig 11.8). Cut the fan shaft and air cleaner dowels to length. Round off the edges of the air cleaner before gluing on the disc and the air cleaner dowels, the longer of which holds the disc in place. Assemble the two pieces of dowel that make up the generator (Fig 11.8) and make a 6mm (¼in) mounting hole in the front of the engine block for it as seen in Photo 9.

13 Round off the sharp corners of the engine block. Shape the distributor with abrasive paper and glue it onto the engine block. Round off the outer edges of the transmission blocks (Fig 11.7) before gluing them onto the engine block (make sure they allow the engine to sit level when installed onto the front axle). Glue on the exhaust stub block and generator. Cut the spark plug lead wires a little longer than you want them, bare them at one end and bend the wire to form a loop. Insert these into the holes in the spark plugs and glue them in with epoxy resin. Finally check that the air cleaner fits neatly and can be easily removed as in Photo 10.

14 Mark up and cut out the exhaust plate, silencer and exhaust pipe stub (Fig 11.8). Round off the outer edges of the exhaust plate and glue it into place as shown in Photo 11. Check that it lines up with the exhaust stub block when the engine is installed.

15 To make the differential, drill a hole 6mm (¼in) in diameter through the centre of a 37mm (1⁷⁄₁₆in) wooden ball, and then, at 90° to it, another hole 12mm (½in) diameter which goes only halfway through. Cut out the drive shaft (Fig 11.8). Fit the rear axle temporarily. Glue together the drive shaft and differential, and the exhaust pipe, silencer and exhaust pipe assembly with epoxy resin. Place both of these in position on the rear axle temporarily while the epoxy resin glue sets, as seen in Photo 11.

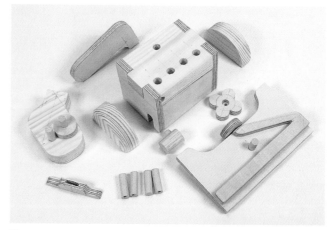

Photo 9 The engine block, base, back, front and sides

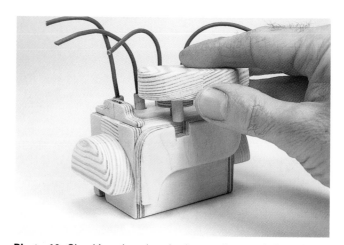

Photo 10 Checking that the air cleaner fits neatly into the engine and can be easily removed.

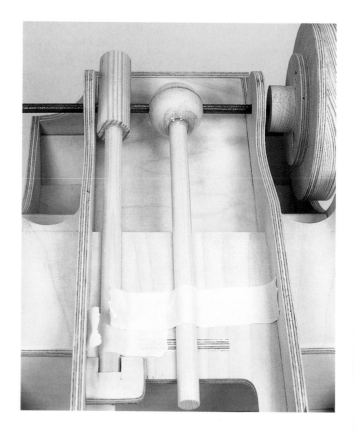

Photo 11 The drive shaft and exhaust pipe assembly placed in position on the rear axle while the glue sets.

16 Make a card template for the brake hubs (Fig 11.9) and mark the axle and wheel bolt centres with a sharp pin held in a pin chuck, as seen in Photo 12. For each brake hub, draw the outer circumference from the axle mark. Drill a 6mm (¼in) hole for the axle and 7mm (⁹⁄₃₂in) holes for the wheel bolts (number plate fixings). Counterbore 12mm (½in) holes into the wheel bolt holes to a depth of no more than 3mm (⅛in), as can be seen in Photo 12. Glue on the hub (Fig 11.9) as also shown in Photo 12 noting it is on the bolt head's side.

17 Using the same template mark up the five wheels (Fig 11.9) and from the axle centre mark out the inner edge of the tyre (Fig 11.9). Drill out the holes as in Step 16. Fix a spring cap to one end of a piece of axle rod and insert it through the axle hole of the wheel. Mark out the perimeter of the spring cap as shown in Photo 13 and then fret out the spring-cap sized hole.

Photo 13 Marking the perimeter of the spring cap. This is then fretted out.

18 You may find it hard to obtain a large enough piece of knot-free pine for the tyres (Fig 11.9). If necessary, you can butt joint together the 15mm (¹⁹⁄₃₂in) pine stock. Mark up the outer and inner perimeters of the tyres onto the pine and cut out the inner section only, as seen in Photo 14. Glue on the tyre, lining it up with the inner perimeter marked on the wheel. Tap fret pins into the waste areas and stack all four wheel-and-tyre assemblies together and clamp them firmly until the glue is set. Finally, cut out around the outer perimeter of the wheels as shown in Photo 14. Smooth the edges of the tyres to about a 2mm (³⁄₃₂in) radius. The procedure for the emergency wheel is the same, except that in this case the tyre is made from 6mm (¼in) plywood.

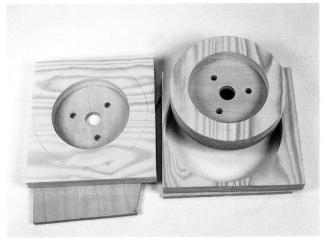

Photo 14 Two stages in the making and fitting of a tyre to a wheel (see Step 18).

19 Cut out and dry assemble the spare wheel latch (Fig 11.10), and temporarily fit it into position with the eccentric disc on the outside as seen in Photo 15. Use the emergency spare wheel as a guide for the 6mm (¼in) counterbored holes for the spare wheel locating posts, which you can now glue in. Cut out the hinge covers (Fig 11.10).

20 Sandwich the 6mm (¼in) and 1.5mm (¹⁄₁₆in) plywood jack inner sections (Fig 11.11) between the outer sections and glue the foot into the slot in the base.

21 Cut out the steering wheel, steering wheel hub, steering pillar, gear unit and gear sticks and handles (Fig 11.10).

22 Paint with white oil-based primer, clear varnish and enamels.

23 Fit an axle, with a spring cap and washer temporarily attached, onto a brake hub. Glue the plastic bolts onto the brake hub with epoxy resin. In order to keep the bolts straight, fit on a wheel as seen in Photo 16, but as soon as the resin starts to set remove the wheel so that they do not stick together. Leave the resin to harden fully. If necessary, you can top up the resin around the bolt head by flowing in some more while heating it with a hairdryer to make it runny. Resin the socket handle (Fig 11.10) into the spanner socket as also seen in Photo 16.

24 Glue the gear sticks and handles into the gear unit and glue this to the centre of the cab floor.

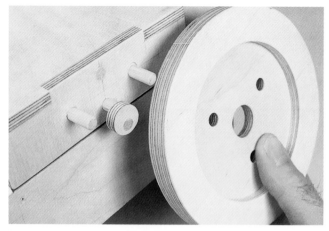

Photo 15 The spare wheel, and the locating posts and latch which hold it in position.

25 Glue the steering wheel, steering pillar, hub and steering shaft together, so that the wheel moves freely and then attach the entire assembly to the front bulkhead.

26 Glue one end of the 6mm (¼in) dowel fan shaft into the counterbored hole in the fan and the other end into the radiator.

27 Trim the spark plug leads to length, expose a little of the wire at the ends and bend it outwards. Fix the ends into the holes in the top of the distributor with epoxy resin made runny by heating it gently with a hairdryer.

28 Glue the spare wheel latch in place as you assembled it in Step 19 and Photo 15.

Photo 16 Fixing the bolts to the brake hub, a wheel and axle fitted temporarily to aid alignment.

29 Fit the wheel axles after cutting to length which is best determined after a trial assembly. When assembling the rear axle note that pieces of neoprene tube are used as spacers between the chassis and the exhaust and differential as seen in Photo 17. Determine the length of the spacers during the trial assembly and cut to length. Slide them onto the axle in their positions between the exhaust, differential and chassis as it is passed through during final assembly. First attach a cap then a steel washer followed by a brake hub and a plastic washer. Insert through the chassis and repeat at the other side, finally tapping on the second cap as seen in Photo 17. Do not rest the vehicle on the wheel bolts, but rest the brake hub on a block of wood as shown.

30 Glue the hinge covers over the bonnet and boot pivots with epoxy resin.

31 Cut out and polish the windscreens (Fig 11.11) (see Cutting acrylic, page 8). Use the holes in the windscreens as guides for drilling 2mm (³⁄₃₂in) pilot holes in the front bulkhead to accept the sheet metal screws. Position the windscreens, and secure them with the screws. Use a small amount of epoxy resin to secure the screws.

32 Cut and shape the balsa wood seat covers (Fig 11.11), then test fit them in the cab before gluing the two parts together. Cover the seat with material, folding it around the back and gluing it on. Finally glue the seats into place in the cab. Add the lettering.

33 Cut out all the pieces for the driver. Glue the shoulder discs onto the inside of the arms, and glue the feet to each side of the lower leg (Fig 11.12). Drill 3mm (⅛in) holes through the arms and shoulders, and counterbore a 6mm (¼in) hole part-way though the arm for the shoulder cord.

34 Drill a 6mm (¼in) hole into a 37mm (1⁷⁄₁₆in) wooden ball for the head and glue in the neck joint dowel along with the neck (Fig 11.12). Drill the holes in the body and use a Gent's saw to cut out the notches where the legs will attach (Fig 11.12) before gluing the head on, as seen in Photo 18.

35 Counterbore 6mm (¼in) holes on the outside of the upper legs for the hip cord. At the bottom of the upper legs, remove the internal areas for the knee joint with a Gent's saw. Test fit the leg parts together, as shown in Photo 18 and adjust if necessary.

36 After painting all the parts for the driver, glue the 3mm (⅛in) dowel knee joints in place. Join the arms and legs onto the body with 2mm (³⁄₃₂in) nylon cord and pull

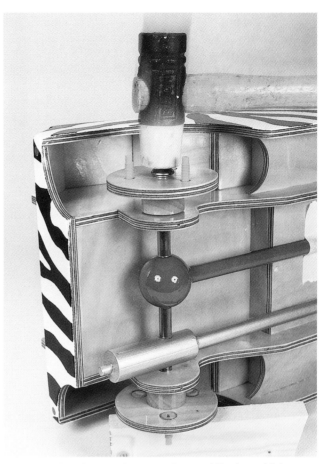

Photo 17 Tapping on the second cap while the vehicle rests on a block of wood.

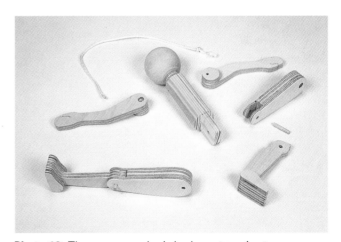

Photo 18 The game warden's body parts, prior to assembly.

as tight as possible. After tying knots on each side push them into the counterbored holes and then fill the holes with epoxy resin. To stiffen the cord, wind thread around it between the body and the limbs.

MARS PATHFINDER GAME

12

In July of 1997 I was fascinated like so many onlookers were when the Mars Pathfinder mission landed successfully on the red planet and proceeded to send back pictures. However not everything went well at first due to the Sojourner Rover becoming hindered by an airbag cushion not fully deflating on landing. The Mars exploration manager at NASA commented at the time that 'The great Galactic Ghoul had to get us somewhere and apparently he has decided to pick on the rover'. So here it is, planet Mars, waiting for up to four young pathfinders to scoop up their precious samples, but not before the little green Martian ghouls have tried to eat them or the dreaded black holes suck them away to reappear somewhere else.

CUTTING LIST

GAME

Top (1)	6mm (¼in) plywood	513 x 513mm (20³/₁₆ x 20³/₁₆in)
Base (1)	6mm (¼in) plywood	570 x 570mm (22⁷/₁₆ x 22⁷/₁₆in)
Pivots (2)	6mm (¼in) plywood	220 x 220mm (5⅝ x 5⅝in)
Dividers 'A' (4)	6mm (¼in) plywood	175 x 55mm (6⅞ x 2⁵/₃₂in)
Dividers 'B' (4)	6mm (¼in) plywood	228 x 55mm (8³¹/₃₂ x 2⁵/₃₂in)
Rims (4)	6mm (¼in) plywood	188 x 134mm (7⅜ x 5⁹/₃₂in)
Balsa wood offcuts		42mm (1¹¹/₁₆in) thick
Balsa wood		6 x 6mm (¼ x ¼in)
Sample disc knob (1)	16mm (⅝in) beech	70mm (2¾in) diameter
	or other hardwood	
Sample disc knob retainer (1)	wooden ball	37mm (1⁷/₁₆in) diameter
Plastic washer (1)	from margarine container	80mm (3⁵/₃₂in) diameter
		with 6mm (¼in) hole
Plastic washer (1)		110mm (4⁵/₁₆in) diameter
		with 6mm (¼in) hole
Wooden balls (20)		19mm (¾in) diameter
Rubber blanking-off grommets (4)		24mm (¹⁵/₁₆in) diameter
Ramps	1mm (¹/₃₂in) cardboard	
Coloured card		
Screw-top plastic container		
Felt		
Dots (4)	Coloured self-adhesive plastic film 14mm (⁹/₁₆in) diameter	
Plastic dice (2)		
Sample disc (1)	2mm (³/₃₂in) transparent acrylic 280mm (11¹/₃₂in) diameter	
Black hole disc (1)	2mm (³/₃₂in) transparent acrylic 360mm (14³/₁₆in) diameter	
Paper		

ROVERS

Chassis sides (8)	6mm (¼in) plywood	72 x 18mm (2²⁷/₃₂ x ¾in)
Chassis top (4)	6mm (¼in) plywood	72 x 34mm (2²⁷/₃₂ x 1¹¹/₃₂in)
Sampler arm part 'A' (4)	6mm (¼in) plywood	88 x 34mm (3½ x 1¹¹/₃₂in)
Sampler arm part 'B' (4)	6mm (¼in) plywood	43 x 34mm (1¹¹/₁₆ x 1¹¹/₃₂in)
Sampler arm part 'C' (4)	6mm (¼in) plywood	25 x 34mm (1 x 1¹¹/₃₂in)
Sampler arm side (8)	6mm (¼in) plywood	90 x 25mm (3¹⁷/₃₂ x 1in)

Wheel hubs (16)	12mm (½in) dowel	18mm (²³⁄₃₂in) long
Centre pivot (1)	6mm (¼in) dowel	100mm (3¹⁵⁄₁₆in) long
Front axles (4)	4.5mm (³⁄₁₆in) dowel	70mm (2¾in) long
Rear axles (4)	4.5mm (³⁄₁₆in) steel nails	70mm (2¾in) long
Wheels (16)	18mm (²³⁄₃₂in) black foam plastic	36mm (1¹³⁄₃₂in) diameter
Scoop prongs (4)	plastic	26 x 30mm (1¹⁄₃₂ x 1³⁄₁₆in)
Hobbies' brass hinges (4)		25mm (1in)
Brass fret pins		6mm (¼in)

MISCELLANEOUS

Acrylic satin varnish

Acrylic satin paints for the game (colours: orange, yellow, pink, magenta, black and white)

Oil-based primer, lacquer and enamels for the rovers and wooden ball samples (colours: silver, red, gold and lime green)

Permanent liner pen for facial features on green samples

Spray Mount adhesive (also sold as Photomount). It is best to use this kind of glue whenever you have to stick paper onto which something has been drawn. Water-based glues cause the paper to stretch and distort the design.

Note: Be aware that some of the components of this toy may present a choking hazard to children of 36 months and under.

CONSTRUCTION

1 Cut out the top from 6mm (¼in) plywood (Fig 12.1) and fret out the 'black holes' and also drill or fret out the 20mm (²⁵⁄₃₂in) holes as seen in Photo 1. Drill out the 6mm (¼in) centre hole in the top and the base (Fig 12.1). I recommend using a drill guide, as shown in Photo 2, to drill a hole accurately in a board this wide.

TIP

Because the parts are so large, it is a good idea to cut the plywood down to a little way from the outline with a powered jigsaw. The final cutting can then proceed in stages by 'nibbling' out in sections (see also Cutting out long pieces of wood, page 7).

---

2 Cut out two 230mm (9in) squares of plywood and mark up the pivot area (Fig 12.2) on one of them. Cut to shape offcut pieces of balsa wood to laminate between the plywood squares, as shown in Fig 12.2. Laminate the ply with the balsa. When the glue has set cut out the pivot area and drill the 6mm (¼in) hole in the centre as shown in Photo 3.

3 Glue the pivot area onto the base using a piece of 6mm (¼in) dowel to locate the centres carefully. Position the pivot area at exactly the angle shown on Fig 12.3.

4 Cut out and dry assemble dividers 'A' and 'B' (Fig 12.2) and the rims (Fig 12.3) onto the base to check and locate their positions as seen in Photo 4. Carefully remove one divider at a time, apply glue and return to its position. Do not glue on the rims yet!

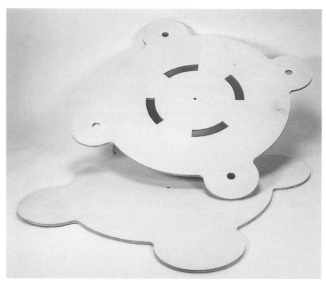

Photo 1 The top with the various fretted and drilled holes that are required.

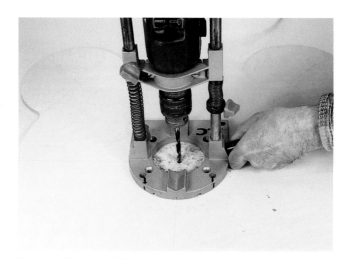

Photo 2 Using a drill guide to drill the 6mm (¼in) centre hole in the top.

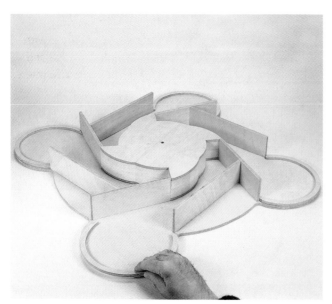

Photo 4 A dry assembly of the base with the rims and dividers 'A' and 'B'.

Photo 3 The pivot area cut out, with a 6mm (¼in) hole drilled in the centre.

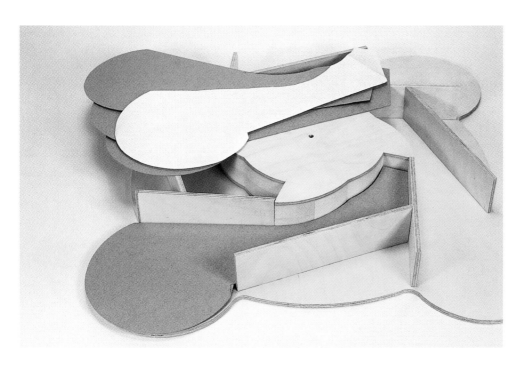

Photo 5 Four sample ramps and the template that was used to draw them.

5 Cut out a paper template of the sample ramp (Fig 12.3) as seen in Photo 5 and check it for fit in each ramp area. Use the template to cut out four sample ramps from 1mm (½2in) cardboard (the material shown here is packing spacers from computer paper boxes). Any variation in shape can be made on the cardboard of each ramp. Note their location and mark accordingly so that they go back in the correct places. An exact fit is not critical, because the sample ball is too large to fall down any tiny gaps.

6 Glue pieces of 6mm (¼in) square-section balsa wood in place to hold the sample ramps at the correct slope and height as shown in Fig 12.4 and Photo 6. Glue the sample ramps in place, paying particular attention to the circular area under the rim (Fig 12.3), which is glued on,

sandwiching the cardboard. Because the cardboard is absorbent, use plenty of glue to ensure a strong bond. Also apply extra glue to the edges of the cardboard ramp to avoid buckling and slipping. Clamp everything firmly while the glue sets, as shown in Photo 6. When set trim the edges of the rims and rub them smooth.

7 Test fit the top and trim the ends of the dividers if necessary so that they are flush with the outer circumference. Paint the ramps with matt black paint or any other dark colour, but don't get paint on any areas that will be glued later.

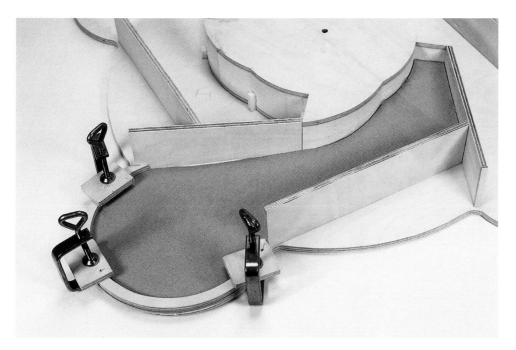

Photo 6 The sample ramps are supported with pieces of balsa wood and sandwiched between the rims and the base.

8 Glue the top in place. Thread a 6mm (¼in) dowel through the centre holes to help align it, and blind pin it to keep it in position. Clamp it firmly, as shown in Photo 7, until the glue is set.

9 To help with marking up the sample and black hole discs (Fig 12.5), mount some thin paper onto the acrylic with Spray Mount, even though it has a protective covering already. This makes it very much easier to draw the shape clearly with drawing instruments. Attach the acrylic to scrap plywood or hardboard using double-sided tape (see Cutting acrylic, page 8). Fret out the round holes and other apertures before cutting out the external shapes as shown in Photo 8 before removing from the backing.

10 Cut out the sample disc knob (Fig 12.6) from beech or similar hardwood and smooth the edges. Make

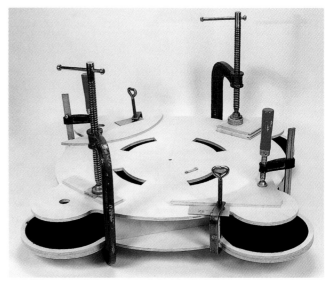

Photo 7 The top clamped in place while the glue sets.

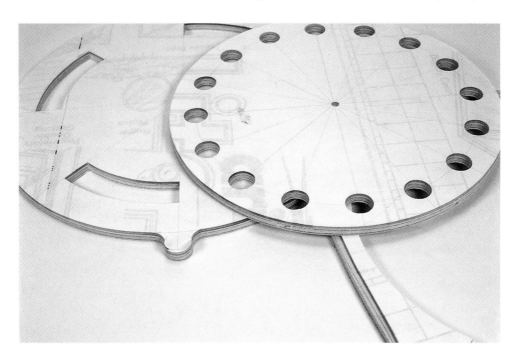

Photo 8 The sample and black hole discs.

two large plastic washers, one 110mm (4⁵⁄₁₆in) in diameter, the other 80mm (3⁵⁄₃₂in) in diameter and both with a 6mm (¼in) diameter centre hole. For the disc knob retainer drill a 6mm (¼in) hole 16mm (⅝in) deep into the centre of the 37mm (1⁷⁄₁₆in) wooden ball.

11 Cut out the rover parts (Fig 12.7) except the scoop prongs, wheels and wheel hubs, noting the bevel cuts required. For sampler arm part 'C' it is best to cut out the scoop portion first or it will be very difficult to handle when you are making the circular cut. Also drill the axle holes in the sides before cutting these out. Glue the sides and top together. Also glue the sampler arm parts together, using masking tape to hold them, as in Photo 9, until the glue is set. Round out the internal area of the scoop, with abrasive paper wrapped around dowelling (see Photo 10), to help the wooden balls roll freely into the sample arm.

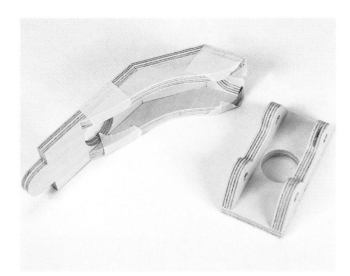

Photo 9 The rover parts. The sample arm parts have been taped together while the glue sets.

Photo 10 Rounding out the inside of the scoop so that the wooden balls can run freely into the sample arm.

12 Cut out the rebate for the brass hinges on the top of the rover chassis, as shown in Fig 12.8. Use a Gent's saw to make the cross cut and remove the waste with a sharp knife.

13 Drill 1mm (¹⁄₃₂in) pilot holes in the rebate for the fret pins. Roughen the back of the hinge and fix it onto the top of the rover with epoxy resin. Tap in the fret pins. When the glue is set, if any pin ends exit underneath, file them down. Place double-sided tape on the upper surface of the hinge to position the sample arm and hold it while you drill 1mm (¹⁄₃₂in) pilot holes, as seen in Photo 11. Remove the tape, and glue and pin the hinge into place as before. Once the glue is set, file down any exposed pin heads (Fig 12.8) and rub down the surface of the chassis top to make the sample arm sit level.

14 Cut out the scoop prongs (Fig 12.7) from thin plastic, such as a margarine tub. Fix four pieces of plastic onto a piece of scrap plywood with double-sided tape, as shown in Photo 12. Mark up the shape and cut them out. Glue the prongs onto the end of their sample arms with epoxy resin, and bind it in place with masking tape until the glue is set. Build up a fillet of resin where the prongs stick proud of the sample arm to reinforce them. When all the glue is fully hardened, rub the underside of the prongs smooth with abrasive paper.

15 To make the wheel hubs (Fig 12.9) drill a 12mm (½in) hole into a block of wood held in the drill vice. Insert a length of 12mm (½in) dowel into the hole as shown. Change to a 5mm (³⁄₁₆in) drill bit and bore out the axle hole. Cut the dowel into 18mm (²³⁄₃₂in) lengths. Cut the rear axles

Photo 11 Drilling pilot holes for the pins that fix the hinge in place.

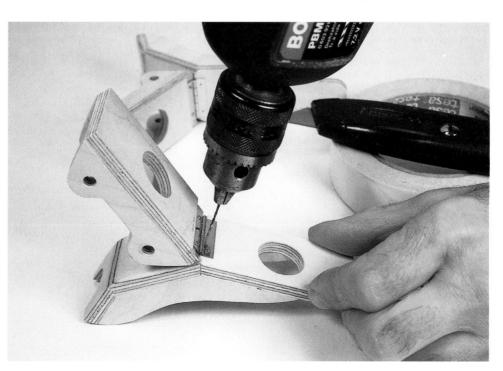

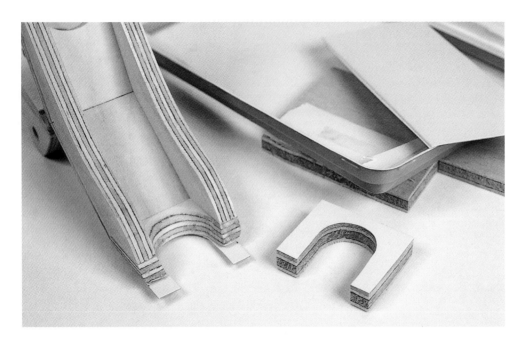

Photo 12 The scoop prongs are made from thin plastic which is stuck to scrap plywood before being cut out.

to length from 4.5mm (³⁄₁₆in) nails as shown in Fig 12.10 and the front axles from 4.5mm (³⁄₁₆in) dowel.

16 Slice some black foam plastic to 18mm (²³⁄₃₂in) thickness (see Cutting foam plastic, page 8). Cut out the wheels (Fig 12.9) using the technique shown in Chapter 2, Paint Stamps. Fret out the hub holes before cutting around the outside.

17 Use acrylic paints for the planet and enamels for the rovers and sample balls.

18 Mark out sixteen divisions on the top with pencil and paint each quadrant with a contrasting transparent colour.

19 Make stamps for the crater patterns (Fig 12.11) as shown in Chapter 2, Paintstamps. Cover the surface with crater patterns. When dry coat the alternate divisions within the quadrants with a darker glaze.

20 Glue the sample disc knob to the sample disc with epoxy resin, aligning the centre holes with a dowel. Fix the grommets onto the black hole disc with a cyanoacrylate glue (super glue) in the positions indicated in Fig 12.5. Stick discs of coloured foil or card inside the grommets with double-sided tape. Make four coloured dots about 14mm (⁹⁄₁₆in) in diameter from self-adhesive coloured plastic film, and stick one between every fourth hole on the sample disc.

21 Place the 110mm (4⁵⁄₁₆in) diameter washer on the top followed by the black hole disc, the 80mm (3⁵⁄₃₂in) diameter washer then the sample disc. Insert the assembled disc knob retaining ball with its dowel pivot through the centre holes and glue it into the base. Gluing

60mm (2³⁄₈in) diameter discs of felt to the underneath of the base will stop the board from slipping on a smooth surface.

22 Glue the wheels onto the hubs with epoxy resin and then glue the hubs onto the axles. The heavier metal axle must go on at the rear of the rover to counterbalance the weight of the sample arm.

23 Photocopy the rules and stick them to the plastic container used for storing the samples and dice.

THE RULES

1 Line up the sample disc and the black hole disc so that the sample balls cannot fall through the black holes. Load the sample balls so that there is one green ball in each player's sector. The rest of the sample balls are then placed on the discs, each player in turn placing one ball in a position of their choice.

2 Throw the dice for the highest number to decide who starts. Then proceed in a clockwise direction around the planet. Each player must first collect one sample from their own sector with their rover and drop it through the hole above their collecting bay. If the sample is not successfully collected it must be returned to its original position.

3 Each player then throws the dice to determine by how many divisions (there are 16 on the board) they will rotate either the sample disc or the black hole disc, or both. The grommet handles on the black hole disc and the coloured dots on the sample disc are used to indicate the movement around the divisions so they can be counted. If, for example, a player throws 10 with the dice, he or she can move the black hole disc 6 divisions and the sample disc 4 divisions in any direction.

4 The players can forego their turn with the sample and black hole discs and take another turn with the rover, collecting or moving samples. You can, for example, drop a green sample into an open black hole so that it goes into another player's collecting bay.

5 The first player to score 8 or above is the winner.

6 If the discs are emptied before the game has finished, return the balls to the pot.

NOTES

A green martian sample eats and cancels all the samples in a player's collecting bay. They must all be returned to the sample disc, except where there are black holes, in positions decided by that player.

A gold sample counts as 2 for scoring purposes.

Samples that roll off the board must be returned to the sample disc.

Samples that drop in to an unused collection bay must be returned to the pot.

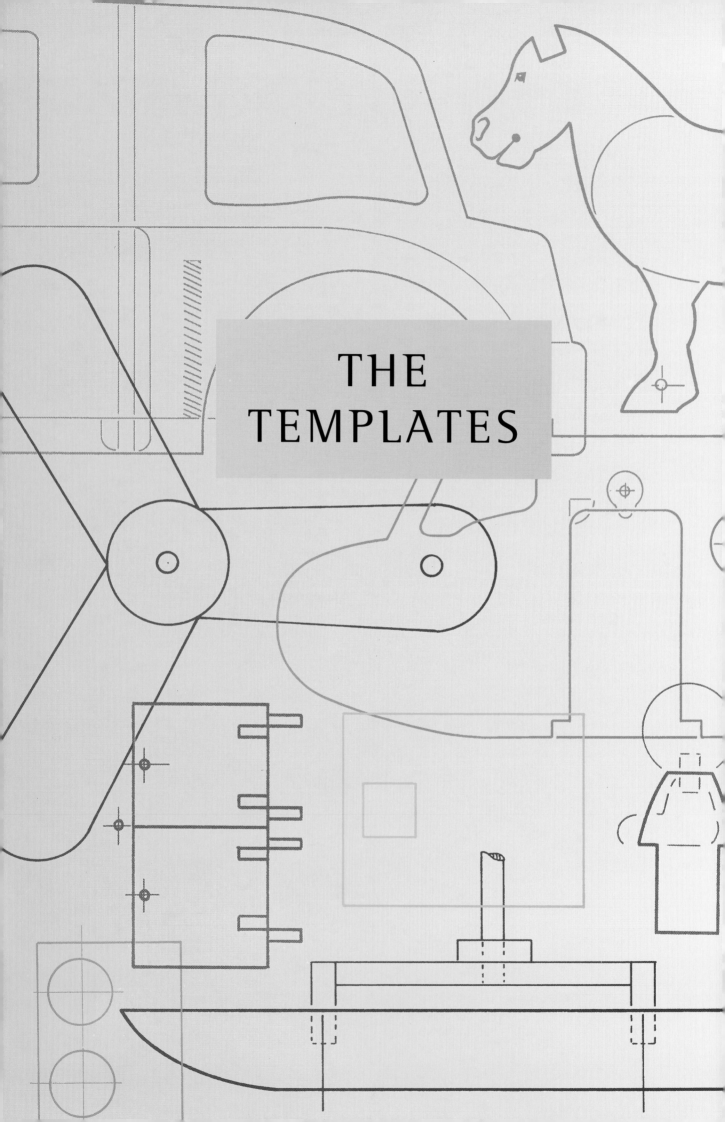

THE
TEMPLATES

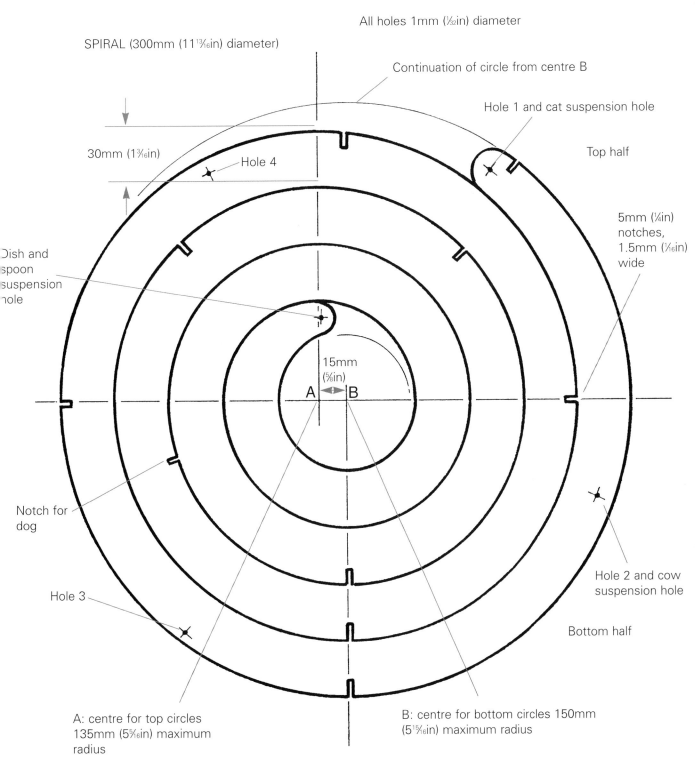

All holes 1mm (½₂in) diameter

SPIRAL (300mm (11¹³⁄₁₆in) diameter)

Continuation of circle from centre B

Hole 1 and cat suspension hole

Top half

30mm (1³⁄₁₆in)

Hole 4

Dish and spoon suspension hole

5mm (¼in) notches, 1.5mm (¹⁄₁₆in) wide

15mm (⅝in)

A   B

Notch for dog

Hole 3

Hole 2 and cow suspension hole

Bottom half

A: centre for top circles 135mm (5⅜in) maximum radius

B: centre for bottom circles 150mm (5¹⁵⁄₁₆in) maximum radius

Fig 3.1 Scale 50%
(Enlarge to 200%)

Fig 3.2 100%   DISH AND SPOON

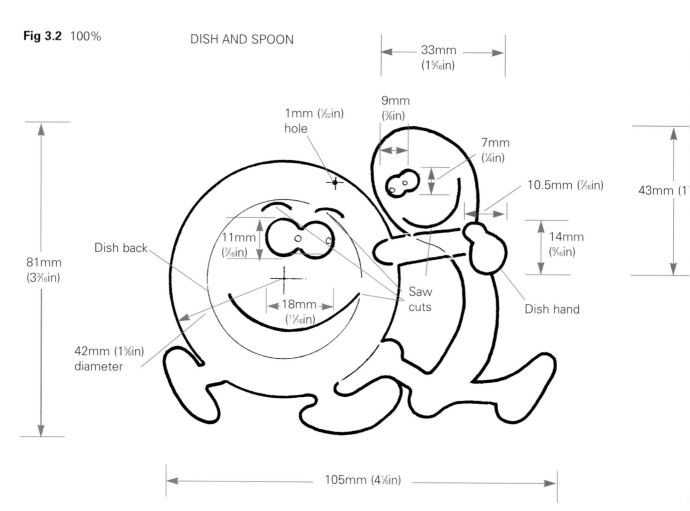

1mm (⅟₃₂in) hole

9mm (⅜in)

7mm (¼in)

33mm (1⅗₁₆in)

10.5mm (⅞₁₆in)

14mm (⅝₁₆in)

43mm (1

Dish back

11mm (⅞₁₆in)

18mm (¹¹⁄₁₆in)

Saw cuts

Dish hand

81mm (3³⁄₁₆in)

42mm (1⅝in) diameter

105mm (4⅛in)

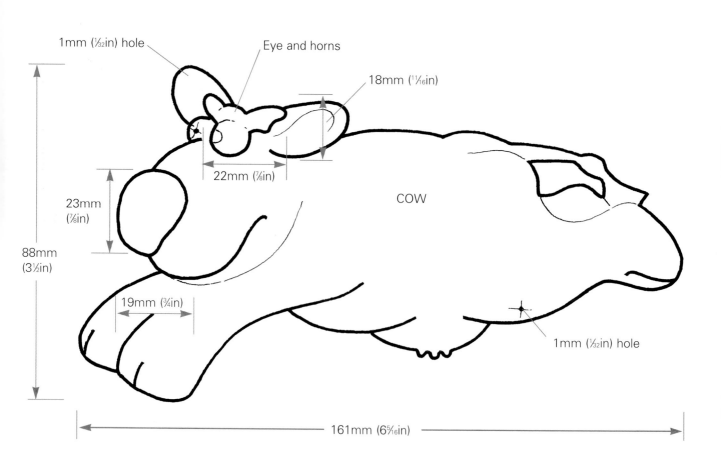

1mm (⅟₃₂in) hole

Eye and horns

18mm (¹¹⁄₁₆in)

22mm (⅞in)

23mm (⅞in)

COW

88mm (3½in)

19mm (¾in)

1mm (⅟₃₂in) hole

161mm (6⅝₁₆in)

112

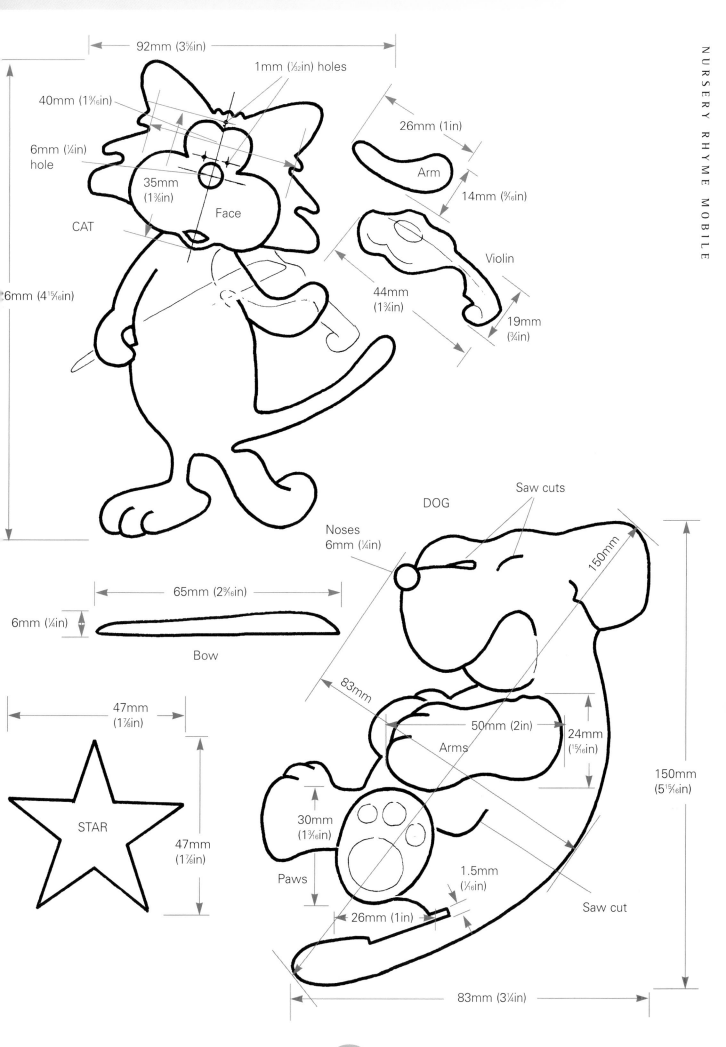

92mm (3⅝in)

1mm (¹⁄₃₂in) holes

40mm (1⁹⁄₁₆in)

6mm (¼in) hole

35mm (1⅜in)

Face

CAT

6mm (4¹⁵⁄₁₆in)

26mm (1in)

Arm

14mm (⁹⁄₁₆in)

Violin

44mm (1¾in)

19mm (¾in)

65mm (2⁹⁄₁₆in)

6mm (¼in)

Bow

47mm (1⅞in)

STAR

47mm (1⅞in)

DOG

Saw cuts

Noses
6mm (¼in)

150mm

83mm

50mm (2in)

Arms

24mm (¹⁵⁄₁₆in)

150mm (5¹⁵⁄₁₆in)

30mm (1³⁄₁₆in)

Paws

1.5mm (¹⁄₁₆in)

Saw cut

26mm (1in)

83mm (3¼in)

Fig 3.2 100%

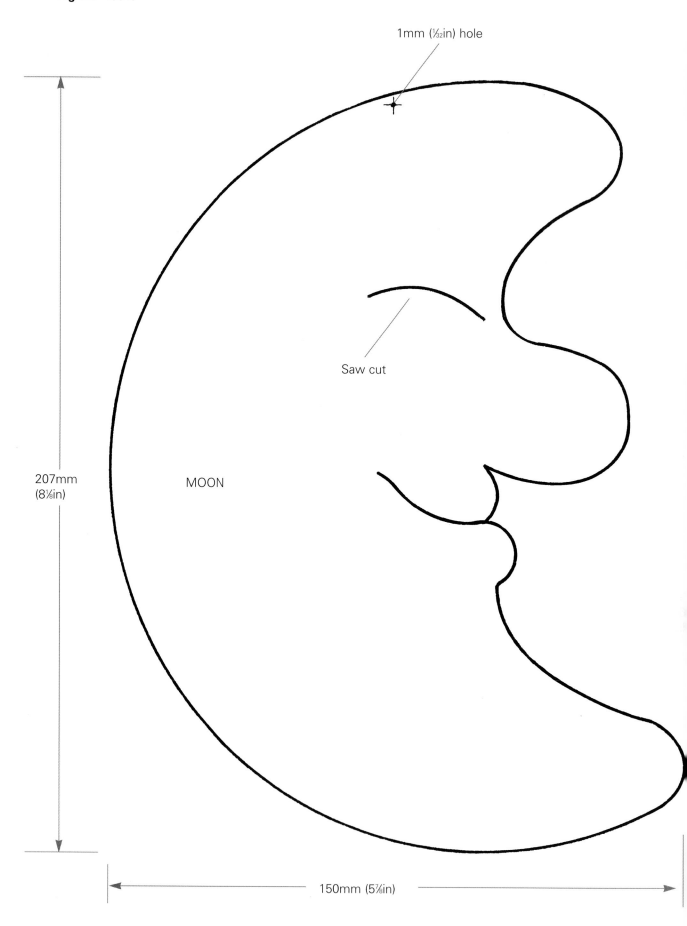

1mm (¹⁄₃₂in) hole

Saw cut

MOON

207mm
(8⅛in)

150mm (5⅞in)

Fig 4.1 100%

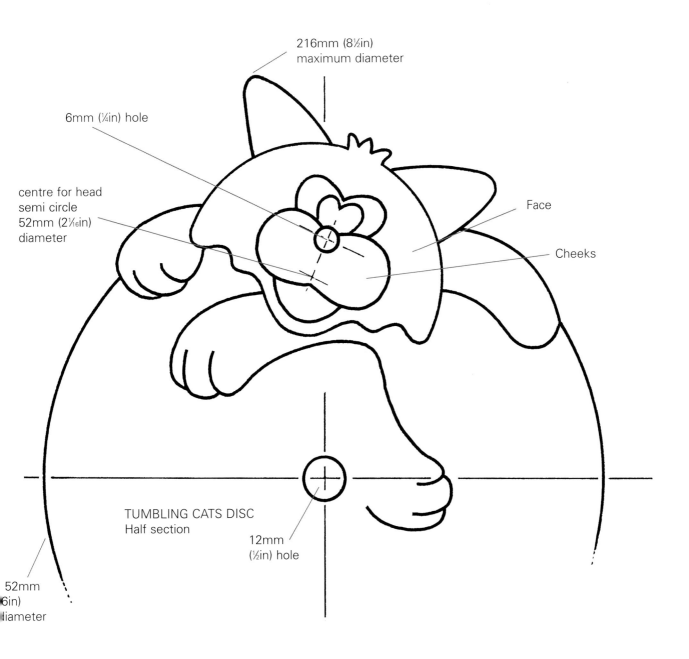

216mm (8½in)
maximum diameter

6mm (¼in) hole

centre for head
semi circle
52mm (2⅟₁₆in)
diameter

Face

Cheeks

TUMBLING CATS DISC
Half section

12mm
(½in) hole

52mm
6in)
diameter

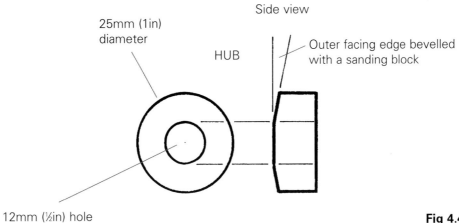

Side view

25mm (1in)
diameter

HUB

Outer facing edge bevelled
with a sanding block

12mm (½in) hole

Fig 4.4 100%

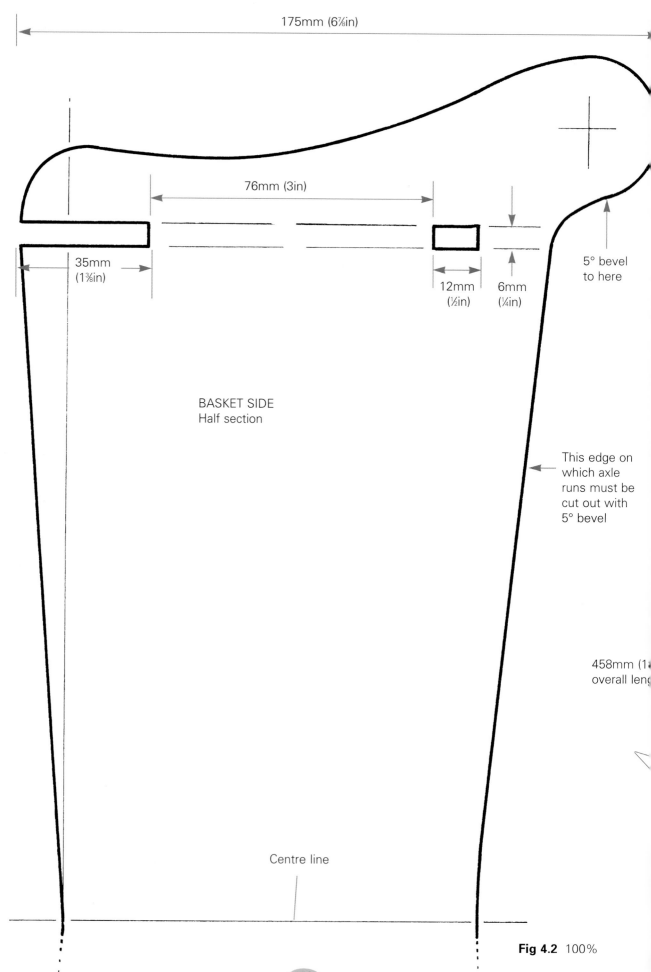

175mm (6⅞in)

76mm (3in)

35mm
(1⅜in)

12mm
(½in)

6mm
(¼in)

5° bevel
to here

BASKET SIDE
Half section

This edge on
which axle
runs must be
cut out with
5° bevel

458mm (1
overall leng

Centre line

Fig 4.2 100%

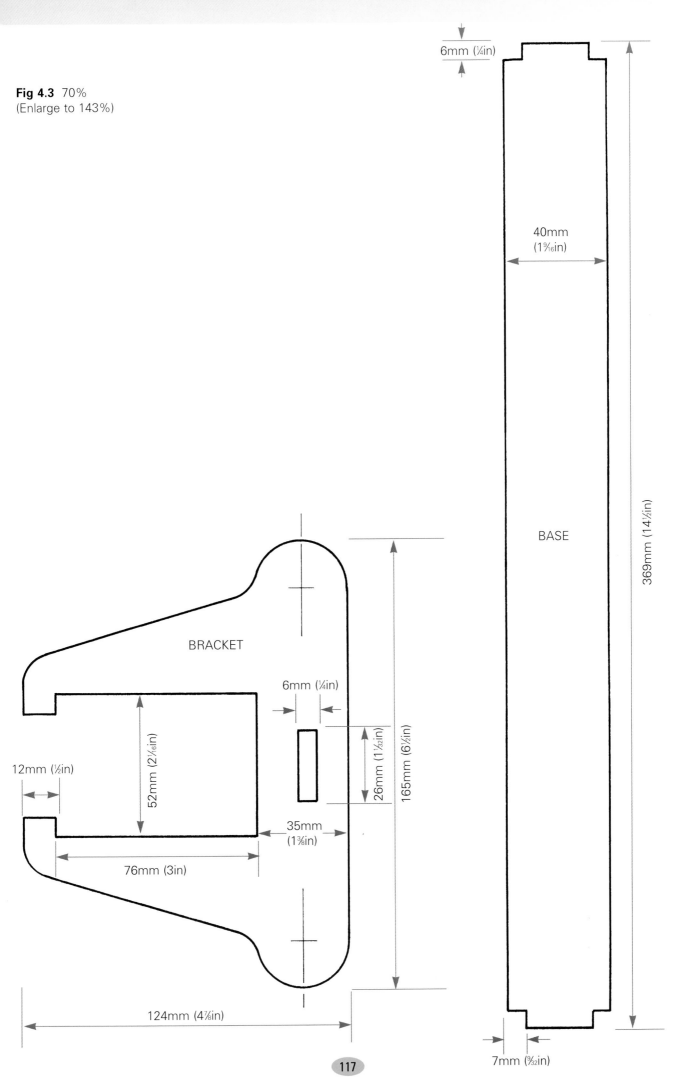

Fig 4.3 70%
(Enlarge to 143%)

6mm (¼in)

40mm
(1⁹⁄₁₆in)

BASE

369mm (14½in)

BRACKET

6mm (¼in)

165mm (6½in)

26mm (1½in)

52mm (2¹⁄₁₆in)

12mm (½in)

35mm
(1³⁄₈in)

76mm (3in)

124mm (4⅞in)

7mm (⁹⁄₃₂in)

117

SCROLLSAW TOYS FOR ALL AGES

Fig 5.1 50% (Enlarge to 200%)

CLOUD AND FRONT
Half sections

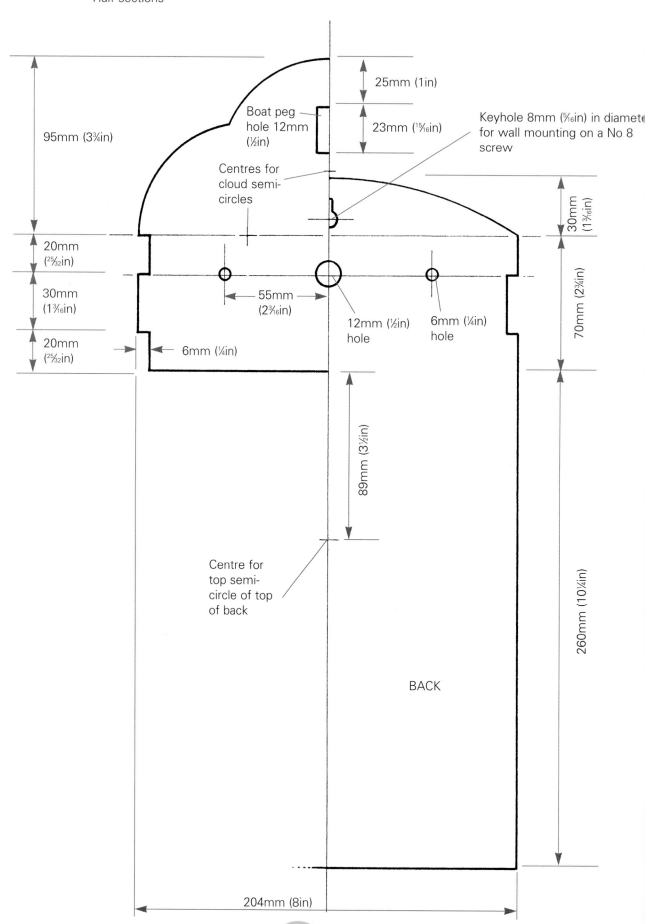

95mm (3¾in)

25mm (1in)

Boat peg
hole 12mm
(½in)

23mm (¹⁵⁄₁₆in)

Keyhole 8mm (⁵⁄₁₆in) in diameter
for wall mounting on a No 8
screw

Centres for
cloud semi-
circles

20mm
(²⁵⁄₃₂in)

30mm
(1¾₆in)

20mm
(²⁵⁄₃₂in)

30mm
(1³⁄₁₆in)

55mm
(2³⁄₁₆in)

12mm (½in)
hole

6mm (¼in)
hole

70mm (2¾in)

6mm (¼in)

89mm (3½in)

Centre for
top semi-
circle of top
of back

260mm (10¼in)

BACK

204mm (8in)

Fig 5.2 100%

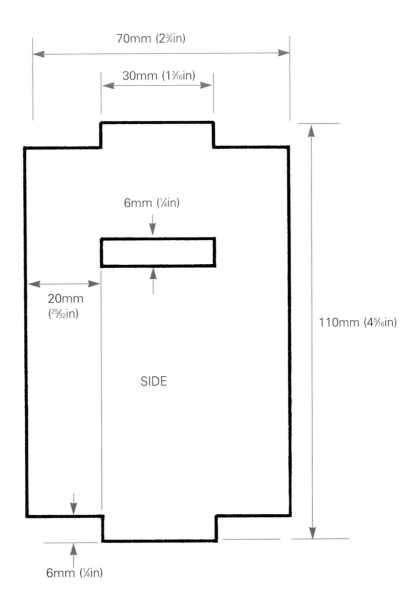

70mm (2¾in)

30mm (1³⁄₁₆in)

6mm (¼in)

20mm
(²⁵⁄₃₂in)

SIDE

110mm (4⁵⁄₁₆in)

6mm (¼in)

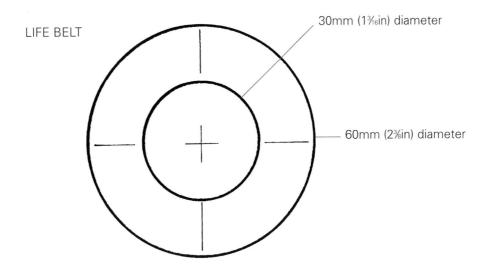

LIFE BELT

30mm (1³⁄₁₆in) diameter

60mm (2³⁄₈in) diameter

Fig 5.6 100%

Fig 5.2 100%

Fig 5.3 100%

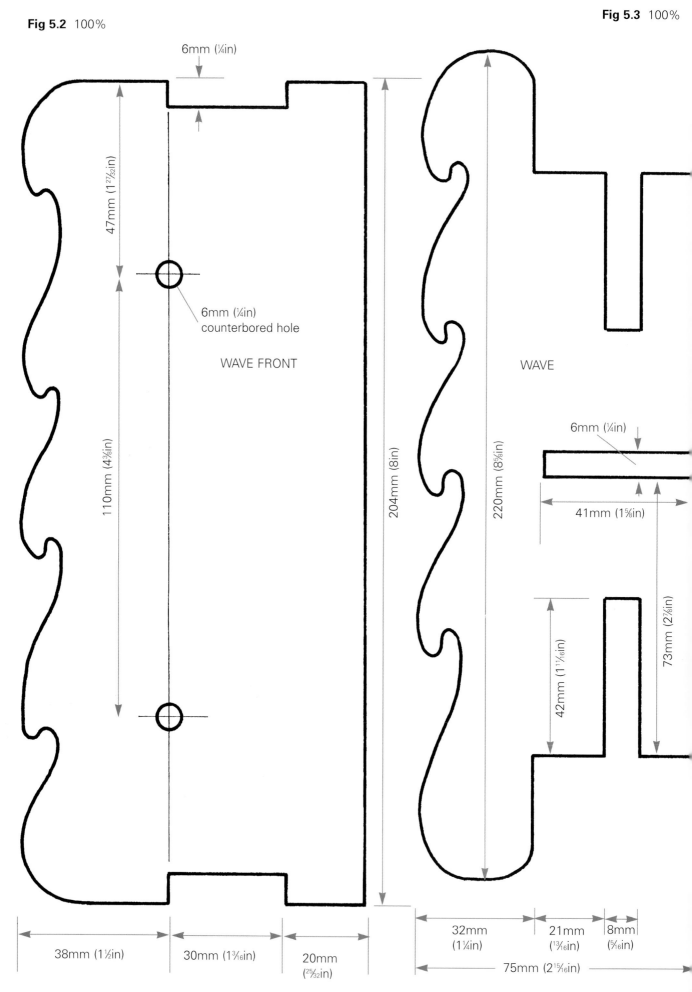

6mm (¼in)

47mm (1²⁷⁄₃₂in)

6mm (¼in)
counterbored hole

WAVE FRONT

WAVE

110mm (4³⁄₈in)

204mm (8in)

220mm (8⁵⁄₈in)

6mm (¼in)

41mm (1⁵⁄₈in)

73mm (2⁷⁄₈in)

42mm (1¹¹⁄₁₆in)

38mm (1½in)

30mm (1³⁄₁₆in)

20mm
(²⁵⁄₃₂in)

32mm
(1¼in)

21mm
(¹³⁄₁₆in)

8mm
(⁵⁄₁₆in)

75mm (2¹⁵⁄₁₆in)

Fig 5.4 100%

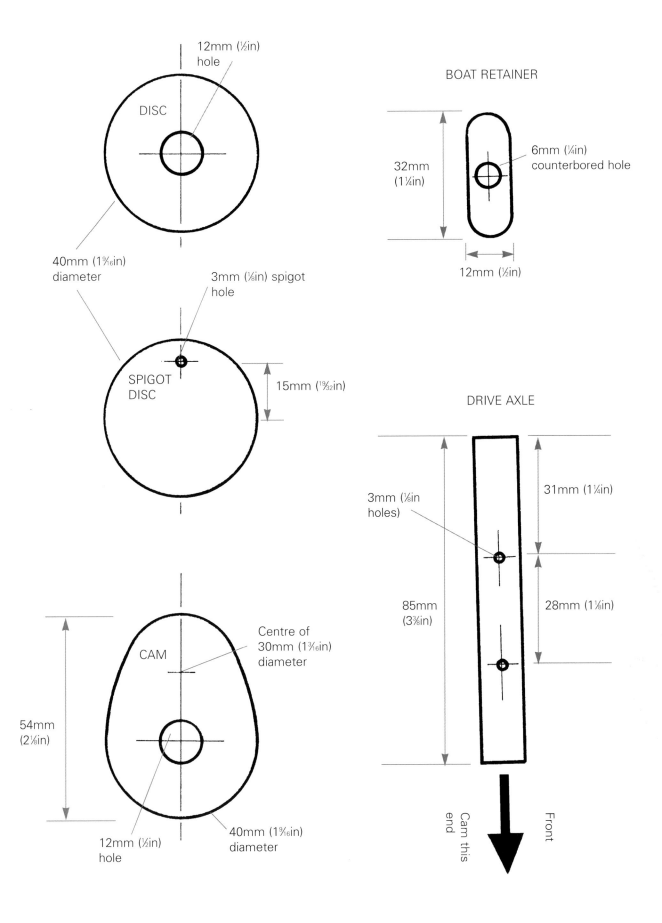

12mm (½in)
hole

DISC

40mm (1⁹⁄₁₆in)
diameter

3mm (⅛in) spigot
hole

SPIGOT
DISC

15mm (¹⁹⁄₃₂in)

CAM

Centre of
30mm (1³⁄₁₆in)
diameter

54mm
(2⅛in)

12mm (½in)
hole

40mm (1⁹⁄₁₆in)
diameter

BOAT RETAINER

32mm
(1¼in)

6mm (¼in)
counterbored hole

12mm (½in)

DRIVE AXLE

3mm (⅛in
holes)

31mm (1¼in)

85mm
(3⅜in)

28mm (1⅛in)

Cam this
end

Front

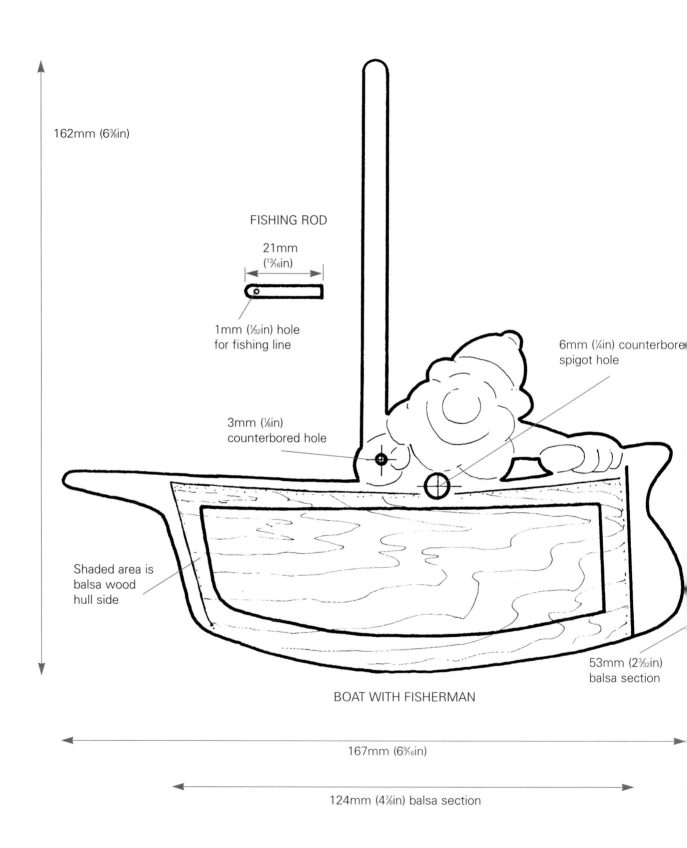

162mm (6⅜in)

FISHING ROD

21mm
(¹³⁄₁₆in)

1mm (¹⁄₃₂in) hole
for fishing line

3mm (⅛in)
counterbored hole

6mm (¼in) counterbore
spigot hole

Shaded area is
balsa wood
hull side

53mm (2³⁄₃₂in)
balsa section

BOAT WITH FISHERMAN

167mm (6⁹⁄₁₆in)

124mm (4⅞in) balsa section

Fig 5.5 100%

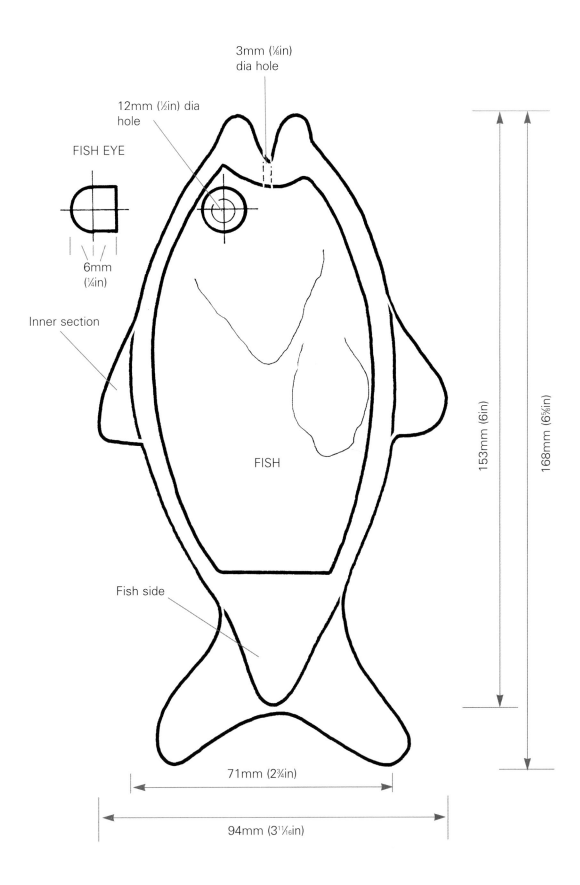

3mm (⅛in)
dia hole

12mm (½in) dia
hole

FISH EYE

6mm
(¼in)

Inner section

FISH

Fish side

153mm (6in)

168mm (6⅝in)

71mm (2¾in)

94mm (3¹¹⁄₁₆in)

Fig 5.6 100%

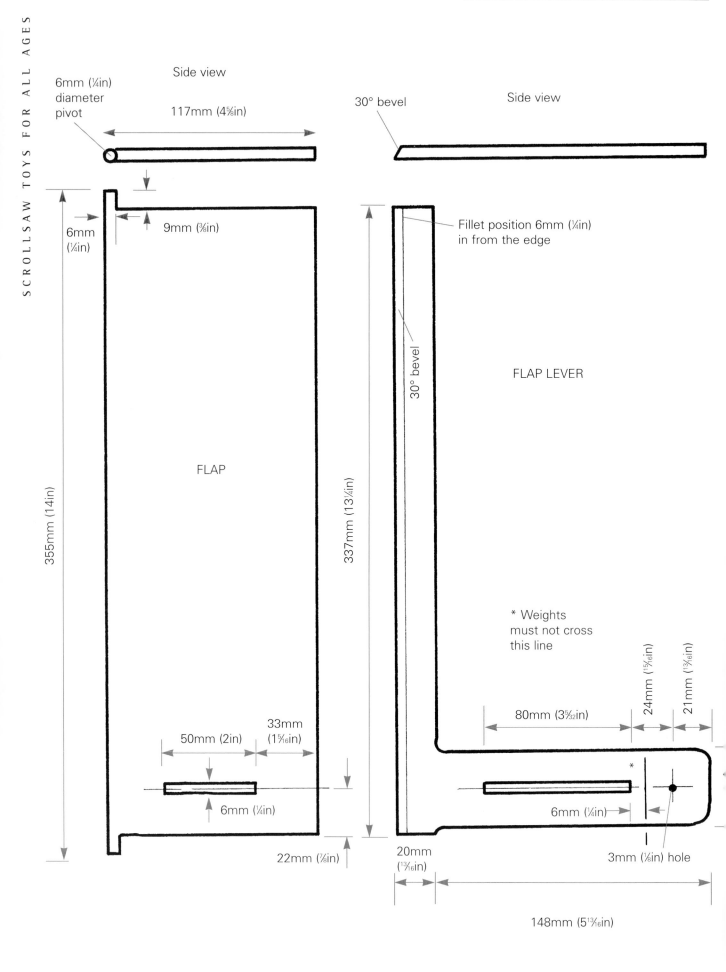

Fig 6.1 50% (Enlarge to 200%)

Fig 6.1 50% (Enlarge to 200%)

Fig 6.2 100%

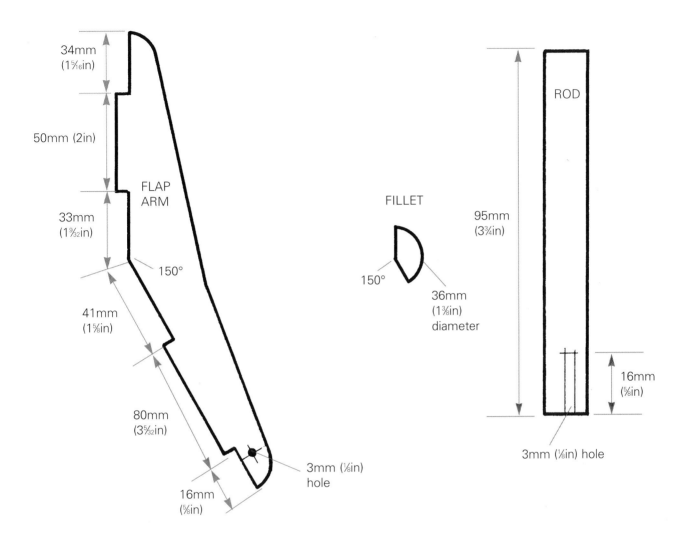

34mm
(1⁵⁄₁₆in)

50mm (2in)

FLAP
ARM

33mm
(1⁹⁄₃₂in)

150°

41mm
(1⁵⁄₈in)

80mm
(3⁵⁄₃₂in)

16mm
(⁵⁄₈in)

3mm (⅛in)
hole

FILLET

150°

36mm
(1⅜in)
diameter

ROD

95mm
(3¾in)

16mm
(⁵⁄₈in)

3mm (⅛in) hole

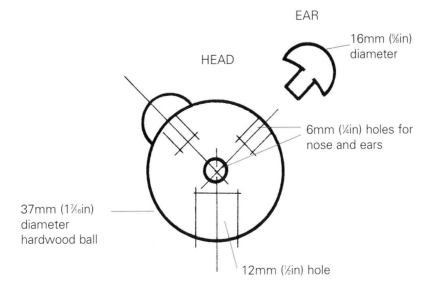

EAR

16mm (⁵⁄₈in)
diameter

HEAD

6mm (¼in) holes for
nose and ears

37mm (1⁷⁄₁₆in)
diameter
hardwood ball

12mm (½in) hole

Fig 6.2 100 %

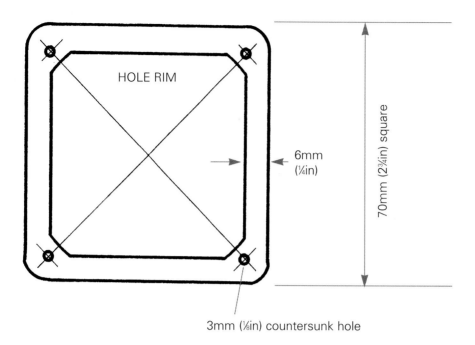

HOLE RIM

6mm
(¼in)

70mm (2¾in) square

3mm (⅛in) countersunk hole

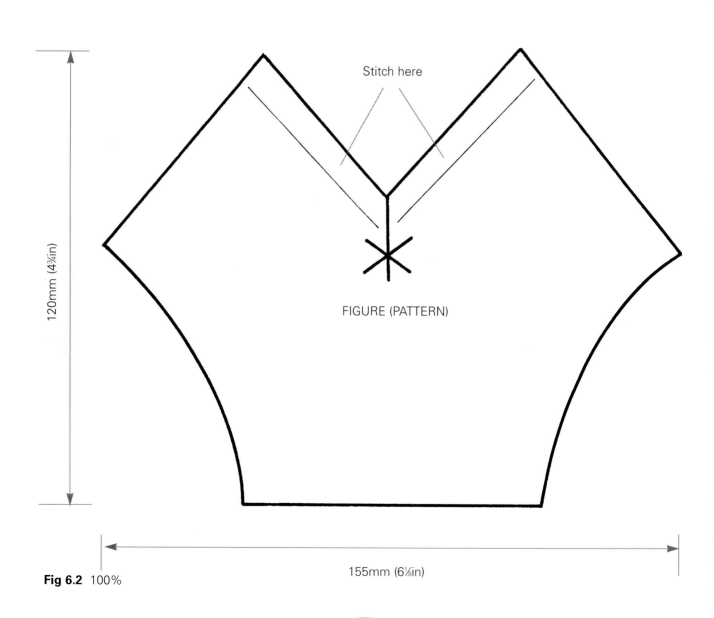

Stitch here

FIGURE (PATTERN)

120mm (4¾in)

155mm (6⅛in)

Fig 6.2 100%

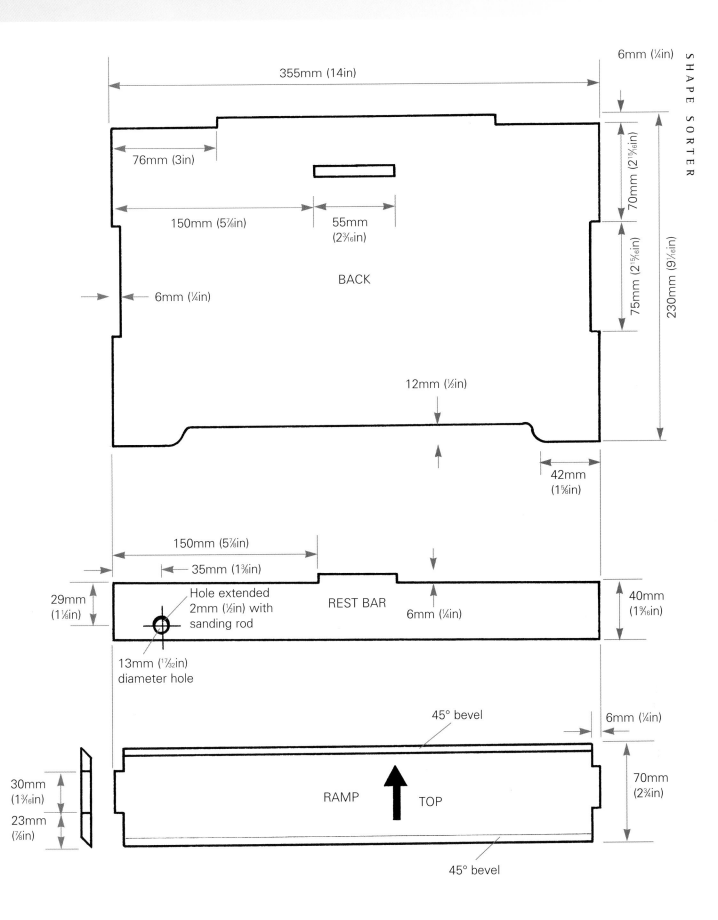

6mm (¼in)

355mm (14in)

76mm (3in)

150mm (5⅞in)

55mm (2³⁄₁₆in)

70mm (2¹⁵⁄₁₆in)

75mm (2¹⁵⁄₁₆in)

230mm (9¹⁄₁₆in)

BACK

6mm (¼in)

12mm (½in)

42mm (1⅝in)

150mm (5⅞in)

35mm (1⅜in)

29mm (1⅛in)

Hole extended 2mm (½in) with sanding rod

REST BAR

6mm (¼in)

40mm (1⁹⁄₁₆in)

13mm (¹⁷⁄₃₂in) diameter hole

45° bevel

6mm (¼in)

30mm (1³⁄₁₆in)

23mm (⅞in)

RAMP

TOP

70mm (2¾in)

45° bevel

Fig 6.3 40%
(Enlarge to 250%)

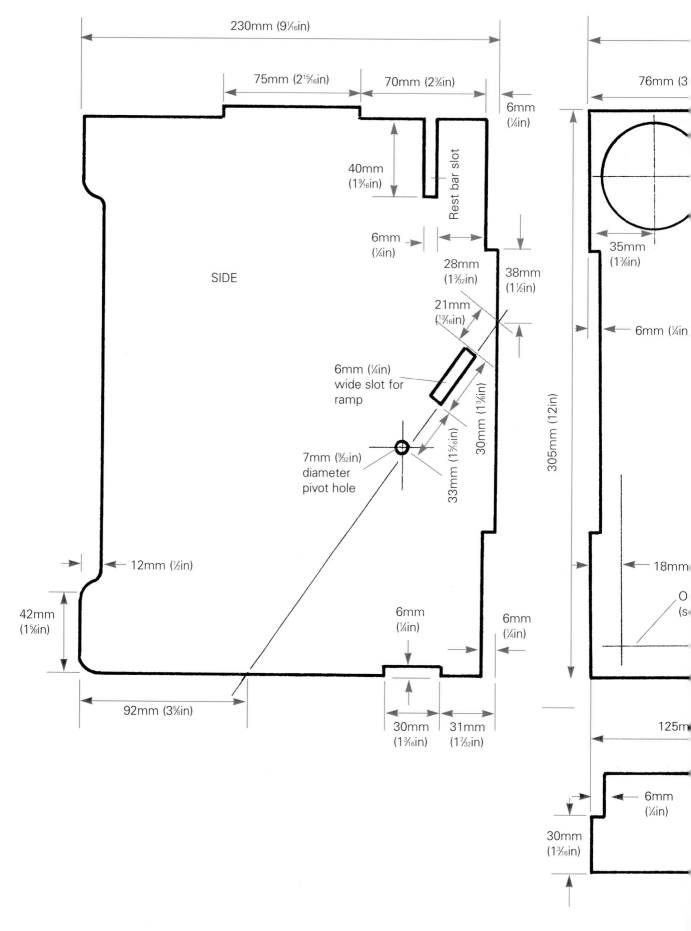

Fig 6.5 50% (Enlarge to 200%)

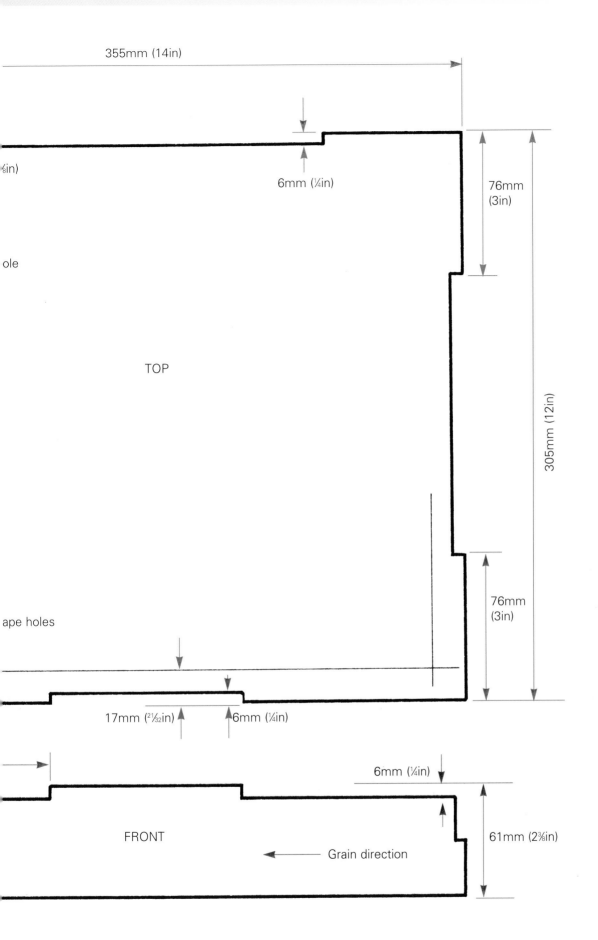

355mm (14in)

6mm (¼in)

%in)

ole

TOP

76mm
(3in)

305mm (12in)

76mm
(3in)

ape holes

17mm (²¹⁄₃₂in)   6mm (¼in)

6mm (¼in)

FRONT

61mm (2⅜in)

Grain direction

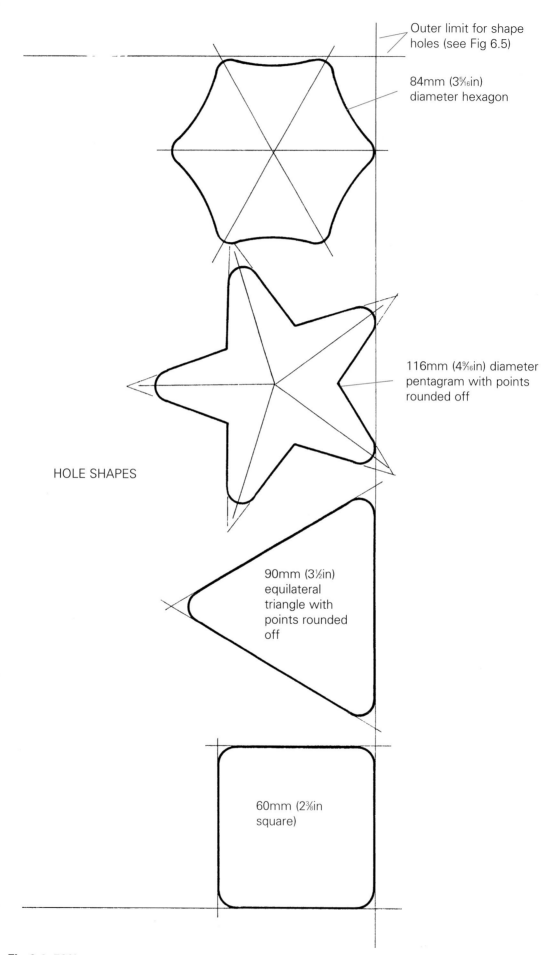

Outer limit for shape holes (see Fig 6.5)

84mm (3⁵⁄₁₆in) diameter hexagon

116mm (4⁹⁄₁₆in) diameter pentagram with points rounded off

HOLE SHAPES

90mm (3½in) equilateral triangle with points rounded off

60mm (2⅜in square)

Fig 6.4 70%
(Enlarge to 143%)

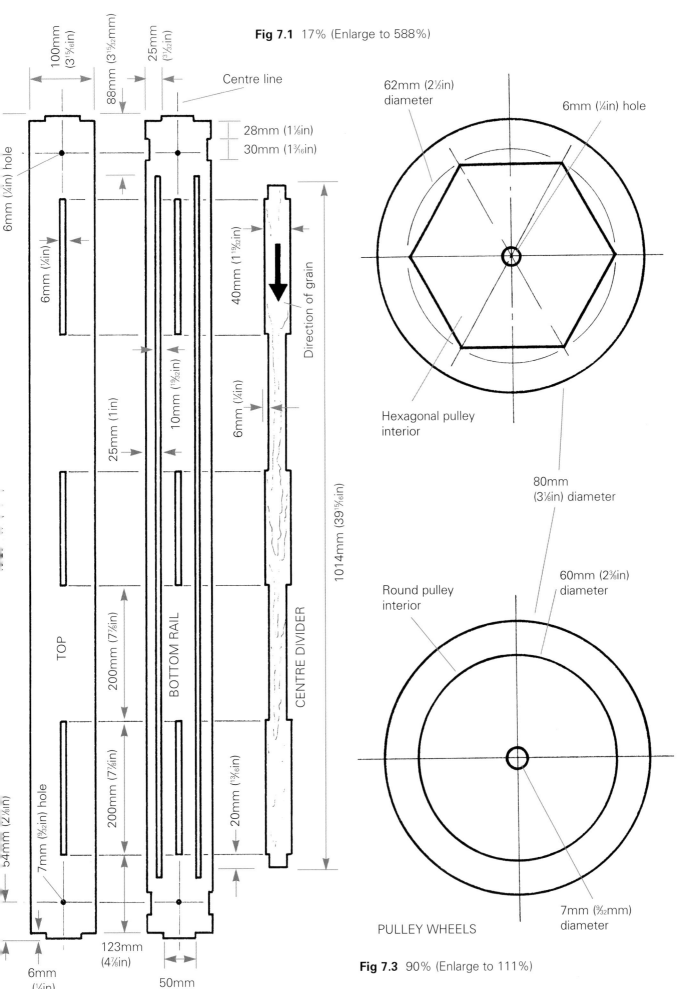

Fig 7.1 17% (Enlarge to 588%)

100mm (3¹⁵⁄₁₆in)

88mm (3¹⁵⁄₃₂mm)

25mm (3½in)

Centre line

28mm (1⅛in)
30mm (1³⁄₁₆in)

6mm (¼in) hole

6mm (¼in)

40mm (1¹⁹⁄₃₂in)

Direction of grain

25mm (1in)

10mm (¹⁹⁄₃₂in)

6mm (¼in)

TOP

200mm (7⅞in)

BOTTOM RAIL

CENTRE DIVIDER

1014mm (39¹⁵⁄₁₆in)

200mm (7⅞in)

20mm (¹³⁄₁₆in)

7mm (⁹⁄₃₂in) hole

54mm (2⅛in)

123mm (4⅞in)

50mm (1³¹⁄₃₂in)

6mm (¼in)

62mm (2½in) diameter

6mm (¼in) hole

Hexagonal pulley interior

80mm (3⅛in) diameter

60mm (2⅜in) diameter

Round pulley interior

7mm (⁹⁄₃₂mm) diameter

PULLEY WHEELS

Fig 7.3 90% (Enlarge to 111%)

Fig 7.2 60%
(Enlarge to 166%)

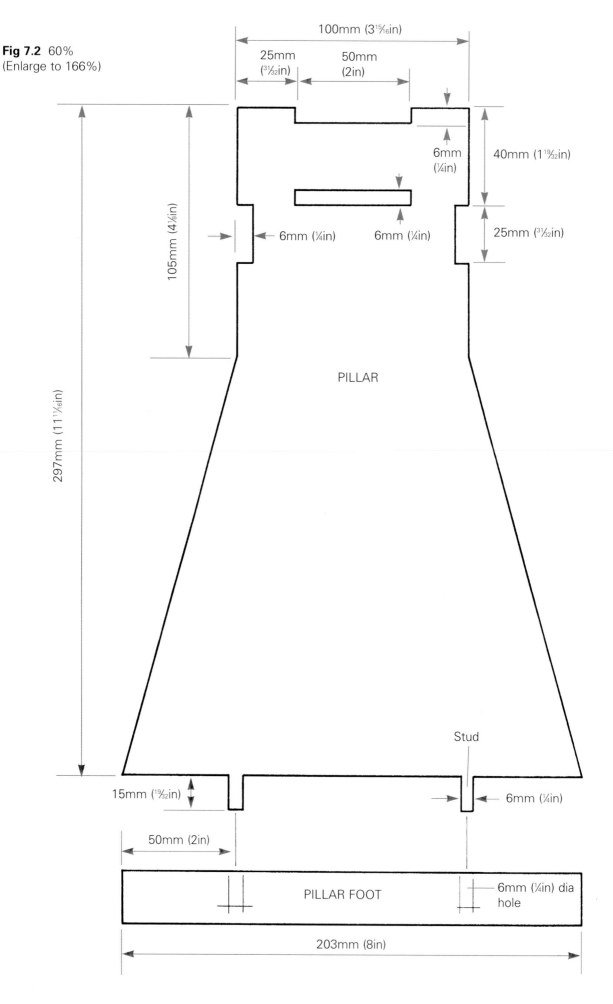

100mm (3¹⁵⁄₁₆in)

25mm (³¹⁄₃₂in)

50mm (2in)

6mm (¼in)

40mm (1¹⁹⁄₃₂in)

6mm (¼in)

6mm (¼in)

25mm (³¹⁄₃₂in)

105mm (4⅛in)

297mm (11¹¹⁄₁₆in)

PILLAR

Stud

15mm (¹⁹⁄₃₂in)

6mm (¼in)

50mm (2in)

PILLAR FOOT

6mm (¼in) dia hole

203mm (8in)

Fig 7.4 100%

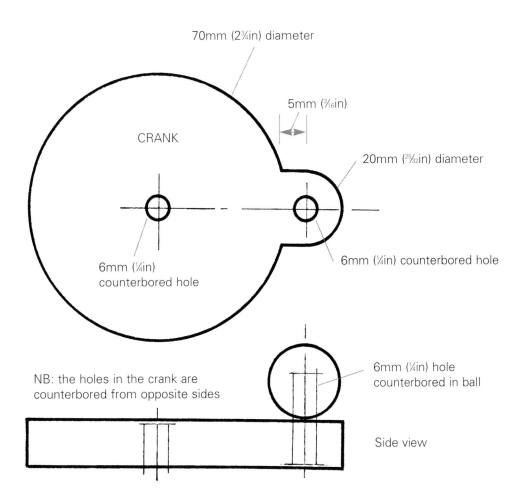

70mm (2¾in) diameter

5mm (³⁄₁₆in)

CRANK

20mm (²⁵⁄₃₂in) diameter

6mm (¼in) counterbored hole

6mm (¼in) counterbored hole

NB: the holes in the crank are counterbored from opposite sides

6mm (¼in) hole counterbored in ball

Side view

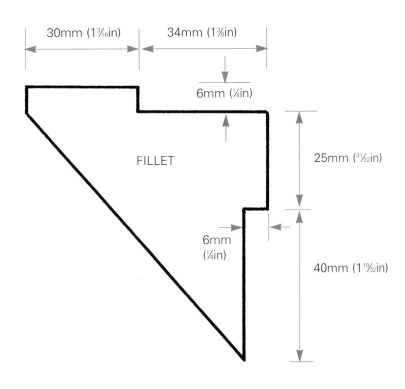

30mm (1³⁄₁₆in)

34mm (1⅜in)

6mm (¼in)

FILLET

25mm (³¹⁄₃₂in)

6mm (¼in)

40mm (1¹⁹⁄₃₂in)

Fig 7.5 100%

133

Fig 7.6 100%

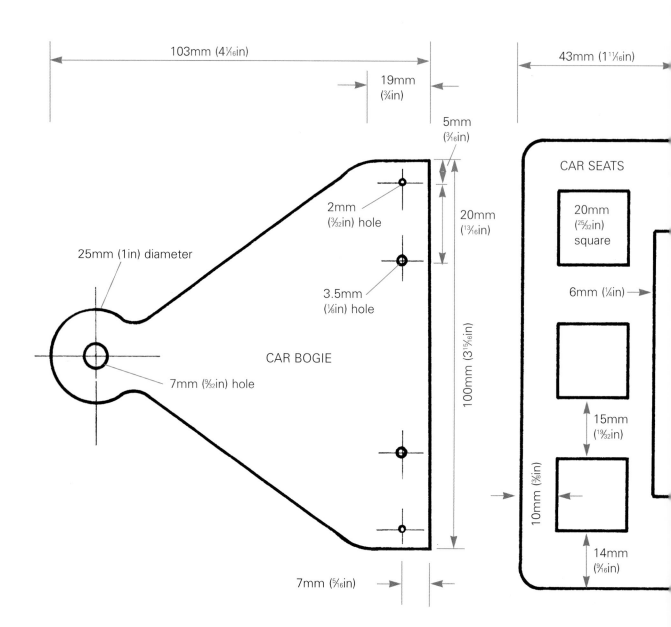

103mm (4¹⁄₁₆in)

19mm (¾in)

43mm (1¹¹⁄₁₆in)

5mm (³⁄₁₆in)

CAR SEATS

2mm (³⁄₃₂in) hole

20mm (¹³⁄₁₆in)

20mm (²⁵⁄₃₂in) square

25mm (1in) diameter

3.5mm (⅛in) hole

6mm (¼in)

CAR BOGIE

100mm (3¹⁵⁄₁₆in)

7mm (⁹⁄₃₂in) hole

15mm (¹⁹⁄₃₂in)

10mm (⅜in)

14mm (⁹⁄₁₆in)

7mm (⁵⁄₁₆in)

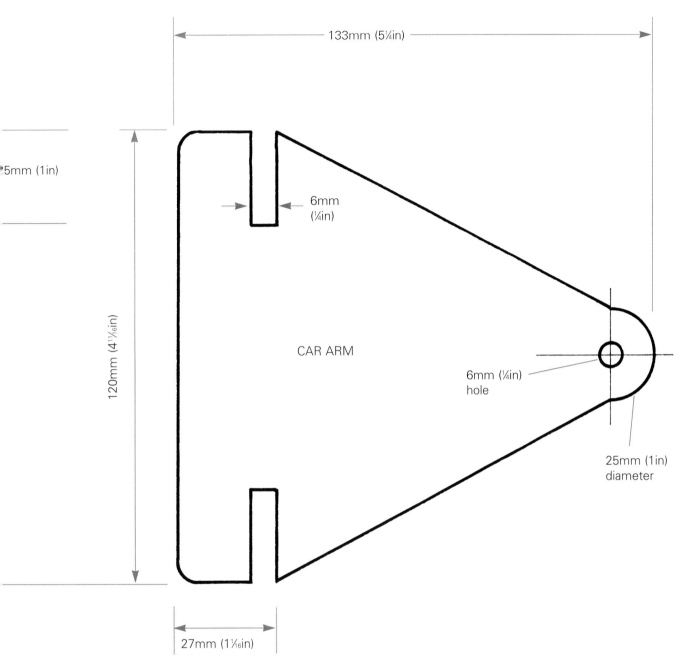

133mm (5¼in)

5mm (1in)

6mm
(¼in)

120mm (4¹¹⁄₁₆in)

CAR ARM

6mm (¼in)
hole

25mm (1in)
diameter

27mm (1¹⁄₁₆in)

Fig 7.6 100%

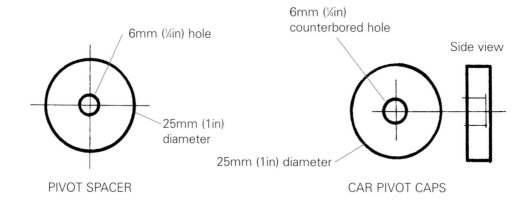

6mm (¼in) hole

6mm (¼in)
counterbored hole

Side view

25mm (1in)
diameter

25mm (1in) diameter

PIVOT SPACER

CAR PIVOT CAPS

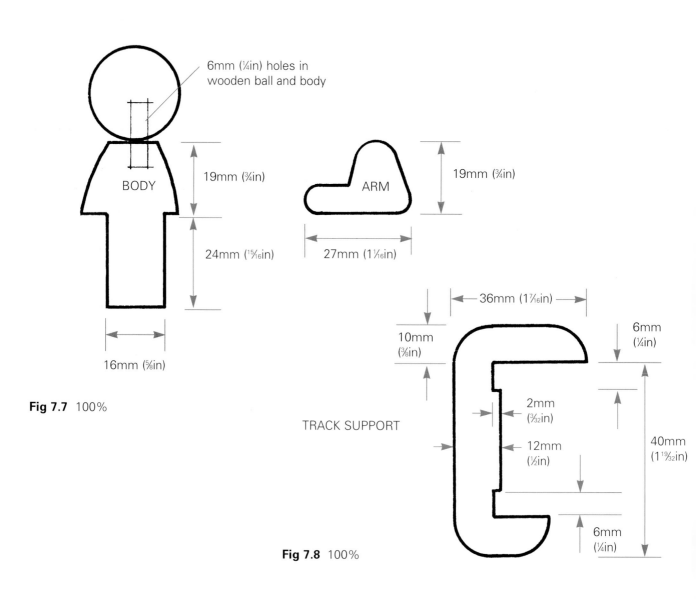

6mm (¼in) holes in
wooden ball and body

BODY

19mm (¾in)

24mm (¹⁵⁄₁₆in)

16mm (⅝in)

Fig 7.7 100%

ARM

19mm (¾in)

27mm (1¹⁄₁₆in)

TRACK SUPPORT

36mm (1⁷⁄₁₆in)

10mm
(⅜in)

2mm
(³⁄₃₂in)

12mm
(½in)

6mm
(¼in)

40mm
(1¹⁹⁄₃₂in)

6mm
(¼in)

Fig 7.8 100%

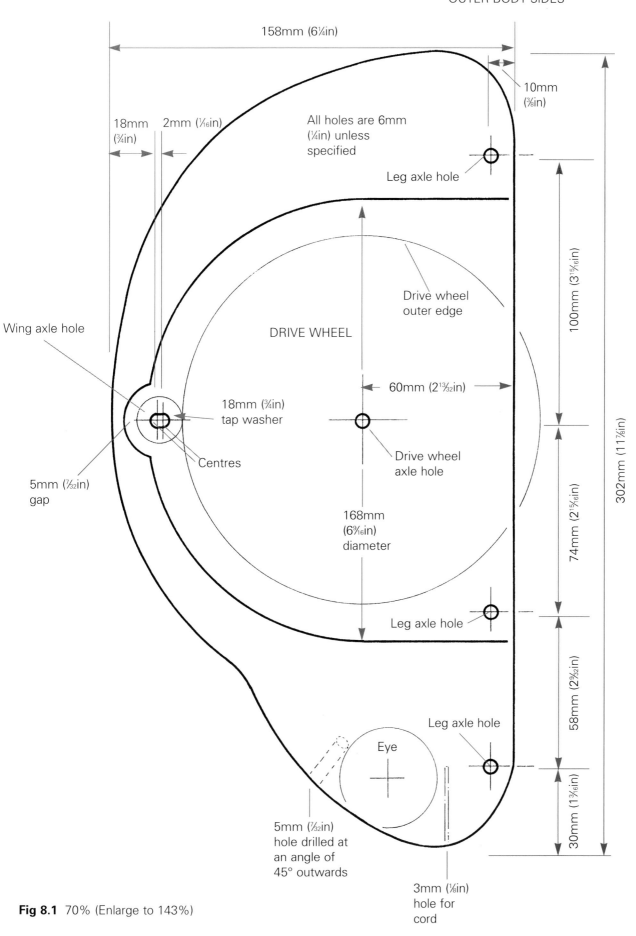

INNER BODY SECTION AND
OUTER BODY SIDES

158mm (6¼in)

10mm
(⅜in)

18mm
(¾in)

2mm (1/16in)

All holes are 6mm
(¼in) unless
specified

Leg axle hole

Wing axle hole

DRIVE WHEEL

Drive wheel
outer edge

100mm (3¹⁵/₁₆in)

18mm (¾in)
tap washer

60mm (2¹³/₃₂in)

Centres

302mm (11⅞in)

5mm (⁷/₃₂in)
gap

Drive wheel
axle hole

168mm
(6⅝in)
diameter

74mm (2¹⁵/₁₆in)

Leg axle hole

58mm (2⁹/₃₂in)

Leg axle hole

Eye

5mm (⁷/₃₂in)
hole drilled at
an angle of
45° outwards

30mm (1³/₁₆in)

3mm (⅛in)
hole for
cord

Fig 8.1 70% (Enlarge to 143%)

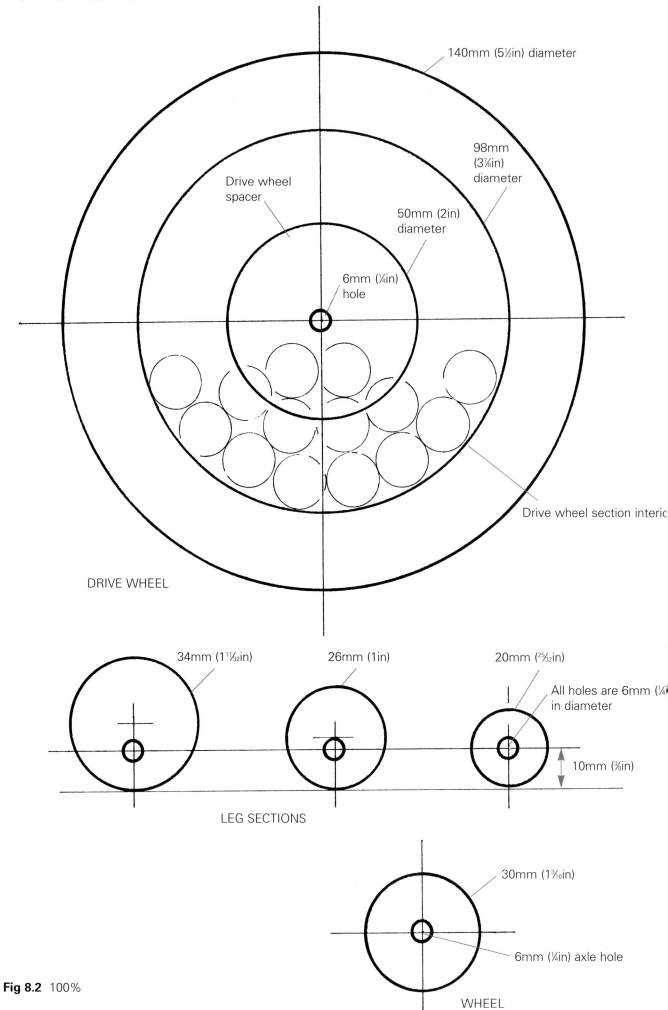

140mm (5½in) diameter

98mm (3⅞in) diameter

Drive wheel spacer

50mm (2in) diameter

6mm (¼in) hole

Drive wheel section interior

DRIVE WHEEL

34mm (1¹¹⁄₃₂in)

26mm (1in)

20mm (²⁵⁄₃₂in)

All holes are 6mm (¼ in diameter

10mm (⅜in)

LEG SECTIONS

30mm (1³⁄₁₆in)

6mm (¼in) axle hole

WHEEL

Fig 8.2 100%

Fig 8.3 100%

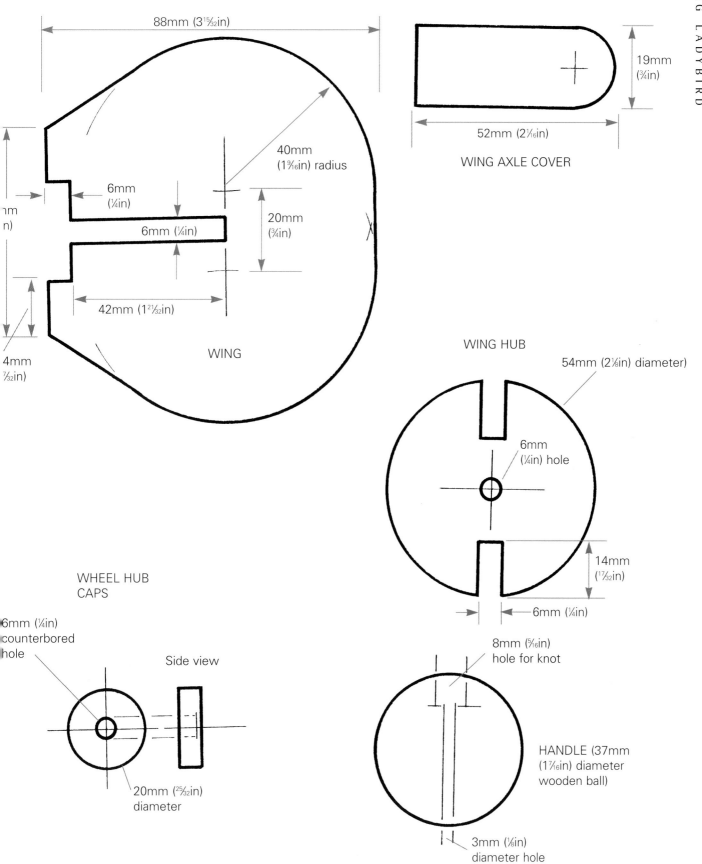

88mm (3¹⁵⁄₃₂in)

40mm
(1⁹⁄₁₆in) radius

6mm
(¼in)

6mm (¼in)

20mm
(¾in)

42mm (1²¹⁄₃₂in)

WING

m
n)

4mm
⁷⁄₃₂in)

19mm
(¾in)

52mm (2¹⁄₁₆in)

WING AXLE COVER

WING HUB

54mm (2¹⁄₈in) diameter)

6mm
(¼in) hole

14mm
(¹⁷⁄₃₂in)

6mm (¼in)

WHEEL HUB
CAPS

6mm (¼in)
counterbored
hole

Side view

20mm (²⁵⁄₃₂in)
diameter

8mm (⁵⁄₁₆in)
hole for knot

HANDLE (37mm
(1⁷⁄₁₆in) diameter
wooden ball)

3mm (⅛in)
diameter hole

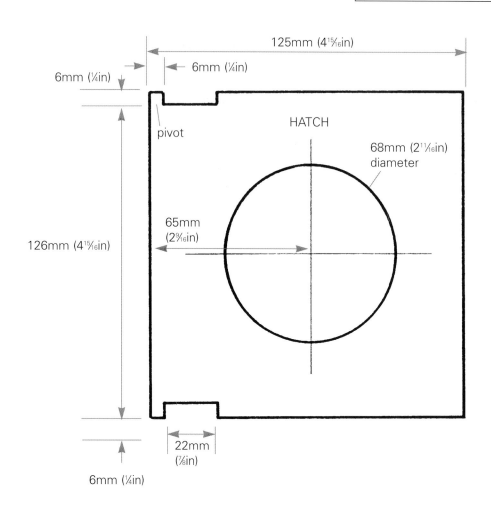

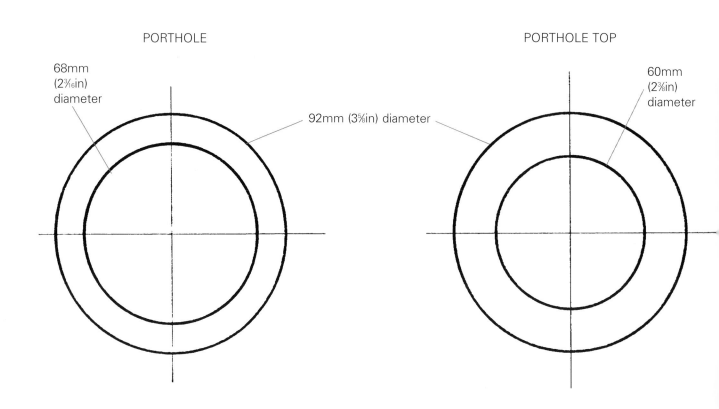

Fig 9.1 70% (Enlarge to 143%)

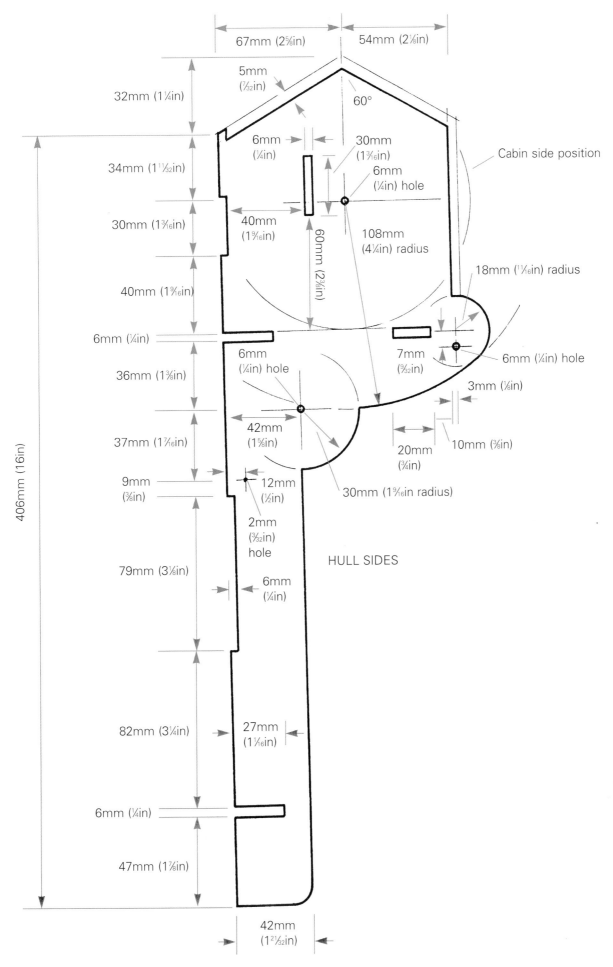

67mm (2⅝in)

54mm (2⅛in)

5mm (⁷⁄₃₂in)

32mm (1¼in)

60°

Cabin side position

6mm (¼in)

30mm (1³⁄₁₆in)

34mm (1¹¹⁄₃₂in)

6mm (¼in) hole

30mm (1³⁄₁₆in)

40mm (1⁹⁄₁₆in)

60mm (2⅜in)

108mm (4¼in) radius

40mm (1⁹⁄₁₆in)

18mm (¹¹⁄₁₆in) radius

6mm (¼in)

6mm (¼in) hole

7mm (⁹⁄₃₂in)

6mm (¼in) hole

36mm (1⅜in)

3mm (⅛in)

42mm (1⅝in)

20mm (¾in)

10mm (⅜in)

37mm (1⁷⁄₁₆in)

30mm (1³⁄₁₆in radius)

9mm (⅜in)

12mm (½in)

2mm (³⁄₃₂in) hole

HULL SIDES

79mm (3⅛in)

6mm (¼in)

406mm (16in)

82mm (3¼in)

27mm (1¹⁄₁₆in)

6mm (¼in)

47mm (1⅞in)

42mm (1²¹⁄₃₂in)

Fig 9.2 50% (Enlarge to 200%)

Fig 9.3 70%
(Enlarge to 143%)

CABIN SIDES

CABIN DISC

83mm (3¼in) diameter

60°

127mm (5in)

67mm (2⅝in)

6mm
(¼in)
hole

67mm
(2⅝in)
radius

38mm (1½in)

105mm (4⅛in)

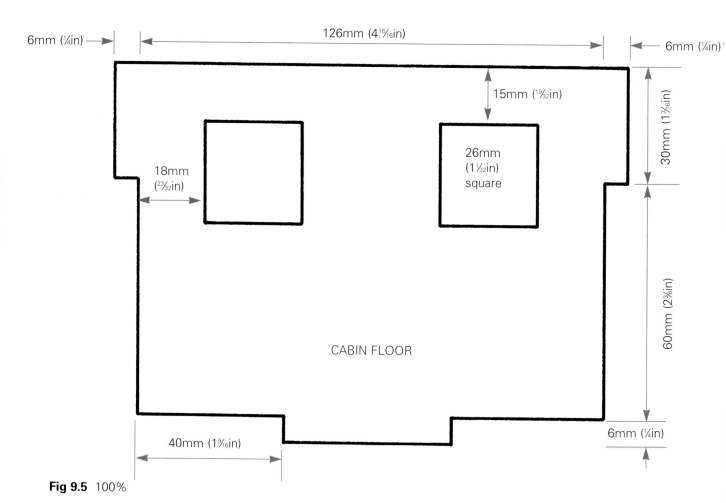

6mm (¼in)

126mm (4¹⁵⁄₁₆in)

6mm (¼in)

15mm (¹⁹⁄₃₂in)

30mm (1³⁄₁₆in)

18mm
(²³⁄₃₂in)

26mm
(1¹⁄₃₂in)
square

60mm (2⅜in)

CABIN FLOOR

40mm (1⁹⁄₁₆in)

6mm (¼in)

Fig 9.5 100%

142

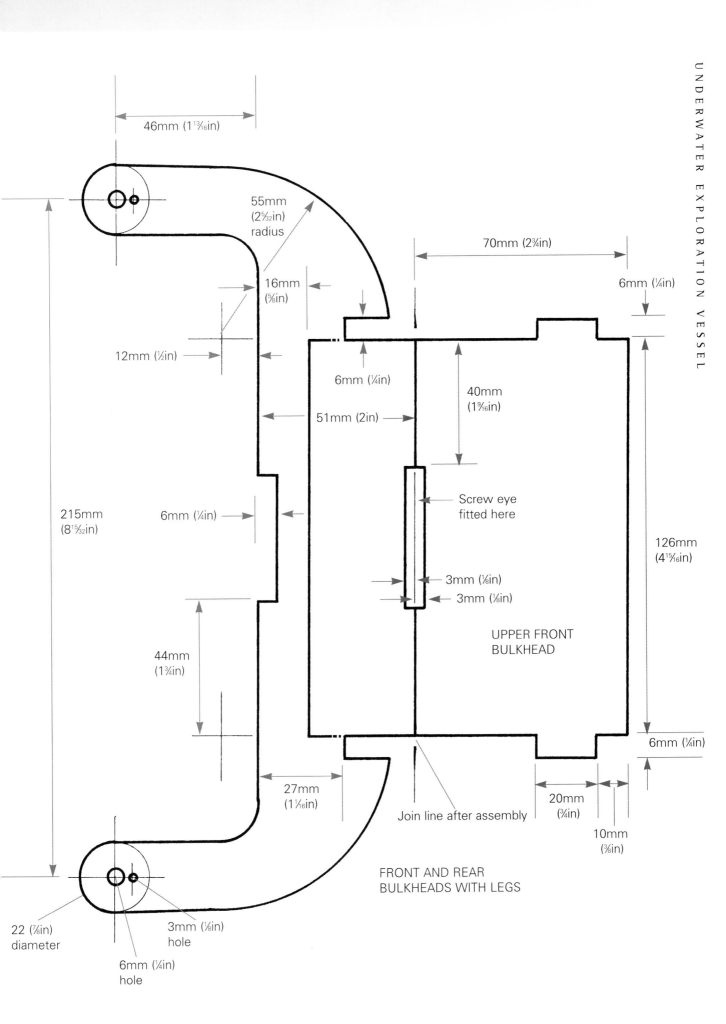

46mm (1¹³⁄₁₆in)

55mm (2⁵⁄₃₂in) radius

70mm (2¾in)

6mm (¼in)

16mm (⅝in)

12mm (½in)

6mm (¼in)

51mm (2in)

40mm (1⁹⁄₁₆in)

215mm (8¹⁵⁄₃₂in)

6mm (¼in)

Screw eye fitted here

126mm (4¹⁵⁄₁₆in)

3mm (⅛in)

3mm (⅛in)

UPPER FRONT BULKHEAD

44mm (1¾in)

27mm (1¹⁄₁₆in)

Join line after assembly

6mm (¼in)

20mm (¾in)

10mm (⅜in)

FRONT AND REAR BULKHEADS WITH LEGS

22 (⅞in) diameter

3mm (⅛in) hole

6mm (¼in) hole

Fig 9.4 83% (Enlarge to 120%)

143

Fig 9.6 50%
(Enlarge to 200%)

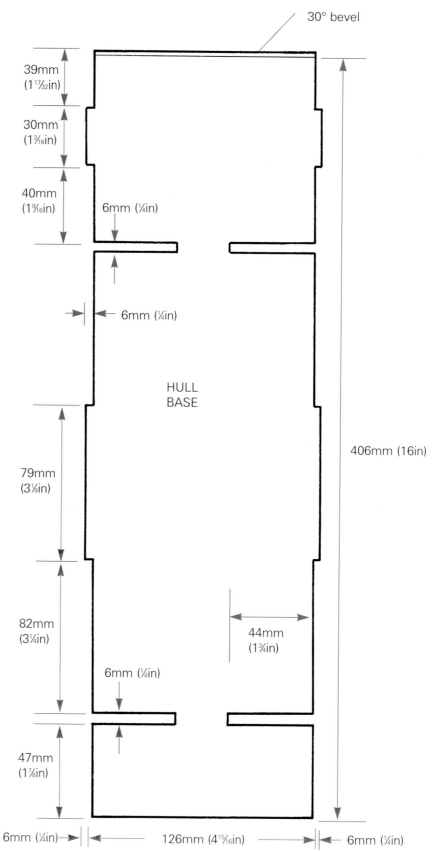

30° bevel

39mm
(1¹⁷⁄₃₂in)

30mm
(1³⁄₁₆in)

40mm
(1⁹⁄₁₆in)

6mm (¼in)

6mm (¼in)

HULL
BASE

406mm (16in)

79mm
(3⅛in)

82mm
(3¼in)

44mm
(1¾in)

6mm (¼in)

47mm
(1⅞in)

6mm (¼in)→ |← 126mm (4¹⁵⁄₁₆in) →| |← 6mm (¼in)

3mm (⅛in) hole
10mm (⅜in) deep

240mm (9⁷⁄₁₆in)

SKID

6mm
(¼in) hole

Fig 9.7 50%
(Enlarge to 200%)

20mm (²⁵⁄₃₂in)

10mm (⅜in)

Fig 9.8 100%

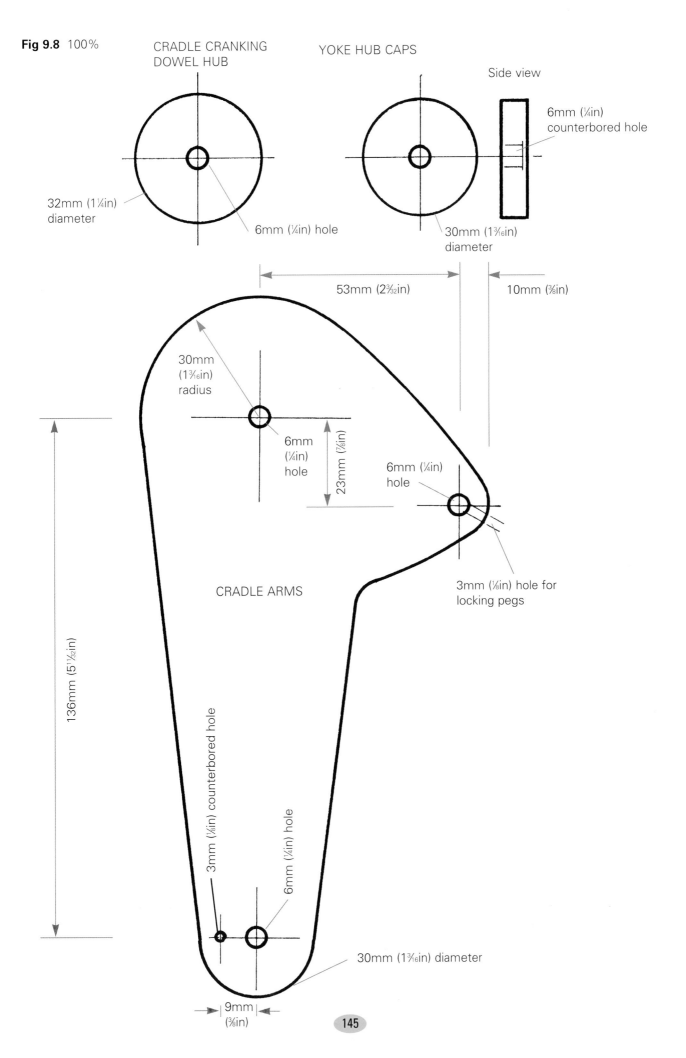

CRADLE CRANKING
DOWEL HUB

YOKE HUB CAPS

Side view

6mm (¼in)
counterbored hole

32mm (1¼in)
diameter

6mm (¼in) hole

30mm (1³⁄₁₆in)
diameter

53mm (2³⁄₃₂in)

10mm (³⁄₈in)

30mm
(1³⁄₁₆in)
radius

6mm
(¼in)
hole

23mm (⁷⁄₈in)

6mm (¼in)
hole

3mm (⅛in) hole for
locking pegs

CRADLE ARMS

136mm (5¹¹⁄₃₂in)

3mm (⅛in) counterbored hole

6mm (¼in) hole

30mm (1³⁄₁₆in) diameter

9mm
(³⁄₈in)

145

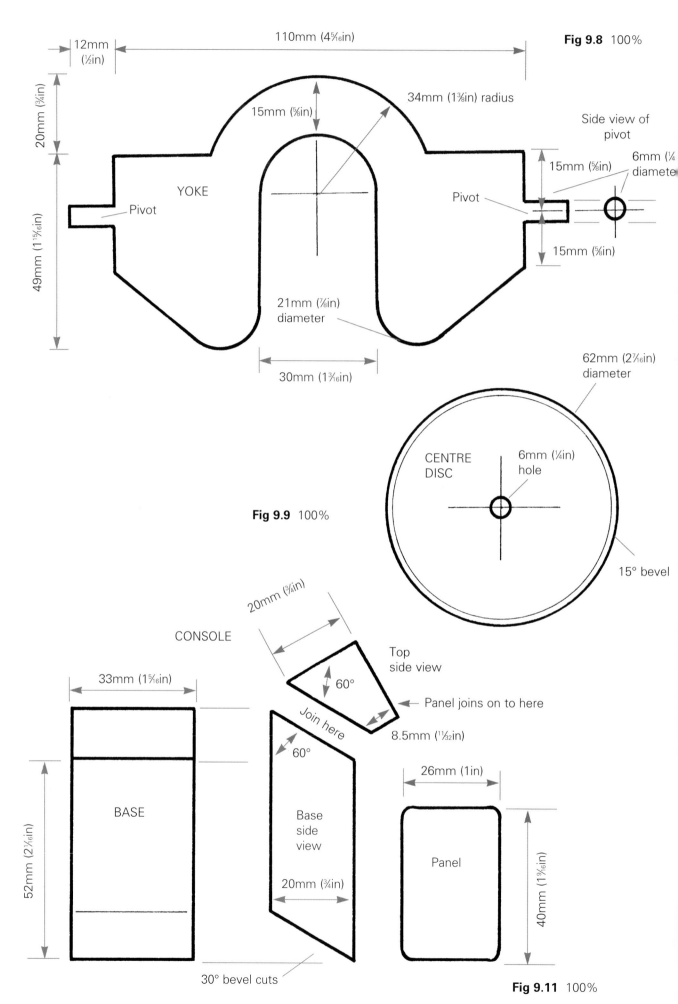

Fig 9.8 100%

12mm (½in)

110mm (4⁵⁄₁₆in)

20mm (¾in)

15mm (⅝in)

34mm (1⅜in) radius

Side view of pivot

6mm (¼ diameter

15mm (⅝in)

YOKE

Pivot

Pivot

15mm (⅝in)

49mm (1¹⁵⁄₁₆in)

21mm (⅞in) diameter

30mm (1³⁄₁₆in)

62mm (2⁷⁄₁₆in) diameter

CENTRE DISC

6mm (¼in) hole

Fig 9.9 100%

15° bevel

20mm (¾in)

CONSOLE

Top side view

60°

Panel joins on to here

33mm (1⁵⁄₁₆in)

8.5mm (1¹⁄₃₂in)

Join here

60°

26mm (1in)

BASE

Base side view

Panel

52mm (2¹⁄₁₆in)

40mm (1⁹⁄₁₆in)

20mm (¾in)

30° bevel cuts

Fig 9.11 100%

146

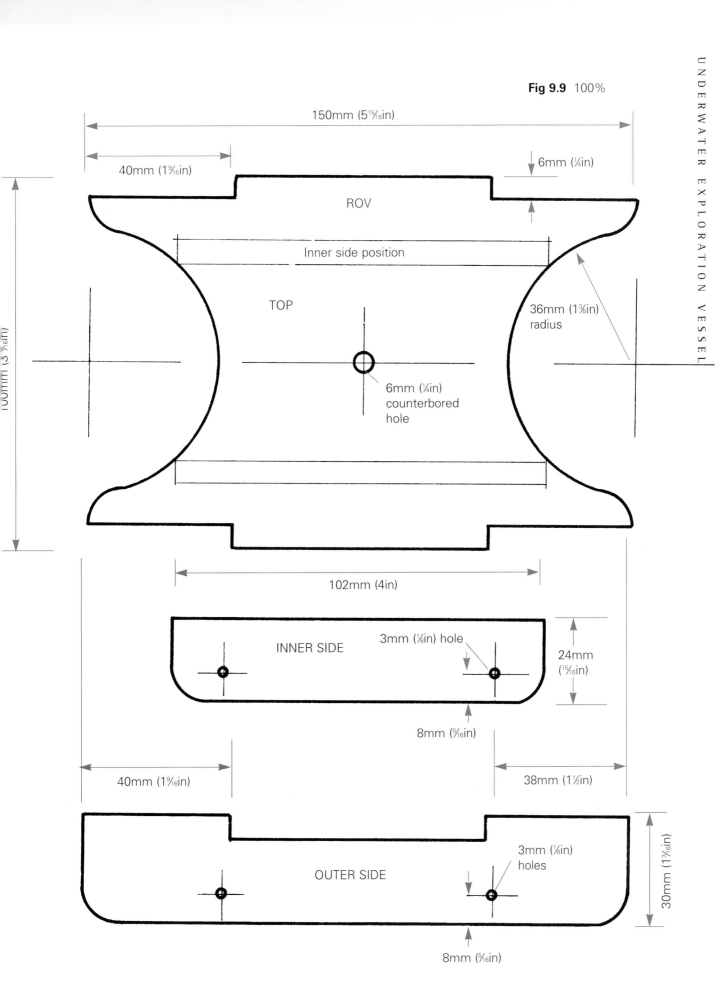

Fig 9.9 100%

150mm (5¹⁵⁄₁₆in)

40mm (1⁹⁄₁₆in)

6mm (¼in)

ROV

Inner side position

TOP

36mm (1⁷⁄₁₆in)
radius

6mm (¼in)
counterbored
hole

100mm (3⁷⁄₁₆in)

102mm (4in)

INNER SIDE

3mm (⅛in) hole

24mm
(¹⁵⁄₁₆in)

8mm (⁵⁄₁₆in)

40mm (1⁹⁄₁₆in)

38mm (1½in)

3mm (⅛in)
holes

OUTER SIDE

30mm (1³⁄₁₆in)

8mm (⁵⁄₁₆in)

Fig 9.12 100%

PROPELLERS

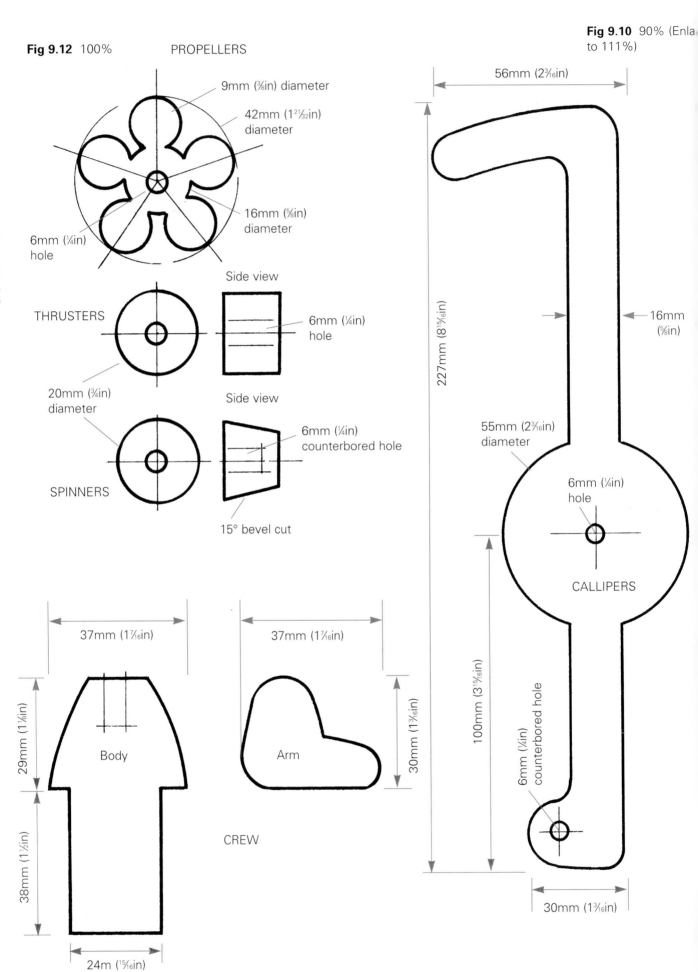

9mm (⅜in) diameter

42mm (1²¹⁄₃₂in) diameter

16mm (⅝in) diameter

6mm (¼in) hole

THRUSTERS

Side view

6mm (¼in) hole

20mm (¾in) diameter

Side view

SPINNERS

6mm (¼in) counterbored hole

15° bevel cut

Fig 9.10 90% (Enlarge to 111%)

56mm (2³⁄₁₆in)

227mm (8¹⁵⁄₁₆in)

16mm (⅝in)

55mm (2³⁄₁₆in) diameter

6mm (¼in) hole

CALLIPERS

100mm (3¹⁵⁄₁₆in)

6mm (¼in) counterbored hole

30mm (1³⁄₁₆in)

37mm (1⁷⁄₁₆in)

29mm (1⅛in)

Body

38mm (1½in)

24m (¹⁵⁄₁₆in)

37mm (1⁷⁄₁₆in)

Arm

30mm (1³⁄₁₆in)

CREW

Fig 9.14 100%

CRANK

Fig 9.13 100%

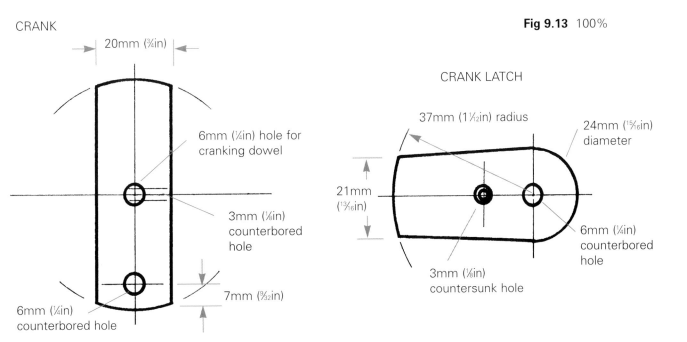

20mm (¾in)

6mm (¼in) hole for cranking dowel

3mm (⅛in) counterbored hole

7mm (⁹⁄₃₂in)

6mm (¼in) counterbored hole

CRANK LATCH

37mm (1½in) radius

24mm (¹⁵⁄₁₆in) diameter

21mm (¹³⁄₁₆in)

6mm (¼in) counterbored hole

3mm (⅛in) countersunk hole

Side view

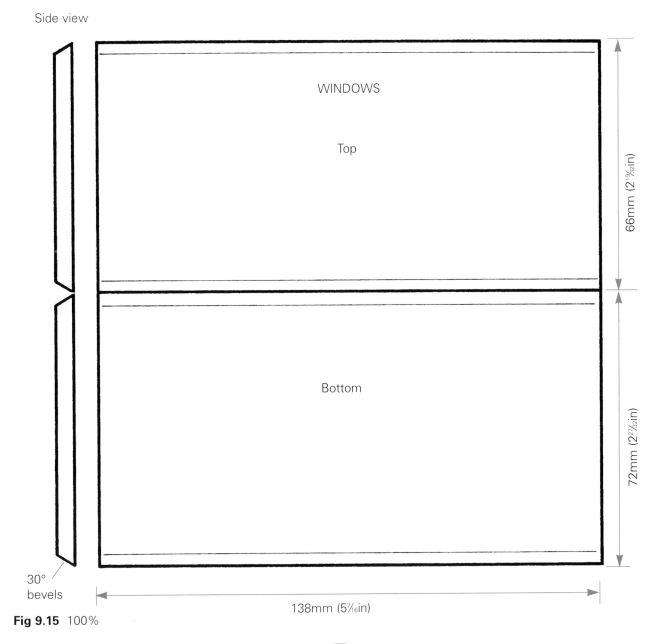

WINDOWS

Top

Bottom

66mm (2¹⁹⁄₃₂in)

72mm (2²⁷⁄₃₂in)

30° bevels

138mm (5⁷⁄₁₆in)

Fig 9.15 100%

Fig 9.16 50% (Enlarge to 200%)

CRADLE CRANKING DOWEL

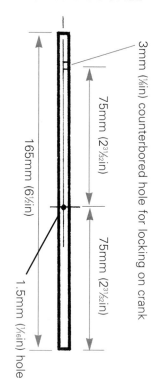

165mm (6½in)

75mm (2³¹⁄₃₂in)

75mm (2³¹⁄₃₂in)

3mm (⅛in) counterbored hole for locking on crank

1.5mm (¹⁄₁₆in) hole

LOCKING HUB

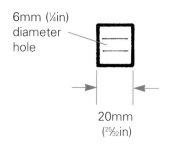

6mm (¼in) diameter hole

20mm (²⁵⁄₃₂in)

Fig 9.16 50%

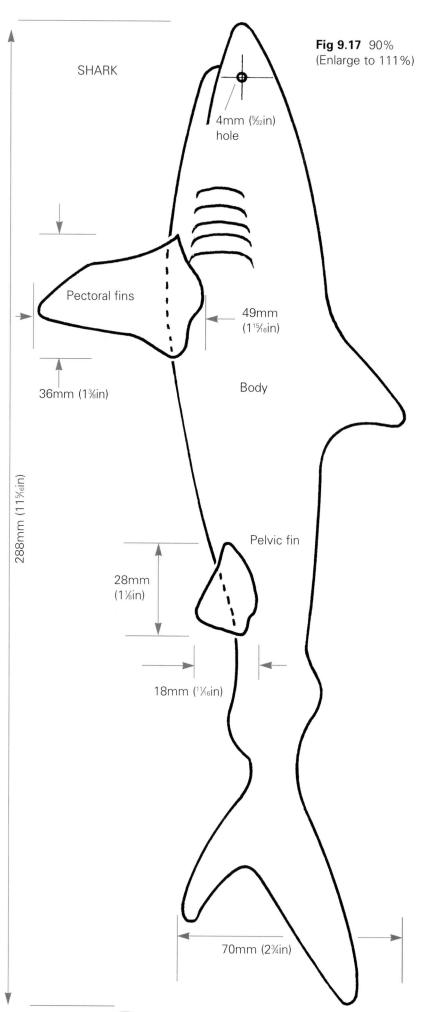

SHARK

Fig 9.17 90% (Enlarge to 111%)

4mm (⁵⁄₃₂in) hole

Pectoral fins

49mm (1¹⁵⁄₁₆in)

Body

36mm (1⅜in)

288mm (11⁵⁄₁₆in)

Pelvic fin

28mm (1⅛in)

18mm (¹¹⁄₁₆in)

70mm (2¾in)

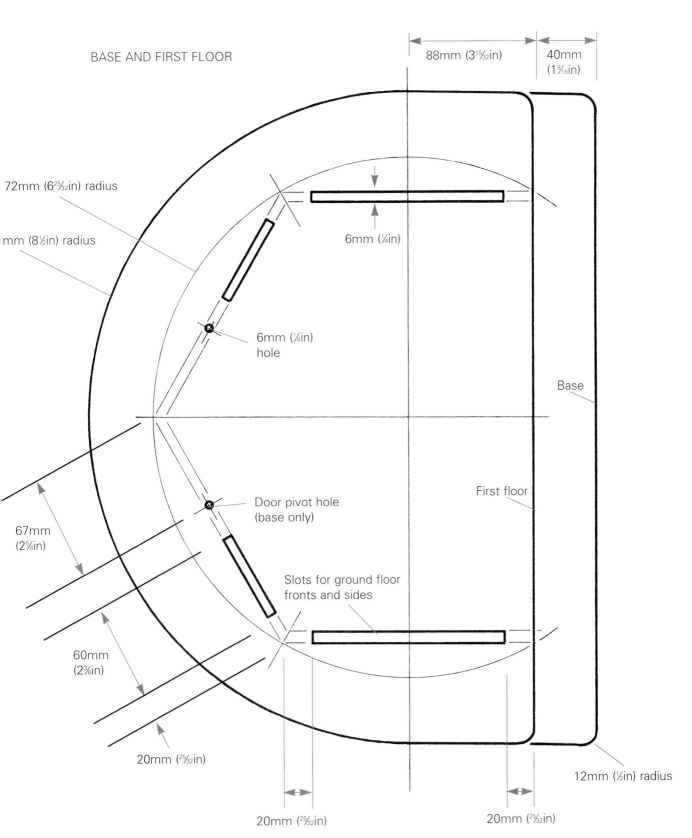

BASE AND FIRST FLOOR

88mm (3¹⁵⁄₃₂in)

40mm (1⁹⁄₁₆in)

72mm (6²⁵⁄₃₂in) radius

mm (8½in) radius

6mm (¼in)

6mm (¼in) hole

Base

67mm (2⅝in)

Door pivot hole (base only)

First floor

60mm (2⅜in)

Slots for ground floor fronts and sides

20mm (²⁵⁄₃₂in)

12mm (½in) radius

20mm (²⁵⁄₃₂in)

20mm (²⁵⁄₃₂in)

Fig 10.1 40% (Enlarge to 250%)

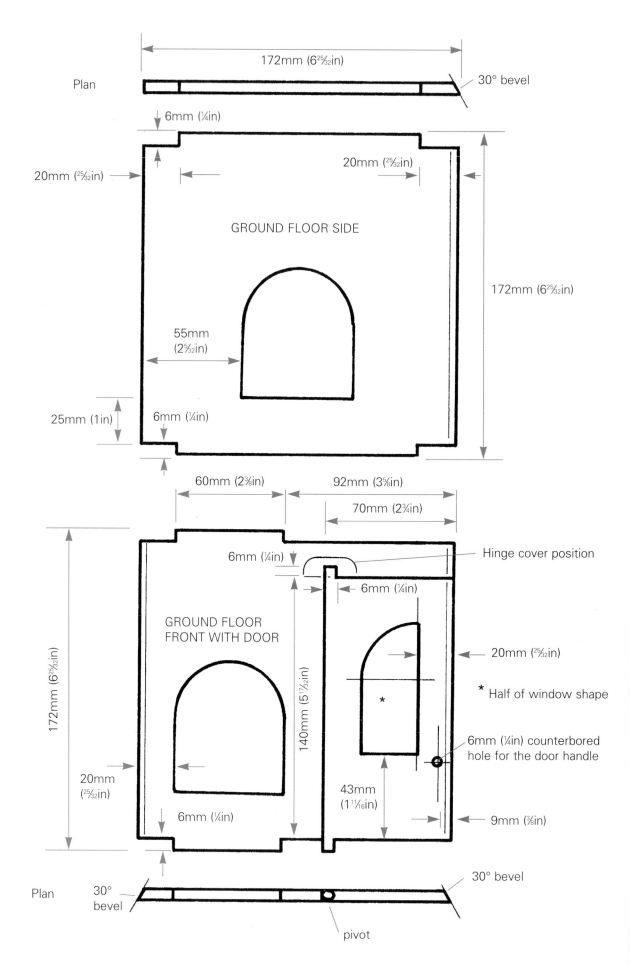

Plan

172mm (6²⁵⁄₃₂in)

30° bevel

6mm (¼in)

20mm (²⁵⁄₃₂in)

20mm (²⁵⁄₃₂in)

GROUND FLOOR SIDE

172mm (6²⁵⁄₃₂in)

55mm (2⁵⁄₃₂in)

25mm (1in)

6mm (¼in)

60mm (2³⁄₈in)

92mm (3⁵⁄₈in)

70mm (2³⁄₄in)

6mm (¼in)

Hinge cover position

6mm (¼in)

GROUND FLOOR FRONT WITH DOOR

172mm (6²⁵⁄₃₂in)

140mm (5¹⁷⁄₃₂in)

20mm (²⁵⁄₃₂in)

* Half of window shape

6mm (¼in) counterbored hole for the door handle

20mm (²⁵⁄₃₂in)

*

43mm (1¹¹⁄₁₆in)

9mm (³⁄₈in)

6mm (¼in)

30° bevel

Plan

30° bevel

30° bevel

pivot

Fig 10.2 50% (Enlarge to 200%)

Fig 10.4 50% (Enlarge to 200%)

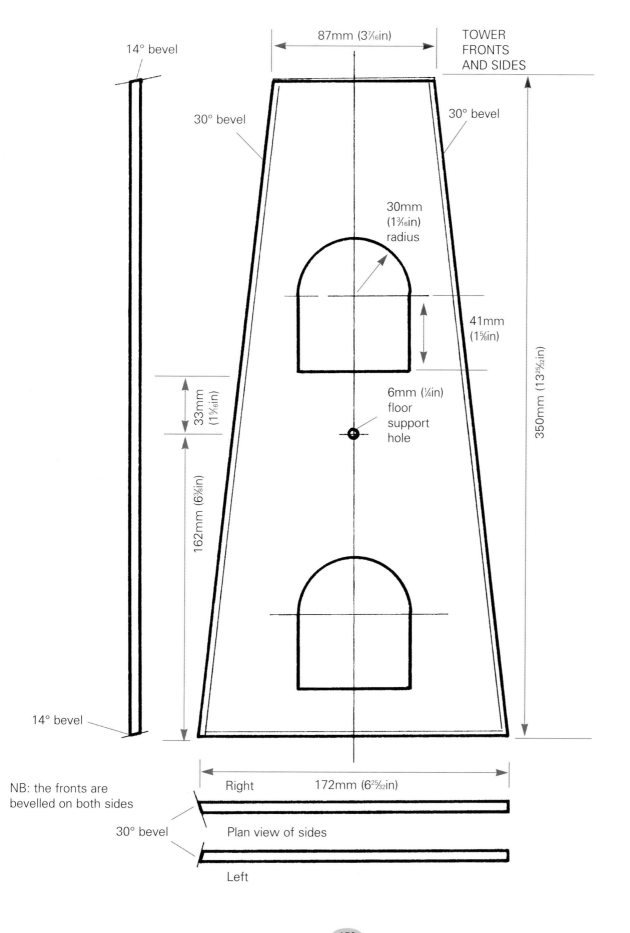

14° bevel

30° bevel

30° bevel

TOWER
FRONTS
AND SIDES

87mm (3⁷⁄₁₆in)

30mm
(1³⁄₁₆in)
radius

41mm
(1⅝in)

350mm (13²⁵⁄₃₂in)

6mm (¼in)
floor
support
hole

33mm
(1⁵⁄₁₆in)

162mm (6⅜in)

14° bevel

NB: the fronts are
bevelled on both sides

30° bevel

Right

172mm (6²⁵⁄₃₂in)

Plan view of sides

Left

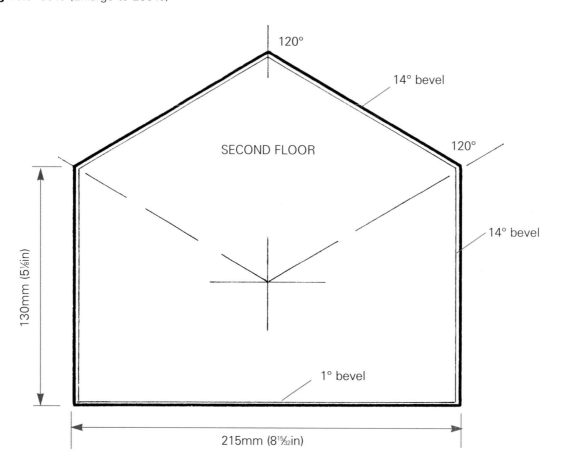

Fig 10.5 50% (Enlarge to 200%)

120°

14° bevel

SECOND FLOOR

120°

14° bevel

130mm (5⅛in)

1° bevel

215mm (8¹⁵⁄₃₂in)

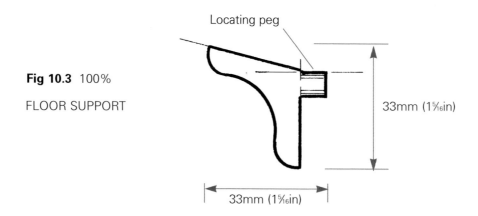

Locating peg

Fig 10.3 100%

FLOOR SUPPORT

33mm (1⁵⁄₁₆in)

33mm (1⁵⁄₁₆in)

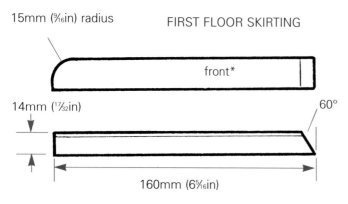

15mm (⅝⁄₁₆in) radius

FIRST FLOOR SKIRTING

front*

14mm (1⁷⁄₃₂in)

60°

160mm (6⁵⁄₁₆in)

Fig 10.6 45% (Enlarge to 222%)

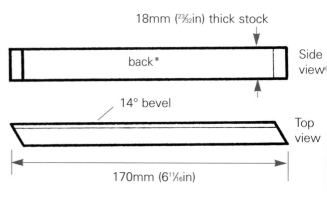

18mm (²³⁄₃₂in) thick stock

back*

Side view

14° bevel

Top view

170mm (6¹¹⁄₁₆in)

* as viewed from open back of windmill

Fig 10.5 50% (Enlarge to 200%)

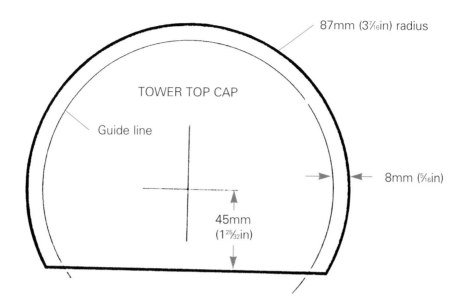

87mm (3⅞in) radius

TOWER TOP CAP

Guide line

8mm (⅚in)

45mm
(1²⁵⁄₃₂in)

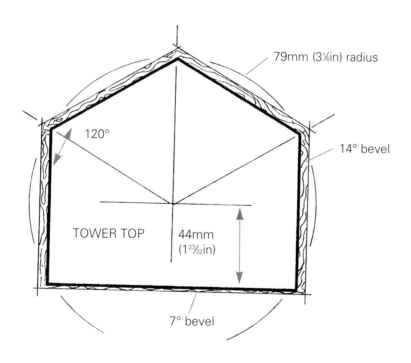

79mm (3⅛in) radius

120°

14° bevel

TOWER TOP   44mm
(1²³⁄₃₂in)

7° bevel

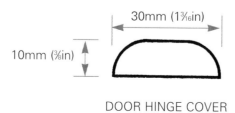

30mm (1³⁄₁₆in)

10mm (⅜in)

DOOR HINGE COVER

Fig 10.7 100%

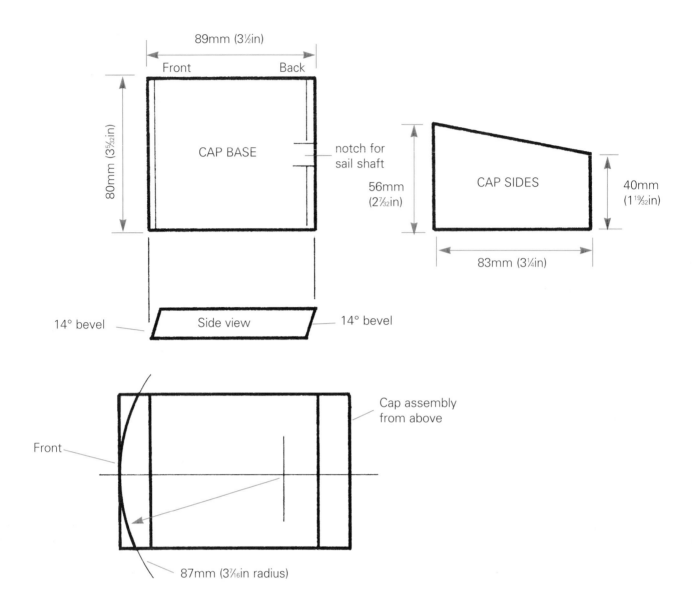

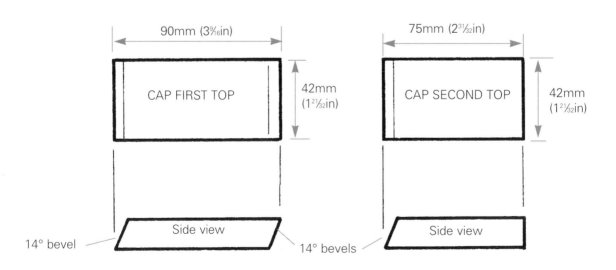

Fig 10.8 50% (Enlarge to 200%)

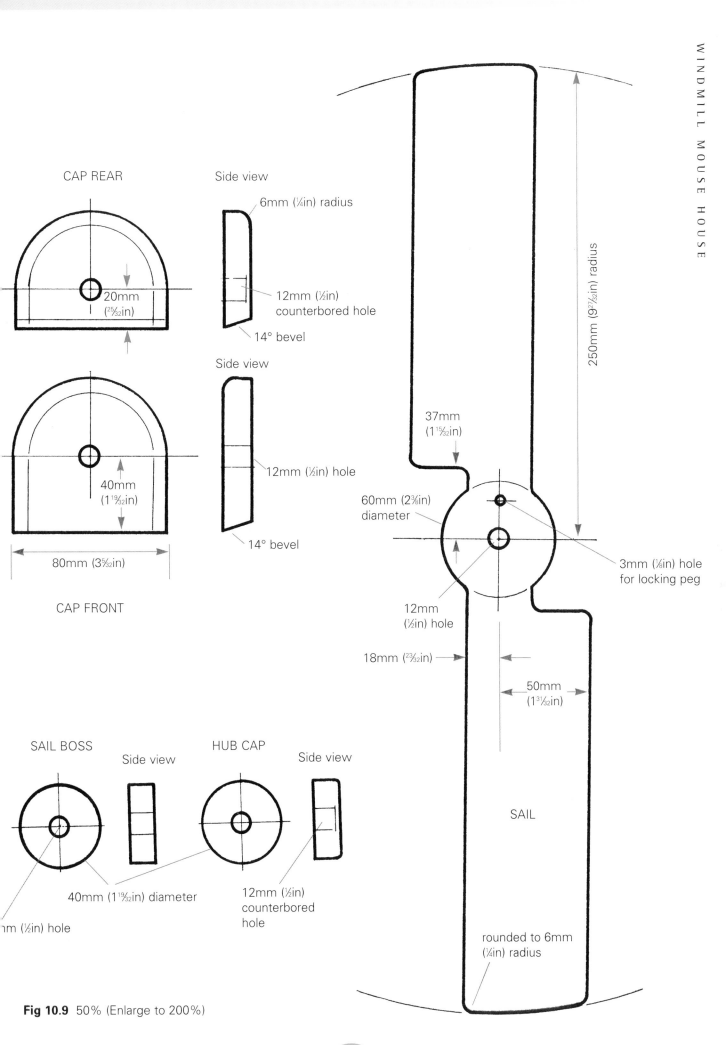

CAP REAR

Side view

6mm (¼in) radius

20mm
(²⁵⁄₃₂in)

12mm (½in)
counterbored hole

14° bevel

Side view

40mm
(1¹⁹⁄₃₂in)

12mm (½in) hole

14° bevel

80mm (3⁵⁄₃₂in)

CAP FRONT

37mm
(1¹⁵⁄₃₂in)

250mm (9²⁷⁄₃₂in) radius

60mm (2³⁄₈in)
diameter

3mm (⅛in) hole
for locking peg

12mm
(½in) hole

18mm (²³⁄₃₂in)

50mm
(1³¹⁄₃₂in)

SAIL

SAIL BOSS

Side view

HUB CAP

Side view

40mm (1¹⁹⁄₃₂in) diameter

12mm (½in)
counterbored
hole

m (½in) hole

rounded to 6mm
(¼in) radius

Fig 10.9 50% (Enlarge to 200%)

MICE

Fig 10.10 100%

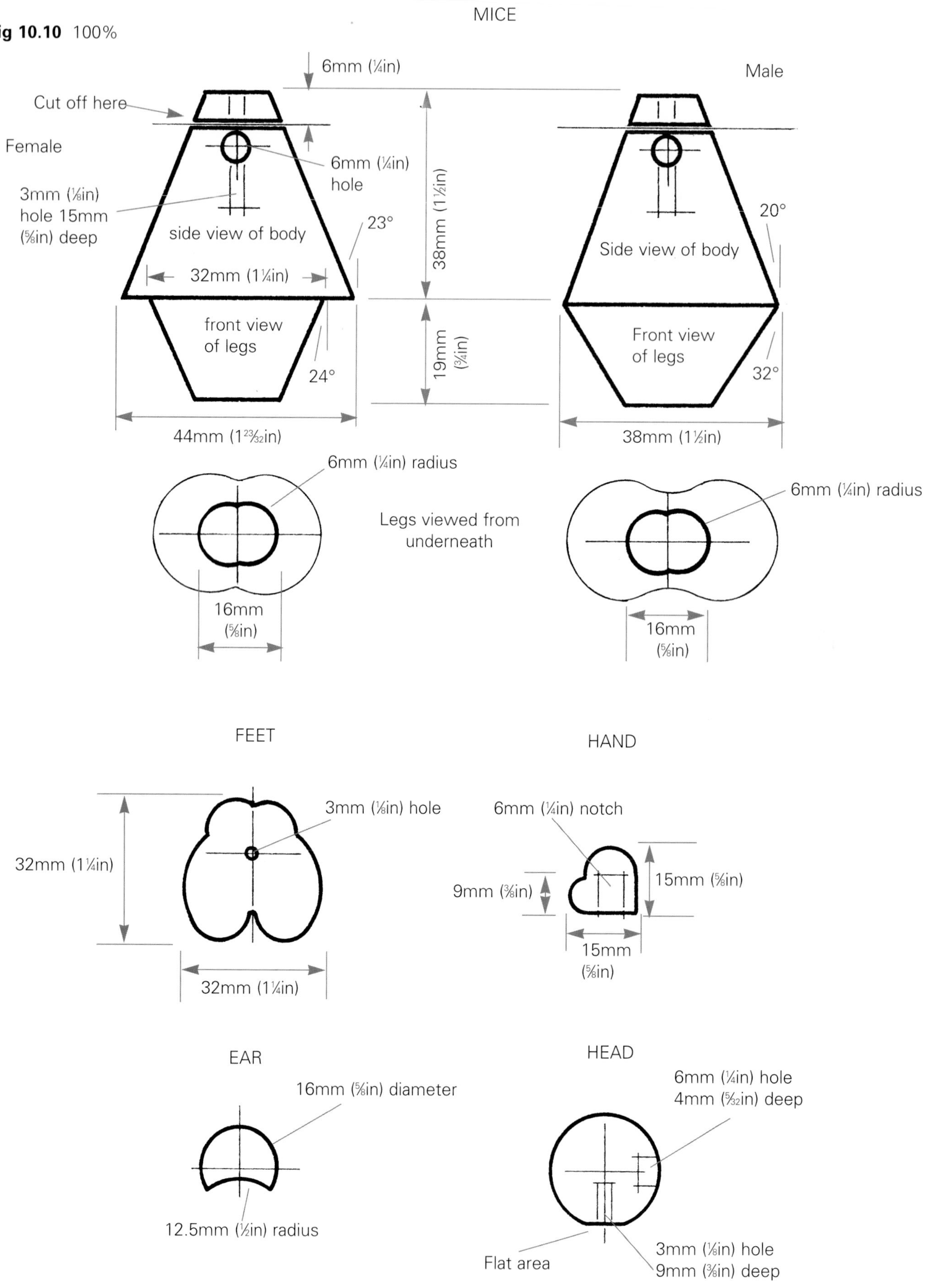

Male

Female

6mm (¼in)

Cut off here

6mm (¼in) hole

3mm (⅛in) hole 15mm (⅝in) deep

side view of body

32mm (1¼in)

23°

38mm (1½in)

Side view of body

20°

front view of legs

24°

19mm (¾in)

Front view of legs

32°

44mm (1²³⁄₃₂in)

38mm (1½in)

6mm (¼in) radius

Legs viewed from underneath

6mm (¼in) radius

16mm (⅝in)

16mm (⅝in)

FEET

HAND

32mm (1¼in)

3mm (⅛in) hole

6mm (¼in) notch

9mm (⅜in)

15mm (⅝in)

15mm (⅝in)

32mm (1¼in)

EAR

HEAD

16mm (⅝in) diameter

6mm (¼in) hole
4mm (⁵⁄₃₂in) deep

12.5mm (½in) radius

Flat area

3mm (⅛in) hole
9mm (⅜in) deep

Fig 11.1 60%
(Enlarge to 166%)

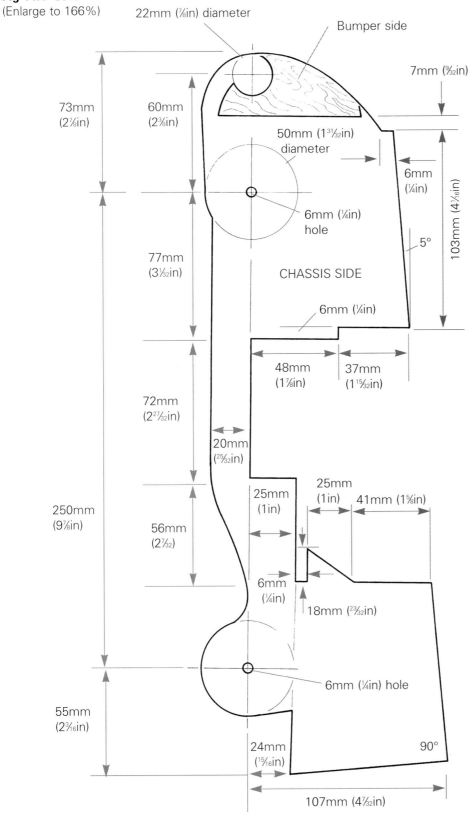

22mm (⅞in) diameter

Bumper side

7mm (⁹⁄₃₂in)

73mm
(2⅞in)

60mm
(2⅜in)

50mm (1³¹⁄₃₂in)
diameter

6mm
(¼in)

6mm (¼in)
hole

103mm (4¹⁄₁₆in)

5°

77mm
(3⅛₂in)

CHASSIS SIDE

6mm (¼in)

48mm
(1⅞in)

37mm
(1¹⁵⁄₃₂in)

72mm
(2²⁷⁄₃₂in)

20mm
(²⁵⁄₃₂in)

25mm
(1in)

25mm
(1in)

41mm (1⅝in)

250mm
(9⅞in)

56mm
(2⁷⁄₃₂)

6mm
(¼in)

18mm (²³⁄₃₂in)

6mm (¼in) hole

55mm
(2³⁄₁₆in)

24mm
(¹⁵⁄₁₆in)

90°

107mm (4⁷⁄₃₂in)

Fig 11.3 100%

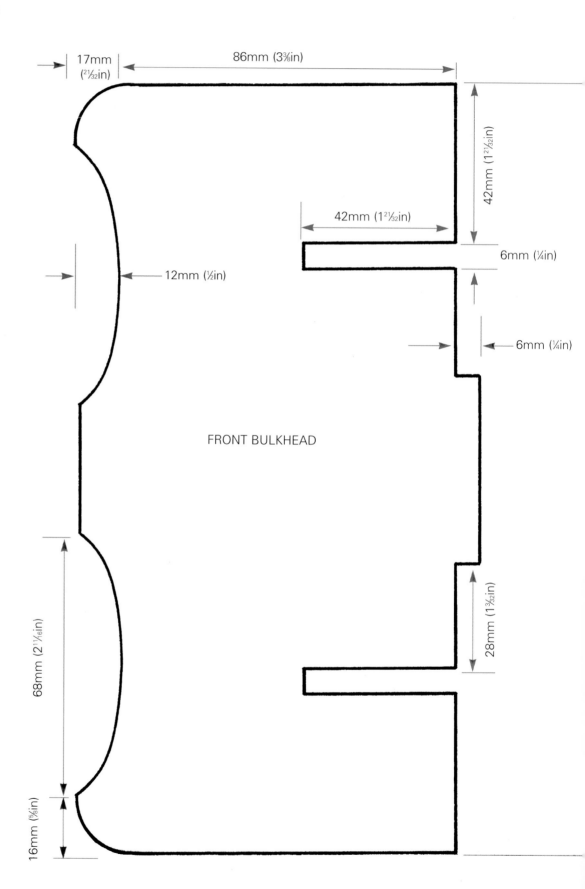

FRONT BULKHEAD

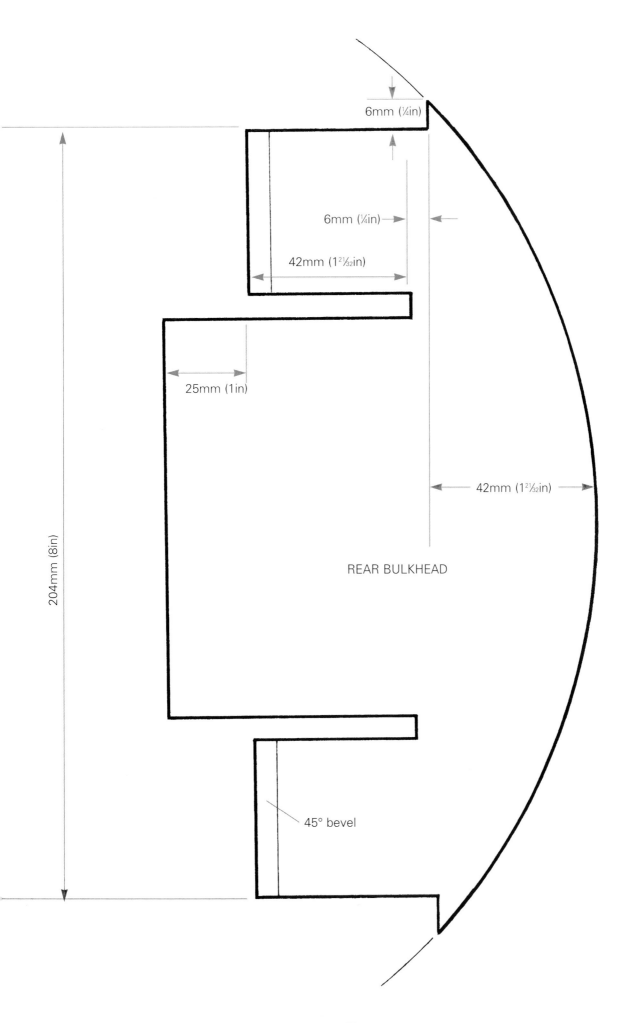

6mm (¼in)

6mm (¼in)

42mm (1²¹⁄₃₂in)

25mm (1in)

42mm (1²¹⁄₃₂in)

REAR BULKHEAD

204mm (8in)

45° bevel

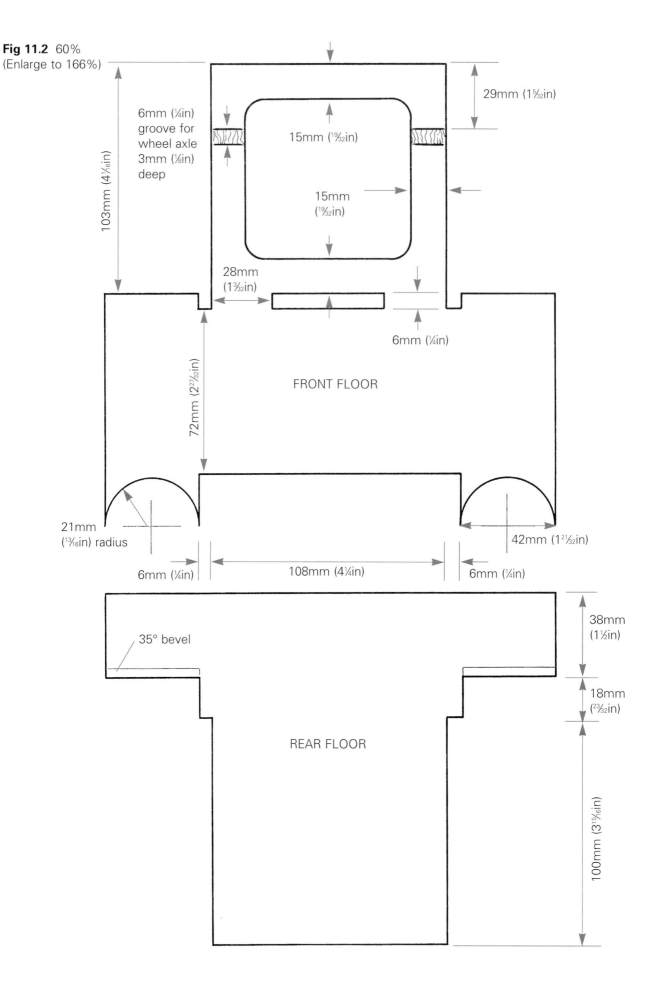

Fig 11.2 60%
(Enlarge to 166%)

29mm (1⁵⁄₃₂in)

6mm (¼in)
groove for
wheel axle
3mm (⅛in)
deep

15mm (¹⁹⁄₃₂in)

15mm
(¹⁹⁄₃₂in)

103mm (4¹⁄₁₆in)

28mm
(1³⁄₃₂in)

6mm (¼in)

FRONT FLOOR

72mm (2²⁷⁄₃₂in)

21mm
(¹³⁄₁₆in) radius

42mm (1²¹⁄₃₂in)

6mm (¼in)

108mm (4¼in)

6mm (¼in)

35° bevel

38mm
(1½in)

18mm
(²³⁄₃₂in)

REAR FLOOR

100mm (3¹⁵⁄₁₆in)

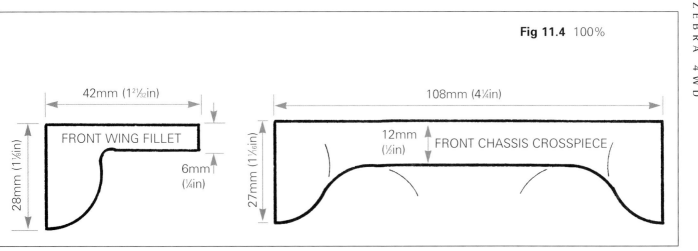

Fig 11.4 100%

FRONT WING FILLET

42mm (1²¹⁄₃₂in)

28mm (1⅛in)

6mm (¼in)

108mm (4¼in)

FRONT CHASSIS CROSSPIECE

12mm (½in)

27mm (1¹⁄₁₆in)

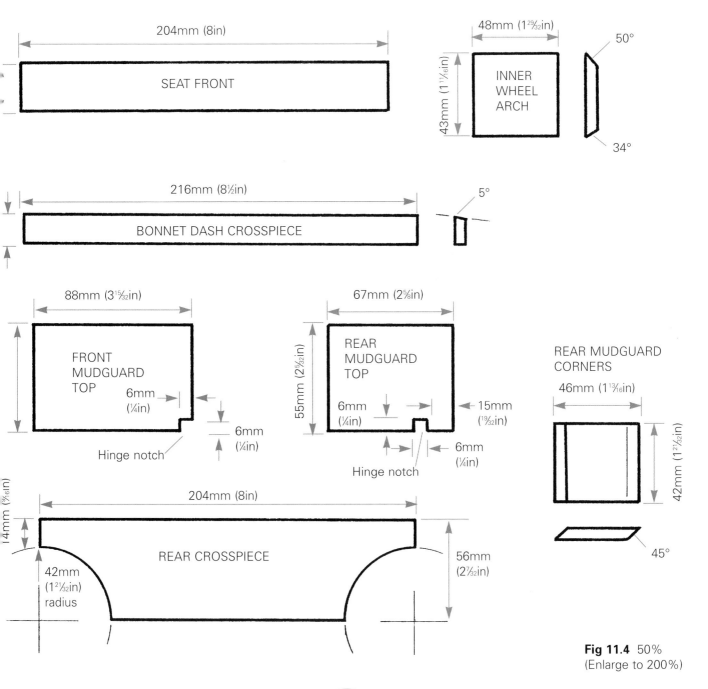

204mm (8in)

SEAT FRONT

48mm (1²⁹⁄₃₂in)

INNER WHEEL ARCH

43mm (1¹¹⁄₁₆in)

50°

34°

216mm (8½in)

BONNET DASH CROSSPIECE

5°

88mm (3¹⁵⁄₃₂in)

FRONT MUDGUARD TOP

6mm (¼in)

6mm (¼in)

Hinge notch

67mm (2⅝in)

REAR MUDGUARD TOP

55mm (2³⁄₁₆in)

6mm (¼in)

15mm (¹⁹⁄₃₂in)

6mm (¼in)

Hinge notch

REAR MUDGUARD CORNERS

46mm (1¹³⁄₁₆in)

42mm (1²¹⁄₃₂in)

45°

14mm (⁹⁄₁₆in)

204mm (8in)

REAR CROSSPIECE

42mm (1²¹⁄₃₂in) radius

56mm (2⅞in)

Fig 11.4 50%
(Enlarge to 200%)

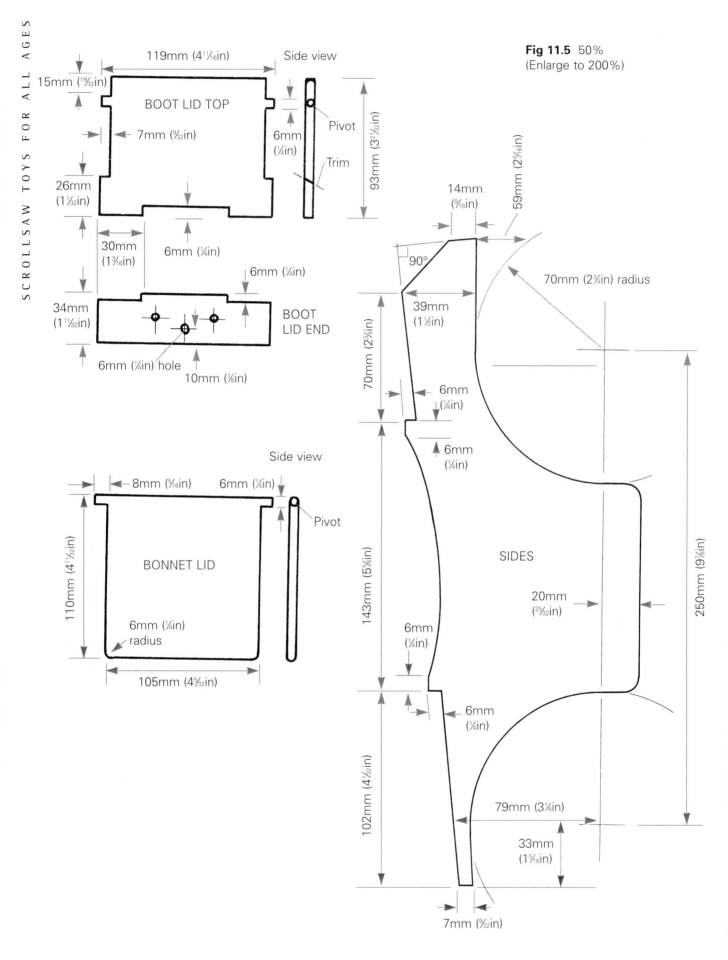

119mm (4¹¹⁄₁₆in)

15mm (¹⁹⁄₃₂in)

Side view

Fig 11.5 50%
(Enlarge to 200%)

BOOT LID TOP

7mm (⁹⁄₃₂in)

Pivot

6mm (¼in)

Trim

93mm (3²¹⁄₃₂in)

26mm (1¹⁄₃₂in)

14mm (⁹⁄₁₆in)

59mm (2⁵⁄₁₆in)

90°

30mm (1³⁄₁₆in)

6mm (¼in)

70mm (2¾in) radius

6mm (¼in)

34mm (1¹¹⁄₃₂in)

BOOT LID END

39mm (1½in)

70mm (2¾in)

6mm (¼in) hole

10mm (⅜in)

6mm (¼in)

6mm (¼in)

Side view

8mm (⁵⁄₁₆in)

6mm (¼in)

6mm (¼in)

143mm (5⅝in)

SIDES

Pivot

110mm (4¹¹⁄₃₂in)

BONNET LID

250mm (9⅞in)

20mm (²⁵⁄₃₂in)

6mm (¼in) radius

6mm (¼in)

105mm (4⁵⁄₃₂in)

102mm (4¹⁄₃₂in)

6mm (¼in)

79mm (3⅛in)

33mm (1⁵⁄₁₆in)

7mm (⁹⁄₃₂in)

Fig11.6 40% (Enlarge to 250%)

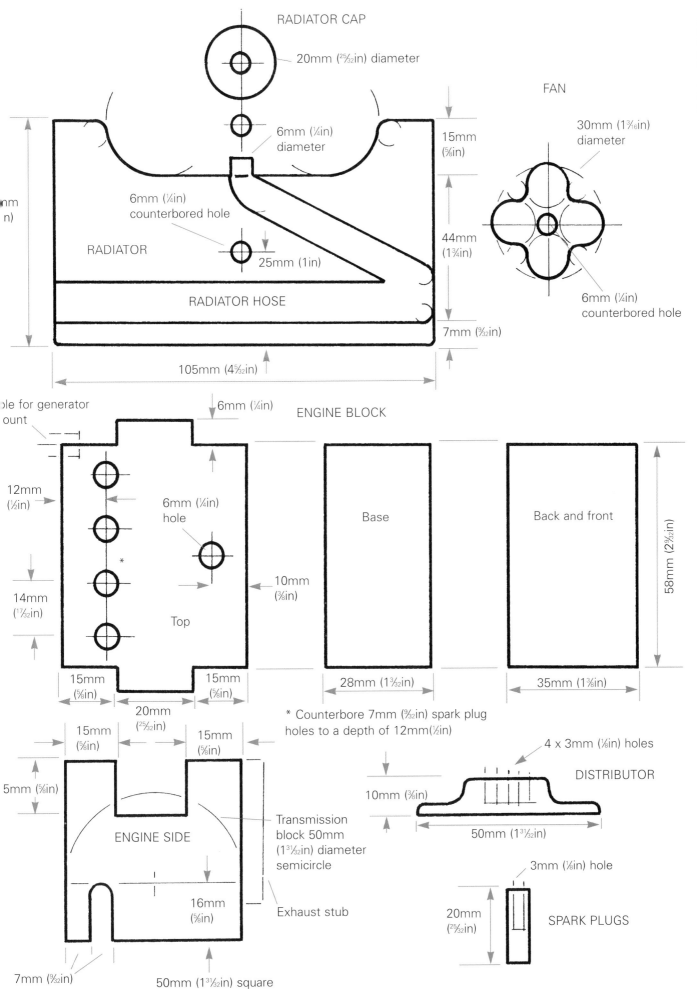

RADIATOR CAP

20mm (²⁵⁄₃₂in) diameter

FAN

30mm (1³⁄₁₆in) diameter

6mm (¼in) diameter

15mm (⅝in)

6mm (¼in) counterbored hole

RADIATOR

6mm (¼in) counterbored hole

44mm (1¾in)

25mm (1in)

RADIATOR HOSE

7mm (⁹⁄₃₂in)

105mm (4⁵⁄₃₂in)

ole for generator ount

6mm (¼in)

ENGINE BLOCK

12mm (½in)

6mm (¼in) hole

Base

Back and front

58mm (2⁹⁄₃₂in)

14mm (¹⁷⁄₃₂in)

10mm (⅜in)

Top

35mm (1⅜in)

15mm (⅝in)

15mm (⅝in)

28mm (1³⁄₃₂in)

20mm (²⁵⁄₃₂in)

* Counterbore 7mm (⁹⁄₃₂in) spark plug holes to a depth of 12mm(½in)

15mm (⅝in)

15mm (⅝in)

4 x 3mm (⅛in) holes

DISTRIBUTOR

5mm (⅝in)

10mm (⅜in)

Transmission block 50mm (1³¹⁄₃₂in) diameter semicircle

ENGINE SIDE

50mm (1³¹⁄₃₂in)

16mm (⅝in)

Exhaust stub

3mm (⅛in) hole

20mm (²⁵⁄₃₂in)

SPARK PLUGS

7mm (⁹⁄₃₂in)

50mm (1³¹⁄₃₂in) square

Fig 11.7 100%

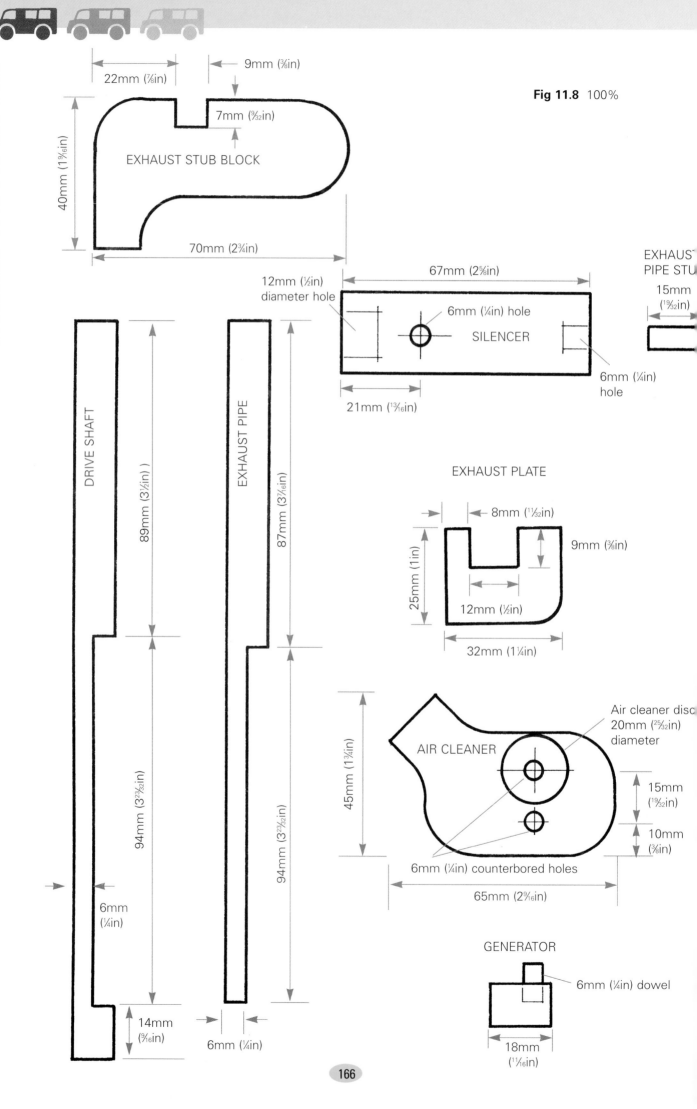

Fig 11.8 100%

22mm (⅞in)

9mm (⅜in)

7mm (⁹⁄₃₂in)

40mm (1⁹⁄₁₆in)

EXHAUST STUB BLOCK

70mm (2¾in)

EXHAUST
PIPE STU

15mm
(¹⁹⁄₃₂in)

67mm (2⅝in)

12mm (½in)
diameter hole

6mm (¼in) hole

SILENCER

21mm (¹³⁄₁₆in)

6mm (¼in)
hole

DRIVE SHAFT

EXHAUST PIPE

89mm (3½in)

87mm (3⁷⁄₁₆in)

94mm (3²³⁄₃₂in)

94mm (3²³⁄₃₂in)

6mm
(¼in)

14mm
(⁹⁄₁₆in)

6mm (¼in)

EXHAUST PLATE

8mm (¹¹⁄₃₂in)

9mm (⅜in)

25mm (1in)

12mm (½in)

32mm (1¼in)

45mm (1¾in)

AIR CLEANER

Air cleaner disc
20mm (²⁵⁄₃₂in)
diameter

15mm
(¹⁹⁄₃₂in)

10mm
(⅜in)

6mm (¼in) counterbored holes

65mm (2⁹⁄₁₆in)

GENERATOR

6mm (¼in) dowel

18mm
(¹¹⁄₁₆in)

WHEELS AND TYRES

Fig 11.9 100%

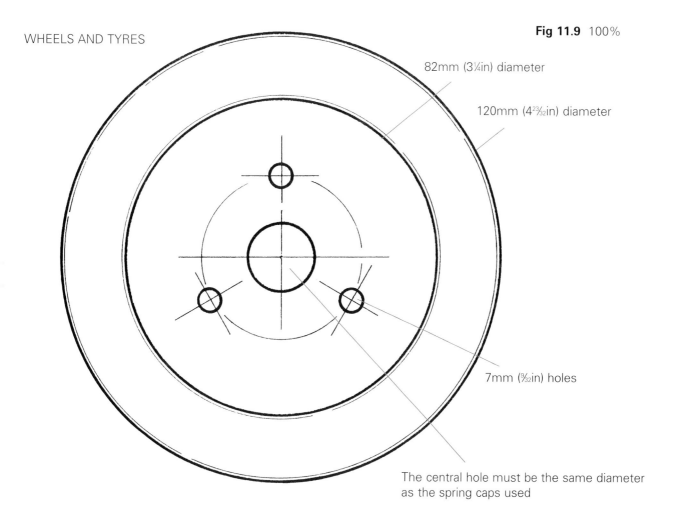

82mm (3¼in) diameter

120mm (4²³⁄₃₂in) diameter

7mm (⁹⁄₃₂in) holes

The central hole must be the same diameter as the spring caps used

BRAKE HUB AND HUB

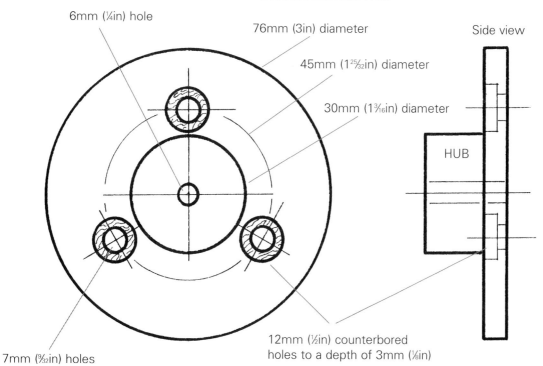

6mm (¼in) hole

76mm (3in) diameter

45mm (1²⁵⁄₃₂in) diameter

30mm (1³⁄₁₆in) diameter

Side view

HUB

7mm (⁹⁄₃₂in) holes

12mm (½in) counterbored holes to a depth of 3mm (⅛in)

SPARE WHEEL LATCH

6mm (¼in)
counterbored holes

14mm (⁹⁄₁₆in) diameter

24mm (¹⁵⁄₁₆in)

SOCKET
HANDLE

20mm (²⁵⁄₃₂in) diameter

9mm (³⁄₈in)

STEERING WHEEL

24mm (¹⁵⁄₁₆in) diameter

60mm (2⅜in) diameter

HUB

View from
side

6mm (¼in)
counterbored hole

6mm (¼in) hole

16mm (⅝in)
diameter

GEAR UNIT

6mm (¼in) holes

20mm
(²⁵⁄₃₂in)
radius

STEERING PILLAR

6mm (¼in) hole

16mm
(⅝in)

41mm (1⅝in)

GEAR STICK AND HANDLE

32mm (1¼in)

18mm
(¹¹⁄₁₆in)

HINGE COVER

25mm (1in)
diameter semi circle

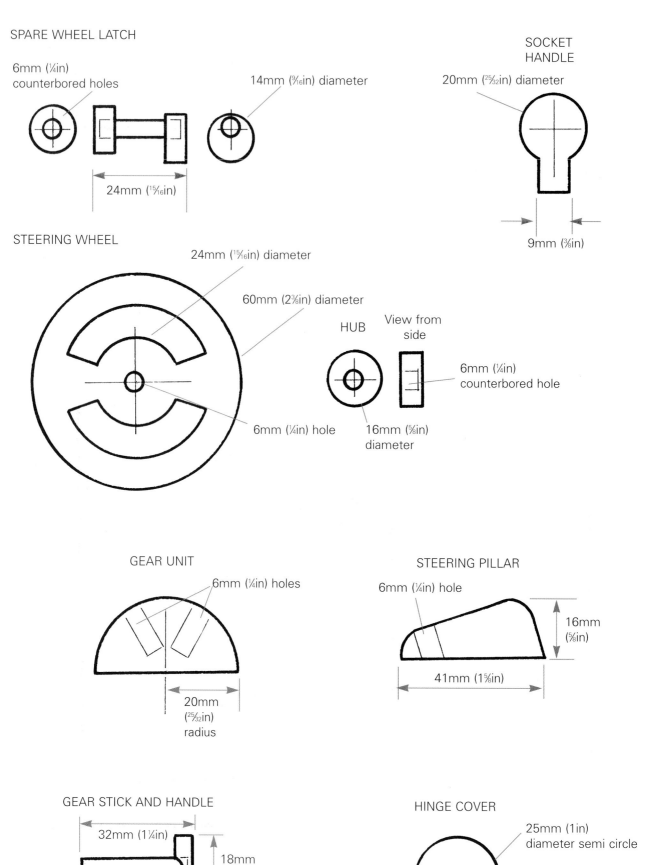

Fig 11.10 100%

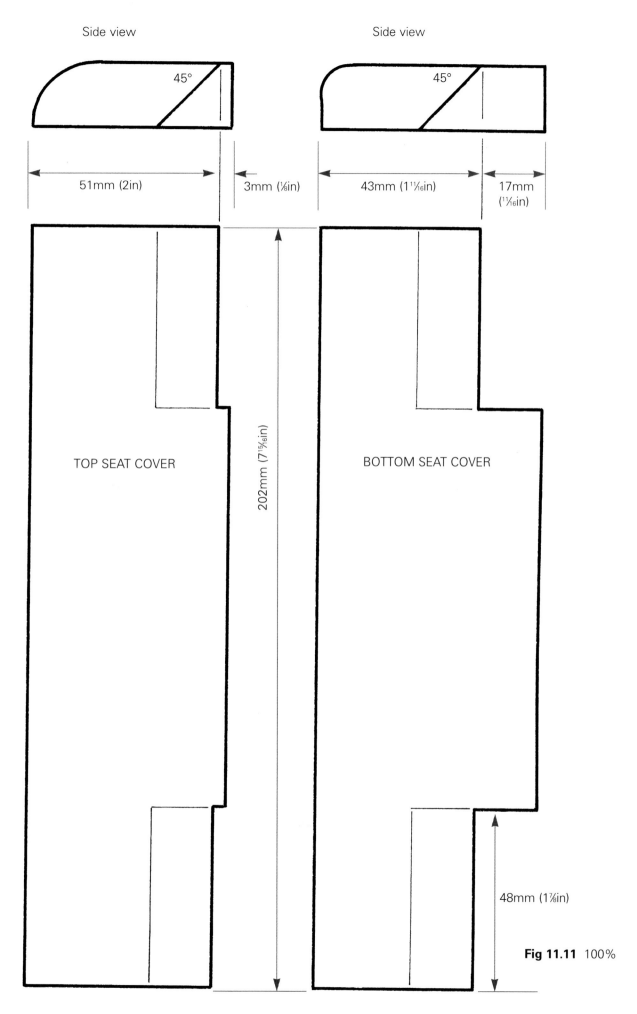

Side view

45°

51mm (2in)

3mm (⅛in)

Side view

45°

43mm (1¹¹⁄₁₆in)

17mm (¹¹⁄₁₆in)

TOP SEAT COVER

BOTTOM SEAT COVER

202mm (7¹⁵⁄₁₆in)

48mm (1⅞in)

Fig 11.11 100%

WINDSCREEN

Fig 11.11 100%

3mm (⅛in) hole

37mm (1⁷⁄₁₆in)

22mm (⅞in)

10mm (⅜in)

7mm (⁹⁄₃₂in)

82mm (3¼in)

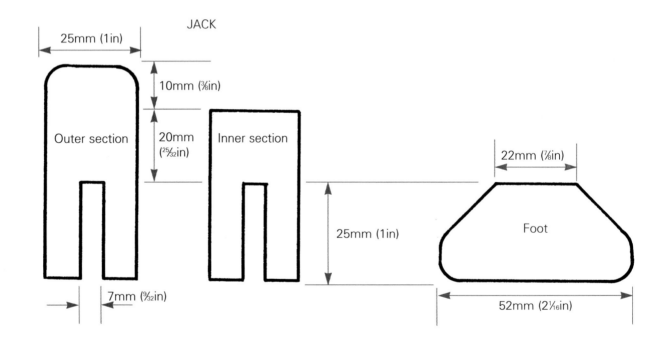

JACK

25mm (1in)

10mm (⅜in)

20mm (²⁵⁄₃₂in)

Outer section

Inner section

25mm (1in)

22mm (⅞in)

Foot

7mm (⁹⁄₃₂in)

52mm (2¹⁄₁₆in)

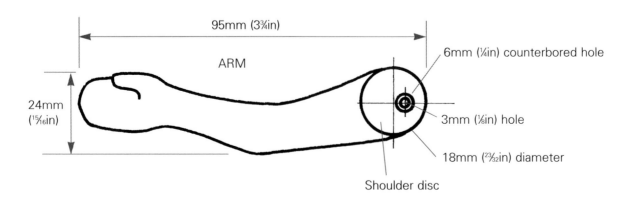

95mm (3¾in)

ARM

24mm (¹⁵⁄₁₆in)

6mm (¼in) counterbored hole

3mm (⅛in) hole

18mm (²³⁄₃₂in) diameter

Shoulder disc

Fig 11.12 100%

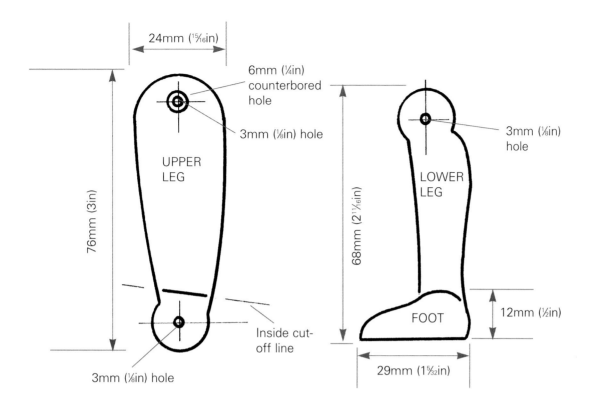

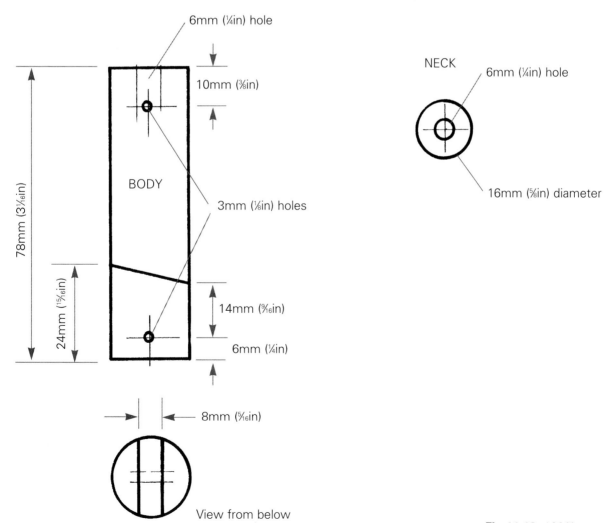

View from below

Fig 11.12 100%

Fig 12.1 35%
(Enlarge to 285%)

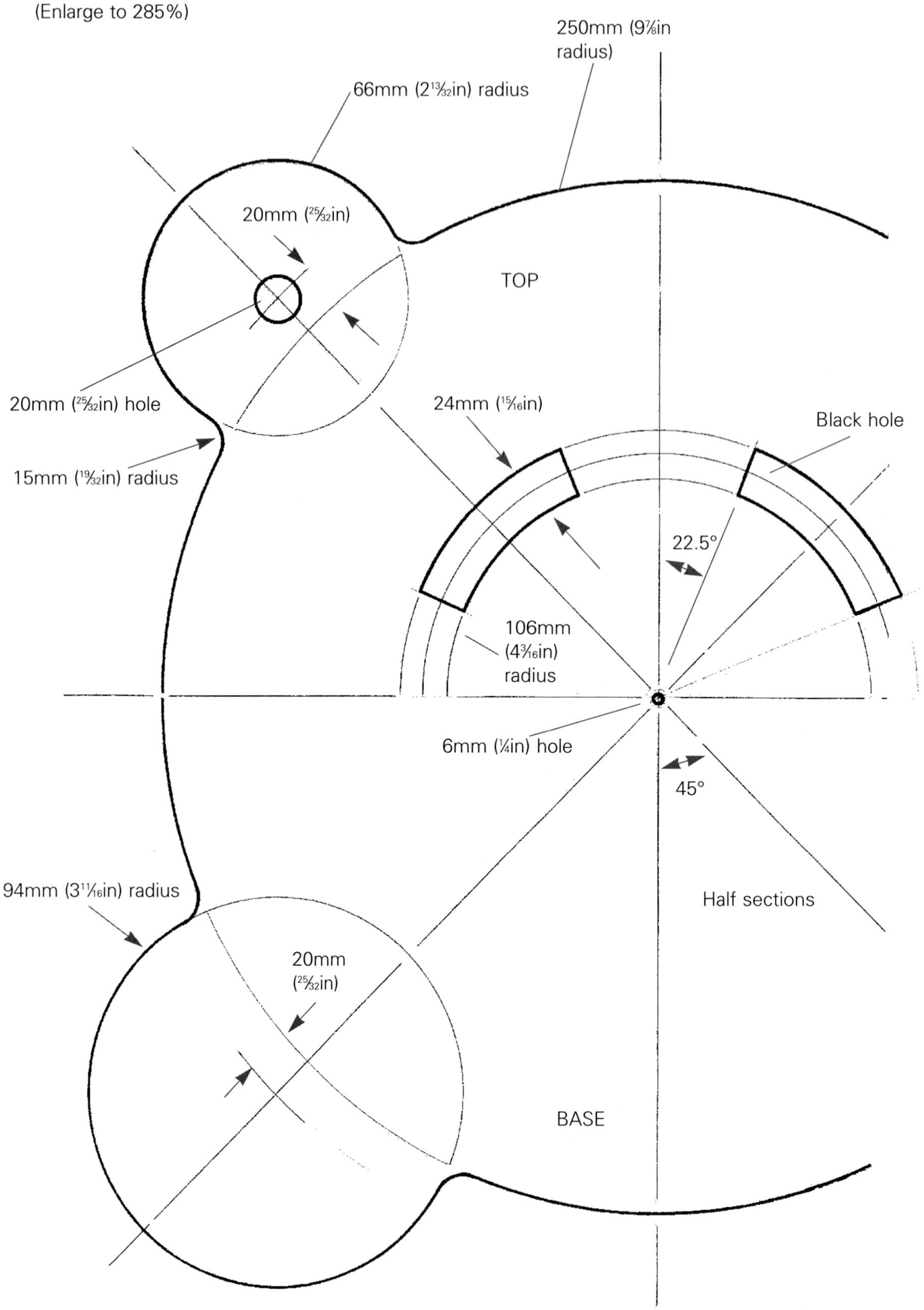

66mm (2¹³⁄₃₂in) radius

250mm (9⅞in radius)

20mm (²⁵⁄₃₂in)

TOP

20mm (²⁵⁄₃₂in) hole

24mm (¹⁵⁄₁₆in)

Black hole

15mm (¹⁹⁄₃₂in) radius

22.5°

106mm (4³⁄₁₆in) radius

6mm (¼in) hole

45°

94mm (3¹¹⁄₁₆in) radius

Half sections

20mm (²⁵⁄₃₂in)

BASE

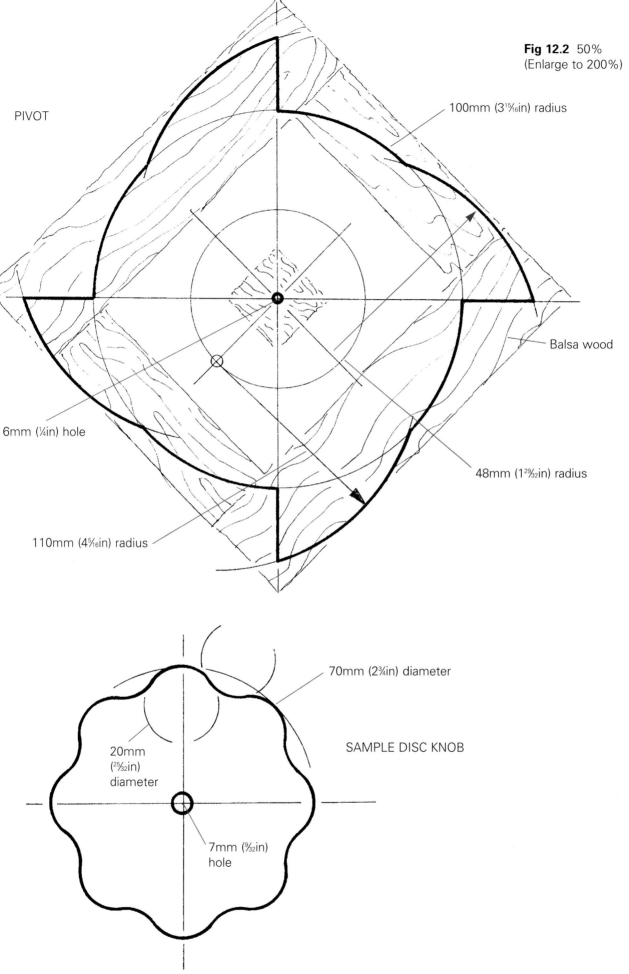

PIVOT

Fig 12.2 50%
(Enlarge to 200%)

100mm (3¹⁵⁄₁₆in) radius

Balsa wood

6mm (¼in) hole

48mm (1²⁹⁄₃₂in) radius

110mm (4⁵⁄₁₆in) radius

70mm (2¾in) diameter

20mm
(²⁵⁄₃₂in)
diameter

SAMPLE DISC KNOB

7mm (⁹⁄₃₂in)
hole

Fig 12.6 100 %

Fig 12.2 50% (Enlarge to 200%)

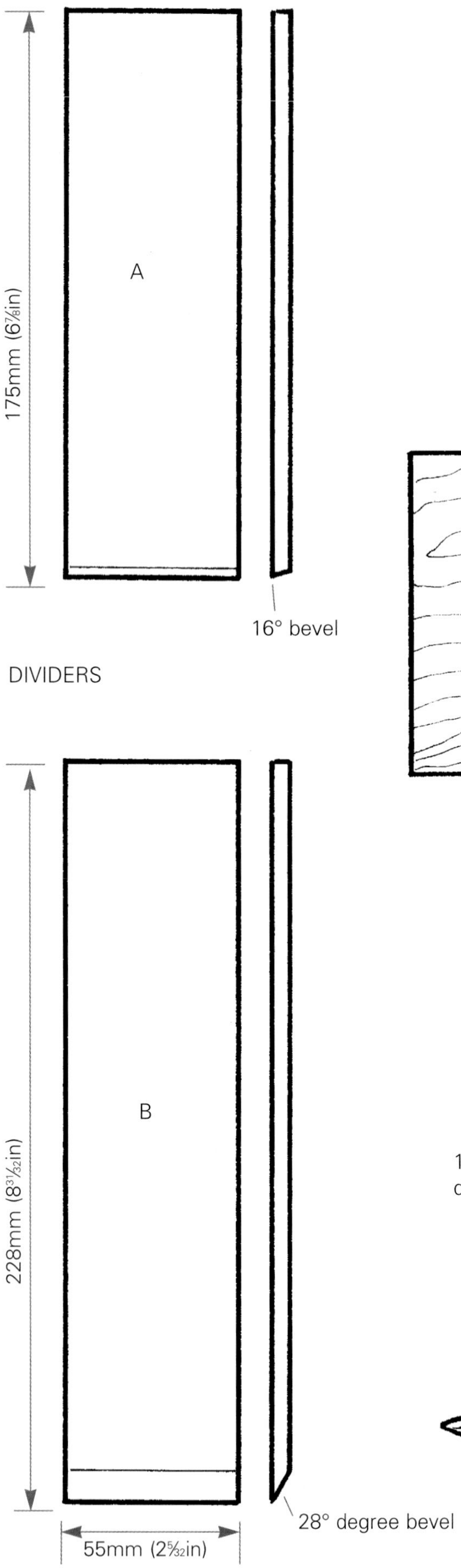

175mm (6⅞in)

A

16° bevel

DIVIDERS

228mm (8³¹⁄₃₂in)

B

55mm (2⁵⁄₃₂in)

28° degree bevel

Fig 12.8

FILING DOWN
HINGE PINS

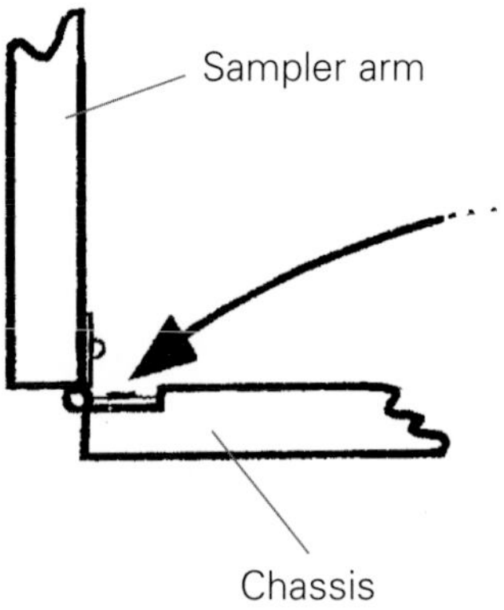

Sampler arm

Chassis

DRILLING HUBS

Fig 12.9 100%

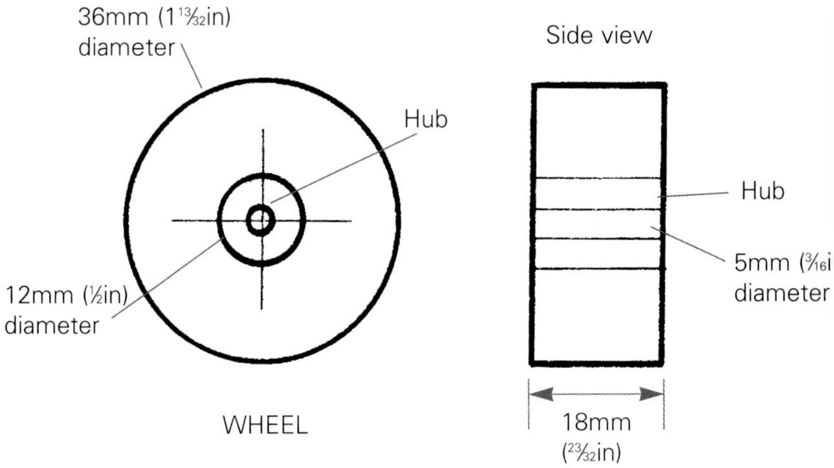

36mm (1¹³⁄₃₂in)
diameter

Side view

Hub

12mm (½in)
diameter

Hub

5mm (³⁄₁₆i
diameter

WHEEL

18mm
(²³⁄₃₂in)

70mm (2¾in)

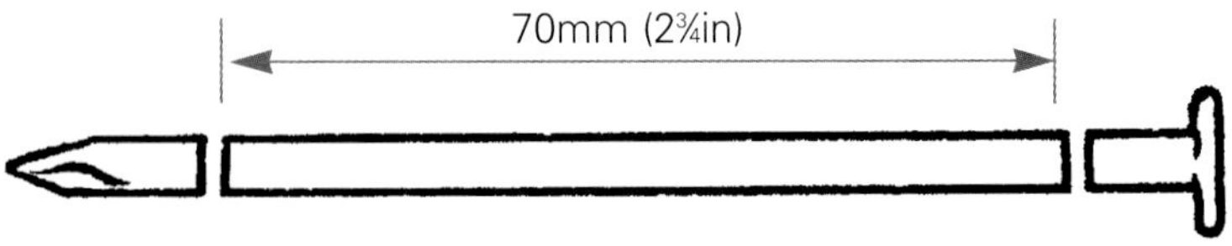

MAKING REAR AXLES FROM NAILS

Fig 12.10 100%

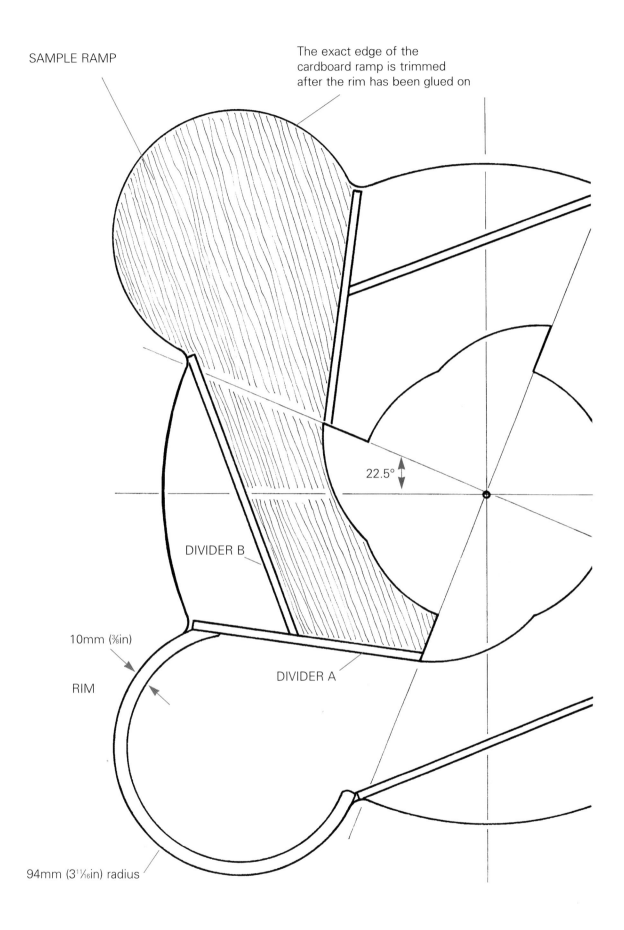

SAMPLE RAMP

The exact edge of the cardboard ramp is trimmed after the rim has been glued on

22.5°

DIVIDER B

10mm (⅜in)

RIM

DIVIDER A

94mm (3¹¹⁄₁₆in) radius

Fig 12.3 33%
(Enlarge to 303%)

RAMP DETAIL

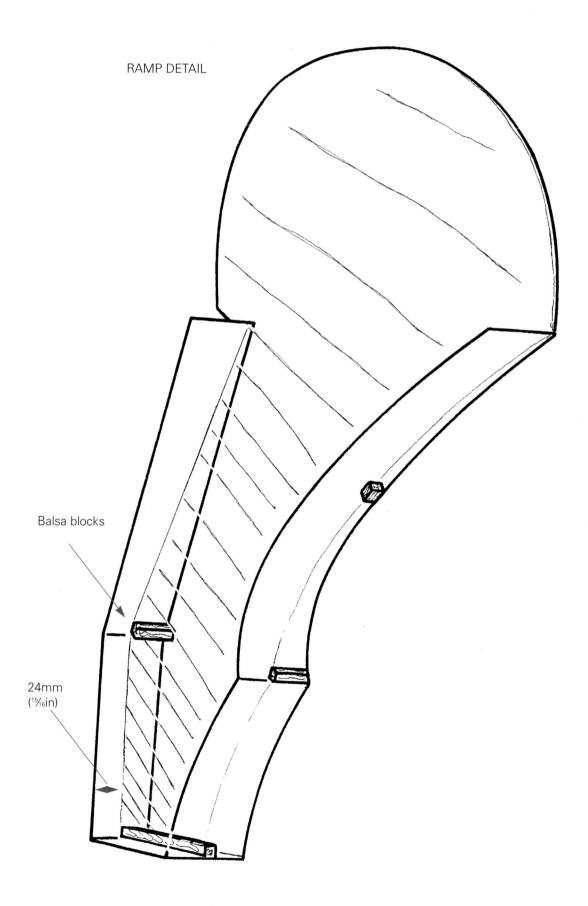

Balsa blocks

24mm
($^{15}/_{16}$in)

Fig 12.4 30% (Enlarge to 333%)

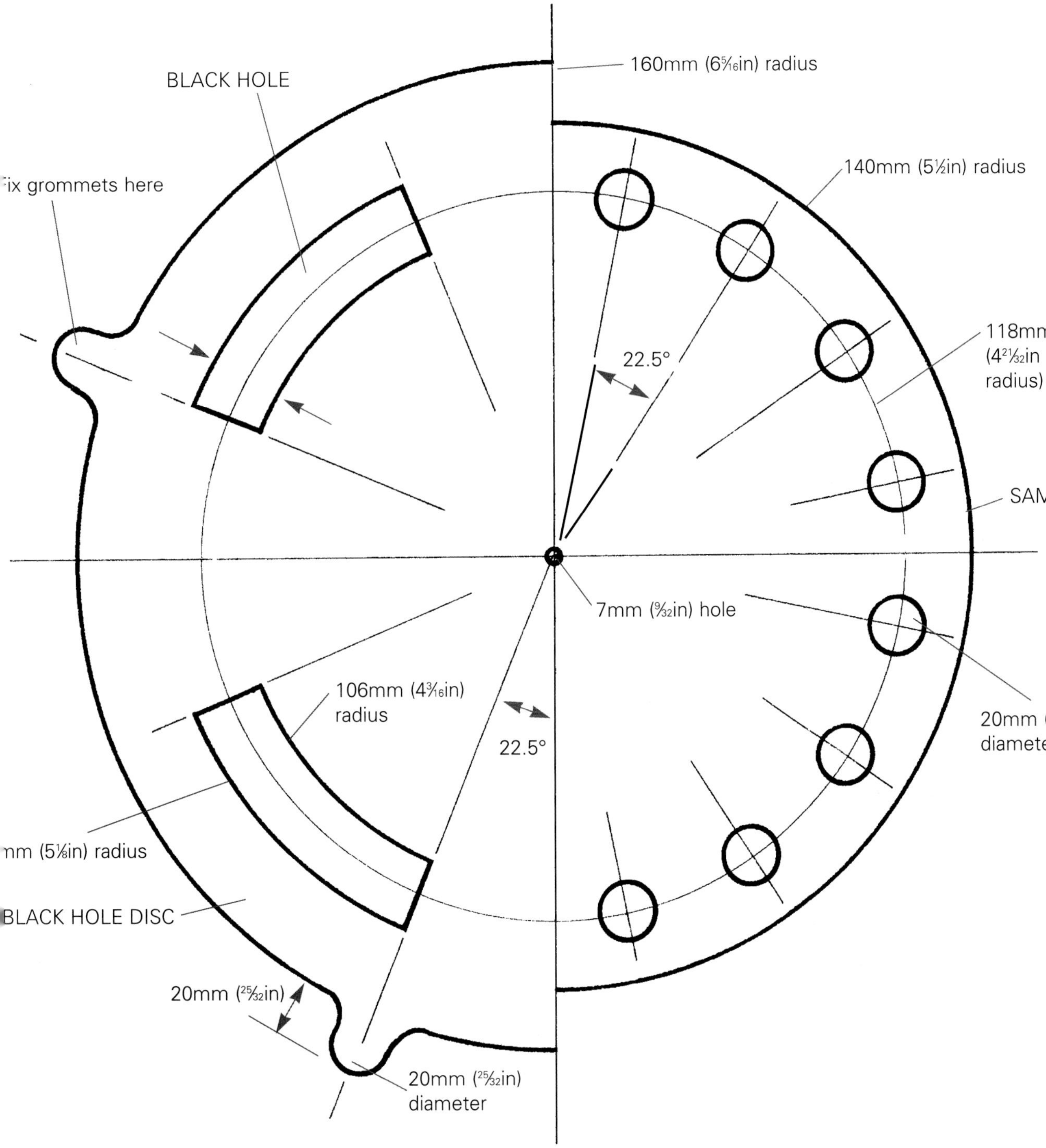

BLACK HOLE

Fix grommets here

160mm (6⁵⁄₁₆in) radius

140mm (5½in) radius

118mm (4²¹⁄₃₂in radius)

22.5°

SAMPLE DISC

7mm (⁹⁄₃₂in) hole

106mm (4³⁄₁₆in) radius

22.5°

20mm (²⁵⁄₃₂in) diameter hole

mm (5⅛in) radius

BLACK HOLE DISC

20mm (²⁵⁄₃₂in)

20mm (²⁵⁄₃₂in) diameter

Fig 12.5 50% (Enlarge to 200%)

ROVER

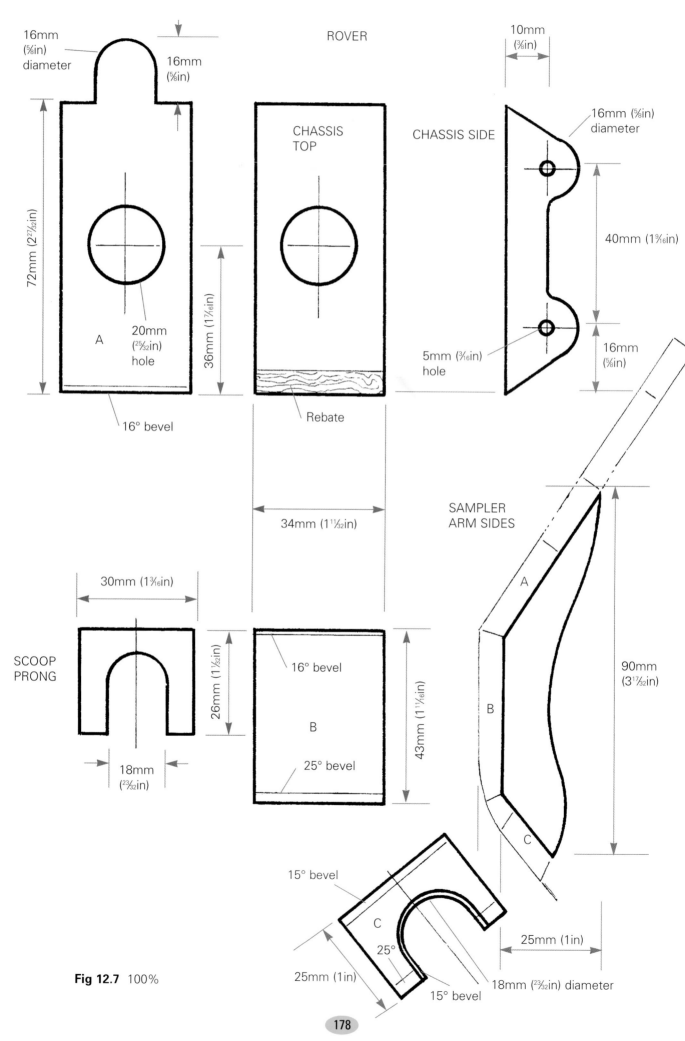

16mm
(⅝in)
diameter

16mm
(⅝in)

72mm (2²⁷⁄₃₂in)

A

20mm
(²⁵⁄₃₂in)
hole

16° bevel

CHASSIS
TOP

36mm (1⁷⁄₁₆in)

Rebate

34mm (1¹¹⁄₃₂in)

10mm
(⅜in)

CHASSIS SIDE

16mm (⅝in)
diameter

40mm (1⁹⁄₁₆in)

5mm (³⁄₁₆in)
hole

16mm
(⅝in)

SAMPLER
ARM SIDES

A

B

C

90mm
(3¹⁷⁄₃₂in)

30mm (1³⁄₁₆in)

SCOOP
PRONG

26mm (1¹⁄₃₂in)

18mm
(²³⁄₃₂in)

16° bevel

B

25° bevel

43mm (1¹¹⁄₁₆in)

15° bevel

C

25°

25mm (1in)

15° bevel

25mm (1in)

18mm (²³⁄₃₂in) diameter

Fig 12.7 100%

CRATER PAINTSTAMPS

Fig12.11 100%

GLOSSARY

ACRYLIC SHEET

Available in various thickness from 1mm upwards. Often known as 'Perspex'(TM) in the UK and as 'Plexiglas'(TM) in the USA and widely used in the sign making trade. Also sold in 2mm (⅛in) thickness sheets in DIY stores as a glazing material.

AXLE

A spindle or rod on which a wheel rotates.

BALSA

Paradoxically a very soft hardwood. It is very useful for filling in small gaps with the aid of PVA glue.

It will not crumble and fall out and is therefore preferable to a decorator's filler.

BEVEL

An angle where two surfaces meet and do not form a right-angle.

BLIND PINNING

A method of temporarily fixing a fret pin in to a piece of work so that the head is left proud enabling it to be easily removed.

BUTT JOINT

A joint where the two surfaces are pushed together with no interlocking parts.

CAM

An elliptical or irregular shaped wheel that converts circular motion into linear motion.

CANDLE WAX

The wax from domestic candles is an ideal lubricant for wooden bearings and pivots. Also helps saw blades to cut through resinous wood.

CHIPBOARD SCREW

A shallow pitch woodscrew with a double spiral and a non tapering shank. It will cut its way into a pilot hole made in composite materials such as plywood and chipboard without splitting it.

COUNTERBORE

A hole that is drilled in to a material but stops short of going all the way through.

COUNTERSINK/COUNTERSUNK SCREWS

Countersinking is carried out by using a conical shaped countersink drill to produce a conical recess at the surface of a screw hole. This enables the flat-topped head of a countersunk screw that tapers 45° into its shank to countersink flush with the wood's surface.

CREPE CORD

A multi stranded silk-like cord, made in many colours for decorative work on garments and furnishings, etc.

CROSS-HALVING JOINT

A simple joint that involves part of a component fitting into a slot or recess cut into another component.

CYANOACRYLATE ADHESIVE

Commonly known as 'super glue'. Ideal for quick repairs and will also join such things as rubber drive belts which makes it unique.

DOUBLE-SIDED TAPE

A tape used for many purposes. It has a removable backing sheet that leaves an adhesive layer on a surface so that another can be joined to it.

DOWEL

A circular section moulding made in hardwood and softwood. These are very useful for making axles, pegs, handles and reinforcing joints and are available in various sizes from 3mm (⅛in) upwards.

DRILL GUIDE

A mobile jig that holds a power drill at 90° to the surface. It has a depth stop guide and can perform many useful functions.

DRY ASSEMBLING

Assembling components without using any adhesive in order to check their fit.

EPOXY RESIN GLUE

The main use of epoxy reason glues is for joining dissimilar materials. They also have good gap-filling qualities. They generally come in two parts that, when mixed together, start a chemical reaction resulting in either a rapid or slow setting depending on the type.

FENCE

A guide that assists material being cut to be accurately moved along at a constant distance from the cutting edge of a tool.

FILLET

A componet or build-up material such as resin adhesive that reinforces the junction where two components meet.

FRET OUT

Making an internal cut by passing the scroll/fretsaw blade through a hole drilled in the material to be cut, relocating the blade in the scroll/fretsaw and cutting out the shape. The blade is detached from the saw again and the workpiece removed.

FRET PIN

A small pin especially made for joining thin materials such as plywood. They can be made of steel or brass.

HOT-MELT GLUE

Delivered from an electrically powered gun; ideal for rapid assembly of dissimilar materials and is very durable.

INVISIBLE THREAD

A very thin black nylon thread for making invisible seams.

JIG

A device designed to hold and locate a component during drilling or cutting and to guide the cutting tool. Also used for repeatedly producing an identical result or design.

JIGSAW

Also known as a sabre saw, it is a hand-held power tool that has a small reciprocating blade that can make curved and internal cuts.

KERF

The slit left behind by a saw blade as it cuts through material.

LIP AND SPUR DRILL BIT

Sometimes referred to as dowel drills. They have a single centre point and two outer cutting spurs. The centre point enables it to be precisely aligned on a previously marked point before drilling starts and will not wander when drilling.

MASKING TAPE

Sometimes called decorator's or automotive tape. It has a paper base enabling it to be cut and trimmed with ease. It is also low tack enabling it to be removed after painting, etc.

PILOT HOLE

A drill hole that is made in wood to aid the accurate positioning and penetration of a screw. It also aids the prevention of splitting.

PIVOT

The male component of a hinge that sits in a matching hole in which it rotates.

PVA ADHESIVE

A one-part PVA emulsion adhesive sometimes referred to as 'white glue'.

SANDING BLOCK

A block of wood or other material around which abrasive paper is wrapped or glued to help in shaping. It makes it easier to get an even line than just using abrasive paper by hand.

SHEET METAL SCREW

A self-tapping screw with a special cutting thread not unlike a chipboard screw. Available in very small sizes and widely used in the automotive trade.

SPIGOT

A protruding peg.

SPRAY MOUNT

Sometimes sold as a photographic mounting medium, it is a petroleum-based adhesive in an aerosol form. Excess can be removed with lighter fluid.

SPRING CAP

A metal dome that contains a spring steel device which only allows a metal rod to enter but not exit, thereby gripping it permanently.

STOCK

The material from which a component is being cut without referring to its type.

TABLE

In the context of this book refers to the platform on which the material rests while being cut on the scrollsaw.

TEMPLATE

A components shape cut out of various materials that is used for guiding drawing or cutting instruments in reproducing the design.

TONGUE AND SLOT JOINTS

Similar to a mortice and tenon where the tongue (tenon) protrudes from a component and fits into the matching slot (mortice) in another component to make a joint.

TWIST DRILL

Looking like a stick of Barley twist candy they are used for drilling holes in metal and a variety of other materials.

WASHERS

A metal disc with a hole in its centre used for load spreading with screw and bolt heads. Can also be made of other materials and can be used on axles for spacing out wheels from the sides of a toy and reducing friction.

ABOUT THE AUTHOR

Ivor Carlyle spent much of his adolescence teaching himself drawing and design at home because the secondary school he first attended banned the subjects on the grounds they were only suitable for girls' schools. He almost failed his Certificate in Secondary Education woodwork exam when the test pieces failed to fit due to a clerical error in the dimensions given in the exam papers. However, due largely to his own efforts he managed to obtain a place at art college and later worked in the aerospace and electronics industry as an industrial photographer. Eventually he set himself up as a freelance illustrator and occasional model maker, covering such diverse subjects as a working model of a watermill to puppet heads and props for advertising photography. An increasing number of nephews and nieces prompted an interest in producing quick and easy-to-make toys. He is also occasionally called on to make items for his wife's Brownie pack holidays. This is his second book for GMC Publications Ltd, the first is entitled *Scrollsaw Toy Projects*. Aside from toy making his other long-standing interests are birdwatching, classical music and opera. He lives with his wife in a busy village near Southampton in Hampshire.

INDEX

Selected titles available from

GMC PUBLICATIONS

BOOKS

Woodworking

Bird Boxes and Feeders for the Garden	David Mackenzie	Pine Furniture Projects for the Home	Dave Mackenzie
Complete Woodfinishing	Ian Hosker	Router Magic: Jigs, Fixtures and Tricks to	
David Charlesworth's Furniture-Making Technique	David Charlesworth	Unleash your Router's Full Potential	Bill Hylton
Furniture & Cabinetmaking Projects	GMC Publications	Routing for Beginners	Anthony Bailey
Furniture Projects	Rod Wales	The Scrollsaw: Twenty Projects	John Everett
Furniture Restoration (Practical Crafts	Kevin Jan Bonner	Sharpening Pocket Reference Book	Jim Kingshott
Furniture Restoration and Repair for Beginners	Kevin Jan Bonner	Sharpening: The Complete Guide	Jim Kingshott
Furniture Restoration Workshop	Kevin Jan Bonner	Space-Saving Furniture Projects	Dave Mackenzie
Green Woodwork	Mike Abbott	Stickmaking: A Complete Course	Andrew Jones & Clive George
Making & Modifying Woodworking Tools	Jim Kingshott	Stickmaking Handbook	Andrew Jones & Clive George
Making Chairs and Tables	GMC Publications	Test Reports: The Router and Furniture & Cabinetmaking	
Making Fine Furniture	Tom Darby		GMC Publications
Making Little Boxes from Wood	John Bennett	Veneering: A Complete Course	Ian Hosker
Making Shaker Furniture	Barry Jackson	Woodfinishing Handbook (Practical Crafts)	Ian Hosker
Making Woodwork Aids and Devices	Robert Wearing	Woodworking with the Router: Professional Router Techniques any	
Minidrill: Fifteen Projects	John Everett	Woodworker can Use	Bill Hylton & Fred Matlack

Toymaking

Fun to Make Wooden Toys & Games	Jeff & Jennie Loader	Scrollsaw Toy Projects	Ivor Carlyle
Making Wooden Toys & Games	Jeff & Jennie Loader	Scrollsaw Toys for All Ages	Ivor Carlyle
Restoring Rocking Horses	Clive Green & Anthony Dew	Wooden Toy Projects	GMC Publications

Dolls' Houses and Miniatures

Architecture for Dolls' Houses	Joyce Percival	Making Georgian Dolls' Houses	Derek Rowbottom
Beginners' Guide to the Dolls' House Hobby	Jean Nisbett	Making Miniature Gardens	Freida Gray
The Complete Dolls' House Book	Jean Nisbett	Making Miniature Oriental Rugs & Carpets	Meik & Ian McNaughton
The Dolls' House 1/24 Scale: A Complete Introduction	Jean Nisbett	Making Period Dolls' House Accessories	Andrea Barham
Dolls' House Accessories, Fixtures and Fittings	Andrea Barham	Making Tudor Dolls' Houses	Derek Rowbottom
Dolls' House Bathrooms: Lots of Little Loos	Patricia King	Making Victorian Dolls' House Furniture	Patricia King
Dolls' House Fireplaces and Stoves	Patricia King	Miniature Bobbin Lace	Roz Snowden
Easy to Make Dolls' House Accessories	Andrea Barham	Miniature Embroidery for the Victorian Dolls' House	Pamela Warner
Heraldic Miniature Knights	Peter Greenhill	Miniature Embroidery for the Georgian Dolls' House	Pamela Warner
Make Your Own Dolls' House Furniture	Maurice Harper	Miniature Needlepoint Carpets	Janet Granger
Making Dolls' House Furniture	Patricia King	The Secrets of the Dolls' House Makers	Jean Nisbett

MAGAZINES

Woodturning • Woodcarving • Furniture & Cabinetmaking • The Router • The Scrollsaw
The Dolls' House Magazine • Creative Crafts for the Home • BusinessMatters • Water Gardening

---

The above represents a selection of the titles currently published or scheduled to be published.
All are available direct from the Publishers or through bookshops, newsagents and specialist retailers.
To place an order, or to obtain a complete catalogue, contact:
GMC Publications,
166 High Street, Lewes, East Sussex BN7 1XU, United Kingdom Tel: 01273 488005 Fax: 01273 478606
Orders by credit card are accepted